This book is fascinating evidence (that) . .  are drawing new and spunky energy from t church, the educational wasteland around them, and ... tion to make evangelical colleges scholarly—in Christ.

James Tunstead Burtchaell author of *The Dying of the Light: The Disengagement of Colleges and Universities from their Christian Churches*

"Jesus Christ is truth" is the powerful cornerstone that an extraordinary group of scholars build upon as they evaluate the future of Christian higher education. It is good news and filled with opportunities and challenges to equip a counterculture to be the light, salt and leaven of our society and the world.

Mark O. Hatfield
Former United States Senator

The authors have isolated the distinctives that must be present in institutions of higher learning if they are to be termed Christian. This is a vital distillation of the challenges faced by Christian institutions in this post-modern age; and in my opinion, nothing short of a wholehearted commitment to these foundational principles will ensure the survival of Christian colleges and their unique contribution to the larger community of higher education. Board members, administration, faculty, and parents should read these pages carefully as personal and institutional decisions are made.

Jay Kesler, President
Taylor University

As we turn the new century, *The Future of Christian Higher Education* provides a timely check-up for those of us who are engaged in Christian higher education. We will all be better at what we do for weighing anew the issues raised in these stimulating essays.

Duane Litfin, President
Wheaton College

THE FUTURE OF
CHRISTIAN
HIGHER
EDUCATION

EDITED BY
DAVID S. DOCKERY & DAVID P. GUSHEE

THE FUTURE OF
CHRISTIAN
HIGHER
EDUCATION

BROADMAN
& HOLMAN
PUBLISHERS
Nashville, Tennesse

0–8054–1682–X

Published by Broadman & Holman Publishers,
Nashville, Tennessee
Acquistions and Development Editor: Leonard G. Goss
Page Design and Typesetting: TF Designs, Mt. Juliet, Tennessee

Dewey Decimal Classification: 378
Subject Heading: EDUCATION/CHRISTIAN HIGHER EDUCATION
Library of Congress Card Catalog Number: 99–12631

Library of Congress Cataloging-in-Publication Data
The future of Christian higher education / David S. Dockery and
David P. Gushee, editors.
    p. Cm.
Includes bibliographical references.
    ISBN 0–8054–1682–X (pbk.)
    1. Church colleges—United States—Congresses. 2. Christian
education—United States—Congresses.
    I. Dockery, David S., 1952– . II. Gushee, David P., 1962– .
LC621.F88 1999
378'.071—dc21   99–12631
                                                             CIP

1 2 3 4 5 03 02 01 00 99

With appreciation
to
Jack and Zan Holmes
Special friends and devoted
partners in Christian higher education

CONTENTS

PREFACE

The future of Christian higher education is bright, filled with great challenges and new opportunities. That was the message of the first National Forum on Christian Higher Education held in Indianapolis, Indiana, in April 1998. That is also the message of this volume.

The chapters in this book include addresses and lectures given at Union University in Jackson, Tennessee, from 1996 to 1998. They include chapel addresses, messages from convocation and commencement exercises, lectures sponsored by the Pew Charitable Trusts and the Staley Lectureships (to whom we express our profound gratitude), and the Conference on the Future of Christian Higher Education, jointly sponsored by Union University's Center for Christian Leadership and the Council for Christian Colleges and Universities. We have made an editorial decision to keep most of the essays in the form in which they were delivered, though personal references, introductions, and greetings have been removed. While this means there is a diversity of styles and formats, we believe you will find a thematic continuity focused on the needs, purposes, mission, direction, and challenges of Christian higher education as we move into the twenty-first century.

We want to thank all who joined us in these efforts to make this volume a reality. We value their friendship and collegiality. We want to express appreciation to Robert Andringa, president of the Council for Christian Colleges and Universities, for his support of this book and for writing the Foreword. We want to thank Broadman & Holman Publishers for their commitment to the future of Christian higher education, particularly James T. Draper, Jr., president of LifeWay Christian Resources of the Southern Baptist Convention, and to Leonard G. Goss and John Landers, editors at Broadman & Holman, who gave helpful guidance and direction to this volume.

Our families have stood beside us through yet another book project. Certainly there will be special rewards in heaven for both Lanese

Dockery and Jeanie Gushee. Cindy Meredith, who coordinated the logistics of the conference on the Union University campus and who patiently worked with us in the editorial process, deserves a special word of commendation and appreciation. We also want to thank Jack and Zan Holmes for their support for the Conference on the Future of Christian Higher Education. Without their friendship and generosity, our initial dreams could not have become reality. We dedicate this volume to them. Finally, we express deep gratitude to our gracious God who has enabled us to pursue this task and who has called us at this time to the mission of Christian higher education. We pray that this work will be used to bring glory to our God and to advance the work of his kingdom.

Soli Deo Gloria
David S. Dockery
David P. Gushee

FOREWORD

ROBERT C. ANDRINGA

When David Dockery invited me to write the Foreword for this much anticipated book, I admit to thinking time was too short to read the entire manuscript and that I would just begin writing. After all, I think about the future of Christian higher education every day! But there was some internal ethic, hopefully biblical, that persuaded me to read all the chapters before going to my PC. I am glad I did. These papers from various chapel, inaugural, and symposium settings clearly left me with more enthusiasm and fact-based confidence not only to write a foreword but also to feel that our great tradition of Christ-centered higher learning was also moving *forward*.

The last of the manuscripts got read very early one Sunday morning. I sat with a blank notepad and asked, "What did this book do for me?" The answers came quite easily and formed a workable outline for my contribution to the book. The key words were *Context . . . Worldview . . . Personal Spirituality . . . Scholarship . . . Community . . . Vision.* You may end up with slightly different mile markers, but these will be the handles by which I recall the contributions of many gifted people to my sense of our future in Christian higher education.

Context

Moving forward is always informed by first looking back. Several authors help us remember that the Christian tradition is unique among all religious traditions in its respect for and support of higher learning. Indeed, most of the great universities of the world were inspired by biblical doctrines of creation, order, the redemption of all things through Christ, the commandment to love God with all our minds, and much more that is tied to a Creator God and living Lord.

Even in America (actually, especially in America) our first institutions of higher learning were distinctly Christ focused. Timothy George quotes Henry Dunster, the first president of Harvard: "The primary purpose of the founding of Harvard was to lay Christ in the bottom as the only foundation of all sound knowledge and learning." Other colonial colleges were born from much the same worldview. In chapter 2, James T. Draper, Jr., adds: "Atheism never once in history built a great educational institution. Why? Atheism always leads to despair."

In my travels to our ninety-one Council member campuses and to many of our twenty-seven affiliate campuses, I occasionally detect a troubling lack of self-esteem among some of our faculty and administrators. We fall into the trap of comparing ourselves on secular yardsticks with larger, more well-endowed institutions with bigger libraries, higher salaries, and better equipped laboratories. This book should call that debilitating attitude to task. History is on our side. We have the tradition. Christians formed the models. The order of creation forms the basis for mathematics, biology, chemistry, and physics. Christian commitment led to great music, meaningful art, and consistent philosophy. It is time to look *forward* with more confidence.

As we allow this book to inform us about the future, then, we need a longer-term view of history than our own lifetimes. The postmodern era of relativism and deconstructionism is quite recent. And what are the results of these forces? Our universities, for the most part, are fragmented and overly specialized; departments have limited academic freedom to dialogue only within narrow and discernible bounds of political correctness; the campus lacks common values; much sense of community is lacking except at football games; and people who take seriously the lordship of Christ are marginalized. It is sad. But many of us received our graduate degrees at such places, and some of the values we learned there are difficult to shed.

This book helps me place our era within the context of two thousand years of history. That perspective really helps us move *forward* in our thinking.

Worldview

We know that everyone has a worldview, whether articulated or simply lived out. We Christ-followers sometimes get impatient when others can't understand how a university offering education from a

Christian worldview is different from other campuses. I've heard at least five hundred people articulate what we are about. Each is somewhat different, but the essence is clear. I've also heard many non-Christians outline their worldviews. Most are half-reasoned views that could not hold water.

Paul reminds us that "natural man does not accept the things of the Spirit of God; for they are foolishness to him, and he cannot understand them, because they are spiritually appraised" (1 Cor. 2:14 NASB). So we must be patient and not judgmental when nonbelievers express impatience or a judgmental attitude toward Christian educators.

You will read several perspectives on our worldview in this book, starting with David S. Dockery's call to consider the Great Commandment as a paradigm for the purpose of our campuses. Since the Great Commandment is my own life purpose statement, it is exciting to see how it plays out in institutional life. If we wait until many secular educators come around to agree with this as a credible foundation for scholarship and learning, we will miss out on the excitement of the living and learning it brings. While we are always ready to share with others the reason for the hope that is within us, let's not wait for consensus. Let's move *forward*.

Personal Spirituality

While this book is focused on organizational futures, it reminds us that to have a Truth-seeking campus requires Truth-seeking individuals. Our brand of excellence requires scholars, staff, and student leaders whose desire is to love the things God loves. There is no substitute. The dimensions of this principle are clearly laid out by Claude Pressnell and David Gushee. Arthur Holmes, as always, shows us how personal character and the integration of faith and learning are inextricably linked. Holmes and Bob Agee show us that character and values do matter. And without people of godly character, one cannot have a Christian college or university.

For me, the book not only underscores this dimension of who we are, but it clearly makes the point that authentic spiritual maturity requires an intentionality we must not ignore. To be a Christian campus in name only—where our words are correct for the evangelical community but our behavior belies another worldview—is to pull us all backward and to lose the vitality that only the Spirit of God, lived out in transformed lives, can bring to the campus. We need to encourage one another to do what only we can do individually—practice the disciplines of spiritual life. Each campus must include in its plans and even its budgets how individual students, faculty, staff, and trustees can be transformed by the renewing of their minds by Christ alone. This is necessary if we are to move *forward.*

Scholarship

Scholarship is our mission. Other organizations led and staffed by Christians focus on health care or world relief or missions or evangelism. We focus on scholarship. Without an unceasing quest for the highest caliber of scholarship, we cannot move forward. Frankly, the commitment to scholarship varies from campus to campus within the Council. Robert Sloan's chapter reminds us that faculties are the heart of our work and that "Christian higher education" means many different things to educators today. Millard Erickson takes us deep into the challenge of Christian scholarship in a postmodern world. Joel Carpenter brings a most articulate historian's perspective on what we have learned and what is yet to be learned to model truly Christian scholarship.

We contend every day with forces that pull us away from the truth-seeking university, whose center is Christ. We need state and federal government approval. We want to be accredited by regional and specialized accrediting agencies. We purchase and assign textbooks that are not written by Christian scholars. We hire faculty members who may love Jesus but who have never been helped to integrate their discipline-based knowledge with the life and mind of a truth seeker. And we invest far too little effort in helping faculty members develop their own "integration theologies" that Christian scholars should have to make good on our promises to students. This area of need is where the Council has focused much of its work for over twenty years through new faculty workshops, supplemental textbooks, discipline-specific seminars, etc. We also try to model for faculty and students what scholarship from this Christ-centered holistic view looks like through our seven semester-study programs in five countries.

Because of the necessarily intense biblical scholarship required beyond one's chosen discipline, the few resources of time and mentors most campuses devote to this dimension of Christian scholarship, and the pull of the guilds to research and write what is acceptable to a majority of peers far removed from the life of faith, we must be more intentional. We must leave behind the notion that Christian scholarship is the same as any scholarship, except that it adds a little something of Christian history or values on top. No, Christian scholarship—authentic, honest, truth-seeking scholarship—is fundamentally different and cannot be faked.

You will get a good impression of what is happening in our brand of scholarship from this book. Surely, as Carpenter and others say, we have come a long way. But we must shuck all remaining vestiges of the anti-intellectualism of Christian fundamentalism and move forward with full confidence that the highest scholarship is honoring to God and, indeed, expected of those who call themselves Christian. We cannot move backward. These capable authors help us to move *forward* in our understanding of Christian scholarship.

Community

It should be difficult to be a loner on any Christian campus. Both Kelly Monroe's intriguing report on how relatively few Christians struggle to have community at Harvard and Ken Elzinga's observations of how blessed Christian students on Christian campuses are compared to Christian students at the University of Virginia who lack a sense of community reminded me that I take this important communal dimension of learning and living for granted. These manuscripts show, once again, that living near other Christians does not guarantee "community."

One dimension of community that Stan Gaede addressed, in part, is how we need to live in unity with ever-increasing diversity in society. This is a big challenge for Christian campuses. We are behind. We are behind in offering women the same opportunities to teach and administer as men. And 60 percent of our students are female! We are behind in building trust with black and Hispanic churches so parents and students learn to have confidence that their skin color makes no difference in being fully accepted in the community of a Christian campus. We are becoming more global in business, government, communications, travel, and learning. Yet some campuses are not yet sure how to reflect the global community in their local communities. Not that we are without progress in these areas. We are moving *forward* in good ways. But society is moving quickly toward a pluralism that our students must experience in the community of learners if we truly want to prepare them to be servant-leaders in the world as it is.

On other levels of community, our campus is far ahead of the pack. We worship together. We care pretty well for individuals in pain. We have role models who demonstrate conflict resolution, asking forgiveness for breaking community standards, reaching and out selflessly to others in need. As you read this book, may I suggest that you keep one question in mind: How do these authors help us move toward more authentic *koinonia* and community? There are many dimensions of that, yet students will be drawn to where they are accepted and feel alive in the midst of community. We must move *forward*, well beyond where we are today.

Vision

I am energized by vision. I also like to solve problems, but only when the solution will contribute to a vision. By now, you can see that this book will contribute significantly to vision.

From my perspective in a national association office, I naturally identify with the chapter by my colleague, Karen Longman. We get excited when we see one of our campuses rally around a clear vision. The energy and hope that flow from a clear vision are unstoppable.

But we also get excited when we see how our campuses—representing a little over 1 percent of total enrollment in American higher education—are learning to collaborate together. We firmly believe that each campus will be more successful in its individual mission when we begin to act together on our common vision for Christ-centered higher learning. As Karen reported, the vision for the Council as a whole is for a world in which Christian higher learning is available for those who seek it. How many could that be? With about 32 percent of the world "Christian," the challenge is one that we can't even dream about without working together. New technologies, for the first time, are making it worthwhile even to talk about such a vision.

Will the challenges of our day create a wider range of visions for our campuses? As I read the Sonju and Dockery chapters on education for business and the professions, I had to ask myself why so few Christian campuses are seriously linking their academic offerings and service with regional economic development priorities. Community colleges have thrived by doing this. Why couldn't we have Bible colleges, liberal arts colleges, seminaries, and several other types of learning enterprises infused with the truth of the gospel and led by people who want to serve God and serve the people? Could some of our own

Council campuses respond more to regional economic development needs and still be rooted in the arts and sciences and continue to be "Christian"? These are questions I hope we can explore.

Another related vision would address the realities of a perpetual learning society. If it is true that workers, on average, will need the equivalent of one year of college every seven years to stay current and employable, that equates to more than twenty million new learners every year—in addition to the fifteen million already enrolled in higher education. Who will serve them? Should many of our current Christian colleges respond to this huge demand for perpetual learning?

My head is full, and my heart is buoyed after reading this book. Visions of what we can be, made all the more palatable by better knowledge of what Christians have done in and for higher education over the centuries, will flow from your interaction with these sixteen diverse writers.

Some books pull me down. Others leave me at the same place I was. This one pulls me *forward* to what we can all become as we love God with all our heart, soul, strength and mind . . . and our neighbors who want to learn with us.

THE FUTURE OF
CHRISTIAN HIGHER EDUCATION:
AN INTRODUCTION

DAVID S. DOCKERY

One year remains before Christian college and university graduates must be equipped to live and work in the twenty-first century. This new century will bring about an expanding world of technology, a changing social context, and a global economy, as well as great spiritual and ethical challenges. Our institutions must move toward these changing times enabled by the rich heritage of higher education throughout the history of Christianity. During the recent past, Christian higher education has faced many challenging transitions and changes. Now we face yet another new day filled with fresh opportunities. Now is the time to refocus our efforts as we think together about the future of Christian higher education.

As we contemplate the future of Christian higher education, we must become focused on and driven by our distinctive mission. We must recognize that we live in a world of rapid and incalculable change. Those who have lived through the twentieth century have seen the world go from horse and buggy to the space shuttle—literally the transformation of transportation. But that has multiplied many times over in recent years. More information has been generated in the last three decades alone than in the previous three thousand years. More than four thousand books are published each day. A single weekday edition of *The New York Times* includes more information than the average person in seventeenth-century England encountered over the course of a lifetime.[1] Such rapid change has not only impacted our lives but also has great implications for our institutions—and for the mission of Christian higher education.

1

Those changes call for us to sense the needs around us. Beyond that we need priestly ears and responsive hearts to help us hear, interpret, and understand our postmodern world.[2]

Our world is now characterized by pluralism, relativism, and the rise of pagan spiritualities. It is a world in which the word *religion* conveys ideas of New Age and Eastern mysticism. This has resulted in a culture that has lost a sense of direction and, moreover, has lost a sense of shame. This loss of shame has caused University of Chicago professor Jean Bethke Elshtain, in her recent volume, *Democracy on Trial*, to conclude that democracy cannot survive without a sense of shame. When shame is lost, the future of democracy is up for grabs.[3]

It is a chaotic world that Will Willimon, dean at Duke University, describes as "one without meaning," suggesting that the current generation of teens and twenty-year-olds is an "abandoned generation."[4] Our society has lost a sense of propriety under the misguided understanding of freedom and individualism. Colgate University professor Barry Alan Shain, in his recent work *The Myth of American Individualism*, argues that American freedom depends on a sense of accountability established by community parameters.[5] It is a day in which the idea of what is right and what is truth has been muffled, if not lost. Secular teachers and writers have increased their efforts to move the minds of this generation away from truth.[6]

At the conclusion of the twentieth century, we face great challenges. While almost 98 percent of Americans claim to believe in God, only 25 percent of the people in this country claim to believe there is any such thing as absolute truth.

Culture watchers as diverse as David Wells, Penny Marler, and George Barna agree that young people are confused about morality because of the pluralism and relativism of our day. Marler, in her book *Unchurched Faith,* suggests that a relativistic youth culture without a core ethical tradition could make for a most troublesome society.

In his most recent book, *God in the Wasteland*, David Wells says that even the small percentage of genuinely committed people are seriously hobbled by their entanglement with modern culture.[7] We must grasp the need of the hour that is to refocus our efforts on the distinctive role of Christian higher education. This effort primarily involves educating and enabling this generation to articulate and live out a commitment to truth that shapes and informs a Christian worldview.[8]

To do so, we must recommit ourselves to the full-orbed implications of the mission of Christian higher education. This will call for

Christian colleges and universities to expand their resource base in terms of both persons and dollars. Some have asked how will we do this. The essays in this book address these concerns from a variety of vantage points.

While each institution must develop its own campus-specific strategy, it is imperative to recognize that restrategizing is essential. In their landmark book _Reengineering the Corporation_, Michael Hammer and James Champy write that the principles laid down more than two centuries ago have shaped the structure, management, and performance of American businesses and institutions throughout the nineteenth and twentieth centuries. Yet due to the continual transformation of the world through rapid change, Hammer and Champy go on to say that the time has come to rethink those principles.[9] Methods that worked well in the past may not be effective in the twenty-first century.

But proponents of change have also learned that one of the biggest barriers to revisioning our future is our past success. Observers have noted that many American companies and institutions are "now performing so badly precisely because they used to perform so well." In other words, a company like IBM became successful because it was uniquely designed for the time in which it prospered. But once that context changed, the insights and processes that once brought success now create challenges. As a result, America's problem—whether in the world of business, health care, or education—is that "it is entering the twenty-first century with companies and institutions designed during the 19th century to work well in the twentieth."[10]

Certainly we must build on past successes and current strengths. Change for change's sake accomplishes nothing! Yet we must ask, "What changes need to be made to make us more effective?"

Not only must we develop a strategy appropriate for our times, but we also need to communicate well our vision and our direction. Thus, beyond the importance of establishing campus-specific strategies is the necessity of communicating those strategies and inviting others to participate with us in carrying out our work.

You may remember the story of the Chevrolet company a few years back. The Chevy Nova was a relatively successful smaller American car for many years. Encouraged by U.S. sales, Chevrolet began to market the American Nova throughout the world. Unfortunately, the Nova did not sell well in Mexico and other Latin American countries. Additional ads were ordered, marketing efforts were stepped up, but sales remained stagnant. Sales directors were baffled. The car had sold well in the American market; why wasn't it selling abroad? When they discovered the answer, it was most embarrassing: *nova* in Spanish means "no go."

The business world is filled with such stories. For example, Perdue Farms expanded its business into Mexico and converted its popular slogan, "It takes a tough man to make a tender chicken" into Spanish. The results were less than desirable. Why? The translation came out, "It takes a virile man to make a chicken affectionate." Not exactly what Frank Perdue had in mind![11]

George Bernard Shaw knew what he was talking about when he said "the greatest problem of communication is the illusion it has been accomplished."[12] Communication is a vitally important aspect in moving toward becoming mission-driven institutions in the twenty-first century. As the folks at Chevrolet and Perdue Farms can tell you, failing to communicate can be costly.

As we work together within the Council for Christian Colleges and Universities and other such combined efforts, we must be willing to do what we have not tried before. Christian higher education must envision new programs, new degrees, new delivery systems, and must take advantage of new opportunities that will come our way. To do so calls for a future-directed mind-set.

If anyone had been asked in 1968 which nation would dominate the world in watchmaking during the 1990s and into the twenty-first century, the answer would have been obvious: Switzerland. The Swiss had dominated the world of watchmaking for the previous sixty years.

The Swiss made the best watches in the world and were committed to constantly refining their expertise. It was the Swiss who developed the minute hand and the second hand. They led the world in discovering better ways to manufacture the gears, mainsprings, and other working parts. They even led the way in waterproofing techniques and self-winding models. By 1968, the Swiss made more than two-thirds of all watches sold in the world and laid claim to as much as 90 percent of all profits.

By 1980, however, they had laid off thousands of watchmakers and were down to less than 10 percent of the world market. Their profit domination dropped to less than 20 percent. Between 1979 and 1981, fifty thousand of the sixty-two thousand Swiss watchmakers lost their jobs.

Why? They had refused a new development—Quartz watches—which had been, ironically, invented by the Swiss. Because it had no mainspring or knob, it was rejected. It was too much of a paradigm shift—too big of a change in worldview—for them to embrace. Seiko adopted it, and along with others became the new leaders in the watch industry.[13]

The lesson of the Swiss watchmakers is profound. A successful, profitable, secure past was destroyed by an unwillingness to consider the future. It involved more than not being able to make predictions about the future, which is likely to happen to anyone at any time. It was a different kind of problem: an inability and an unwillingness to be *future-directed* in outlook.

The twenty-first century will continue to need great Christian liberal arts colleges and universities, perhaps more than ever. We need liberal arts colleges and universities that are unapologetically Christian and church-related. We must revise what it means to be a part of a learning community that is dedicated to academic excellence, faithful to Christian convictions, devoted to the gospel of Jesus Christ and the veracity of Holy Scriptures, where students will be educated and equipped for responsible service and leadership.[14]

As you read the essays and addresses in this volume, you will sense a common theme. There is a call to build institutions primarily devoted to excellence in teaching and creativity in learning but also committed to research, publication, and performance. Such a challenge will require energy and dedication of the highest order.

What is common among all the addresses is the need to keep Christian higher education distinctively Christian. That will involve remaining focused on our essential purpose. There is an old story about a lighthouse keeper who worked on a rocky stretch of coastline. Once a month he would receive a new supply of oil to keep the light burning so that the ships would be protected as they sailed near the rocky coast. Being close to the shore, he received many visitors. One night a woman from the nearby village came and begged him for some of his oil to keep her family warm. Another time a father asked for some to use in his lamp. Another needed some to lubricate a wheel. Since all the requests seemed legitimate, the lighthouse keeper tried to please everyone and grant the requests of all.

Toward the end of the month, his supply of oil was very low. Soon it was gone, and one night the light on the lighthouse went out. As a result, that evening several ships were wrecked, and countless numbers of lives were lost. When the authorities investigated, the man was very apologetic. He told them he was just trying to be helpful with the oil. Their reply to his excuses was simple and to the point. You were given oil for one purpose and one purpose only—to keep the light burning.[15] The story demonstrates that even good things, which are not a part of our essential mission, may at times divert us from our highest purposes.

At this time we must take seriously the call to develop Christian minds. The tensions often created between academic excellence and piety, between scholarship and teaching, between academic pursuits and revealed truth, between the academy and the church, will always be with us. But we can only address these challenges and bridge the tensions with both-and answers. Either-or dichotomies will not advance the cause of Christian higher education at this *kairos* moment. The issues of truth, the call to teach and mentor, and the vision to think and live Christianly are at this time our highest priorities.

It is a challenging and lofty task to which we have been called. Christian higher education at this moment faces marvelous opportunities to strengthen both our academic commitments and our Christian devotion, to develop Christian minds, Christian hearts, and Christian hands to build great Christian colleges and universities.[16]

Let us pray that we can all faithfully respond to the call to refocus on the integration of faith and learning, committed to the education of students in areas of content, character, competencies, and convictional worldviews, thus producing students who will be servant leaders and change agents in the world.[17] That is the challenge for the future of Christian higher education.

Chapter 1

THE GREAT COMMANDMENT AS A PARADIGM FOR CHRISTIAN HIGHER EDUCATION

DAVID S. DOCKERY

The Challenges and Opportunities

We stand on the doorstep of a new century with great hopefulness but simultaneously with an awareness of the changing times in which we live. Values clarification will certainly rage into the third millennium. Educational issues will continue to be compounded by social issues such as poverty, the breakdown of families, and the ravages of crime, drugs, and AIDS.[1] We hear James Mecklenburger, director of the Institute for the Transfer of Technology to Education, loudly proclaim the opportunities that modern technology presents, suggesting that "Information Technology is the most powerful educational force since chalk."[2] Yet others see more serious challenges.[3] The high technology age is here, bringing both blessing and curse. Thus the question is not "high tech" or "no tech." We must remember that "high tech" is not enough. "High touch" is mandatory for followers of Jesus. For Jesus as the Master Teacher first called his followers to be "with him" before he sent them out on mission. Christian higher education must seek to take advantage of these new opportunities that will facilitate learning, break down traditional barriers, and bring new and powerful information our way. We recognize the high-tech world as a useful servant but a horrible master. More important questions even than the use of technology loom larger for us today. We must ask: What is education for, or more specifically, what is Christian education for, and what are the common values we want to share with the next generation?[4]

7

The restlessness that characterizes much of Western society evidences the enormous changes in our country and in our world. Leith Anderson says these changes "promise to be greater than the invention of the printing press, greater than the Industrial Revolution."[5] At the heart of these paradigmatic changes, we see that truth, morality, and interpretative frameworks are being ignored if not rejected. The challenges posed for Christian higher education by these cultural shifts are formidable indeed.[6] Throughout education and culture, the very existence of objective truth is being challenged. We observe this in the academy in the poststructuralism of Lyotard,[7] the deconstructionism of Derrida,[8] the radical subjectivism of Foucault,[9] the reader-focused hermeneutic of Stanley Fish[10]; it is even found in popular culture, exemplified in the lyrics of country music artists like Diamond Rio singing that "it's all interpretation, if you want to know the truth you have to read between the lines."[11] A normative view of truth and a Christian worldview are rejected or devalued, seemingly lost in our contemporary culture.

Recently, a high-profile culture watcher observed this impact on Christians, noting that "an unbelievably small proportion of believers have what is called a Christian worldview . . . and because [most Christians] don't think like Christians, they can't act like Christians. Because they don't act like Christians, they can't have much impact on the world in which they live."[12]

The Call: Toward a Great Commandment Model

Christian higher education has an opportunity at this unique time in history to step forward as a leader in the larger field of higher education to prepare students to enter the changing world of the twenty-first century. In order to answer this call, we must prioritize our commitment to the words of Jesus called the Great Commandment (Matt. 22:36–40). Here we are told to love God with our hearts, our minds, our souls—and to love others completely. Jesus' words refer to a wholehearted devotion to God with every aspect of our being, from whatever angle we choose to consider it—emotionally, volitionally, or cognitively. This kind of "love" for God will then result in obedience to all He has commanded.[13] These words of Jesus serve as the foundational framework for us to carry out our mission to our changing postmodern world.

The purpose of Christian institutions is to educate students so they will be prepared for the vocation to which God has called them, enabled and equipped with the competencies necessary to think Christianly and to perform skillfully in the world, equipped to be servant leaders who impact the world as change agents based on a full-orbed Christian worldview and lifeview. Thus we are called to be Great Commandment schools.

The first and greatest commandment makes it plain that we are to love God with our minds. As T. S. Eliot so appropriately expressed: "The purpose of a Christian education would not be merely to make men and women pious Christians: a system which aimed too rigidly at this end alone would become only obscurantist. A Christian education must primarily teach people to be able to think in Christian categories."[14]

Unfortunately, at times our efforts parallel those of the pastor who was told by a church member, "You don't know how much your sermons have meant to my husband since he lost his mind."

Thus we want to love God with hearts, souls, and minds as well. Learning to think Christianly impacts our homes, our businesses, our health-care agencies, our schools, our social structures, our recreation, and, yes, our churches, too. To love God with our minds means that we think differently about the way we live and love, the way we worship and serve, the way we work to earn our livelihood, and the way we learn and teach.

As we prepare to enter the twenty-first century, we need more than new and novel ideas and enhanced programs; we need distinctively Christian thinking, the kind of tough-minded thinking that results in distinctly different action. To achieve this end, we need to hear afresh the significance of Jesus' words for us. For as T. S. Eliot said: to love God with our minds suggests, "to be able to think in Christian categories."[15] This means being able to define and hold to a worldview and lifeview grounded in the truth of God's revelation to us. It means seeing life and learning from a Christian vantage point; it means thinking with the mind of Christ. This involves the whole of our human personality. Our mind is to be renewed, our emotions purified, our conscience kept clear, and our will surrendered to God's will. Applying the Great Commandment entails all that we know of ourselves being committed to all that we know of God.[16]

The Twentieth-Century Demise

Never before in America has it been so important to awaken our institutions of higher learning to the significance of these words of Jesus for us. For as George Marsden has suggested in his groundbreaking work, *The Soul of the American University*, we have moved from a time of "Protestant establishment" to one of "established unbelief."[17] Russell Chandler adds that colleges and universities affiliated with mainline Protestant denominations are in for a hard time, with both budget blues and an erosion into secularization. He argues that the secular slide is already well under way and destined to be virtually complete by 2001.[18] Mark Schwehn contends that the modern university has forgotten its spiritual foundations.[19] University of Chicago professor Dorothy Bass laments that most church-affiliated colleges and universities have become so totally secularized that it is hard to know a church-affiliated college when you see one.[20] Similarly, James T. Burtchaell has shown us the disappointing outcome when Christian colleges and universities disengage from their supporting churches and distinctive missions. While some are not so pessimistic, it is generally the case that higher education in America has shifted from a vantage point where the knowledge of God provides the context for all forms of human knowledge to one that is hostile to Christianity. Today the focus of the university tends to be one in which the "uses of the university are merely for better knowledge and higher skills."[21]

Clark Kerr, former president of the University of California, has proudly noted in his newly revised volume that the vision of Christian higher education has been shattered forever, with empirical thinking taking the place of moral philosophy and research the place of teaching.[22] What Clark Kerr wrongly sees as healthy positive gains are more rightly interpreted in Bill Readings' new Harvard University Press work as signs of decay. In fact, Readings declares that the University has become an autonomous bureaucratic institution—a ruined institution—without a grand narrative of culture to carry out its work.[23]

On the contrary, regardless of the directionless musings of such postmoderns as Derrida and Lyotard, I would suggest that there is a metanarrative, a larger story, to shape our thinking and learning, and that it is found in the words of Jesus: the Great Commandment.

The problems with the modern university have moved beyond the loss of moral philosophy or the rise of autonomous bureaucracies or even the "political correctness" of the academic elite. The problem is deeper. We have lost the "uni" in uni-versity. We have lost sight of the foundational questions.

Toward a Recovery of the Christian Foundation

In the late 1800s, nothing matched the financial and political dominance of the railroad. Trains completely dominated the transportation industry of the United States, moving both people and goods throughout the country.

Then a new discovery came along—the car; and incredibly, the railroad industry failed to take advantage of its unique position to own its development. The automotive revolution was happening everywhere, but the railroad industry failed to use its industry dominance to take hold of the opportunity.

The leaders of the transportation industry did not take advantage of one of the greatest transportation developments in the history of the modern world. Tom Peters, in his book *In Search of Excellence,* points out the reason: industry leaders didn't understand what business they were in. They thought they were in the train business when, in fact, they were in the transportation business. Time passed them by, as did opportunity. They couldn't see what their real purpose was. They failed to ask themselves any of the foundational questions.

For the railroad industry leaders, foundational questions would have included: What business are we in? What is the goal of our efforts? Answering such questions would have led them to realize they were not really in the railroad business at all. They were in the transportation business. Their ultimate goal was not the preservation of a particular system of transportation, but transportation itself. [24]

A more contemporary example of this problem was pointed out by Ron Pobuda of the National Audiovisual Association, who said, "If *Sports Illustrated* magazine understood it was in the sports information business, not the publishing business, then two decades ago we would have had the Sports Illustrated Channel, not ESPN."[25]

This is the power of a foundational question: it gets underneath momentary methods, tools, and fads, keeping an organization focused on its most basic identity and objective.

The Primary Purpose of Christian Higher Education

Our primary purpose is not just the educating of business, nursing, art, music, or science students in the latest fads. Nor is it bound to certain methods of delivering this information. For our goal is not just the teaching of certain subject matter. No. It is both broader and more basic than that.

In recent days, David Damrosch, professor of English and comparative literature at Columbia University in New York City, has penned a sane and sound analysis of the specific challenges facing higher education at the conclusion of the twentieth century. His work, entitled *We Scholars: Changing the Culture of the University*, proposes several reforms meant to alter the culture of American academic life.[26] He recognizes the changes that have been brought about in higher education with the rise and expansion of disciplines. Yet he proposes that the problem we face is not necessarily increasing academic specialization; it is the lack of interrelatedness between the disciplines. This unwillingness to relate disciplines to one another has resulted in a fragmentation of knowledge. The fragmentation of knowledge should alarm all committed to Christian higher education, for it strikes at the foundation of our purpose!

Damrosch calls for an interdisciplinary community approach to teaching and research, simultaneously generalizing and specializing. He discourages the isolationism of the academy and urges that the university reshape itself by working in concert even across established field boundaries. He rightly recognizes that disciplinary fragmentation dates only from decisions made a century ago when the American university assumed its current form. Damrosch's suggestions are noble and helpful but shortsighted. They fail to address the most important aspect of the problem, which is not specialization, but specialization brought on by fragmentation of knowledge. This has resulted in a false dichotomy between the life of the mind and the life of faith. It is here that Christian institutions seeking to put into practice the implications of the Great Commandment can enter this important conversation.

I would suggest that the starting point of loving God with our minds—thinking Christianly—points us to a unity of knowledge, a seamless whole because all true knowledge flows from the one Creator to his one creation. Thus, specific bodies of knowledge relate to each other not just because scholars work together in community, not just because interdisciplinary work broadens our knowledge, but also because all truth is God's truth, composing a single universe of knowledge.[27]

For Christian colleges and universities to become truly Great Commandment institutions does not mean that we will blur disciplinary boundaries—not at all! It means that we will take our varying, and at times seemingly conflicting, approaches and traditions, and seek to interpret and explain our subject matter under the lordship of the Creator God, the revealer of all Truth. If we can learn to integrate faith thoroughly with our various disciplines, drawing on the long Christian tradition to do so, we can restore coherence to learning.

Then will education not only mean the passing on of content to our students, but it will also mean the shaping of character, and it will move toward the development and construction of a convictional worldview and lifeview by which we can see, learn, and interpret the world from the vantage point of God's revelation to us. We must therefore seek to build a Christian liberal arts university where men and women can be introduced to an understanding and appreciation of God, his creation and grace, and humanity's place of privilege and responsibility in God's world.

Understanding and Appreciating Our Heritage

It might be helpful to realize that the goal of Christian education, rightly understood for the past two thousand years, has been this integration of faith and knowledge. The starting point for this integration has rested on the foundation of the words of Jesus' Great Commandment and the wisdom literature of the Hebrew Scriptures, which reminds us that the fear of the Lord is the beginning of knowledge, wisdom, and understanding (Prov. 1:7; Ps. 111:10; Job 28:28). Thus, the beginning point for thinking, learning, and teaching is our reverence before God the Father Almighty, Maker of heaven and earth.

The search for knowledge, the quest for truth—phrases so familiar as to be cliches in education—must not be uttered carelessly. For when we speak of such from the Christian perspective, we speak of God who is omniscience, God who is Truth. From this foundation has followed a legacy of those committed to a passion for learning based on the supposition that all truth is God's truth. Thus, as Christians related together in a learning community, we all as faculty, students, staff, and administrators are to seek to take every thought captive to Christ and love God with all our minds.[28]

Perhaps Justin Martyr, a Christian philosopher in the second century (A.D. 100–165), was the first in postapostolic times to articulate the need for the integration of faith and learning. He said that whatever has been uttered aright by any person in any place belongs to us

Christians.[29] In Alexandria in the next century, both Clement and Origen instructed their converts not only in doctrine but also in science, literature, and philosophy.[30] Augustine, in the fifth century, in *On Christian Doctrine,* penned the thought that every true and good Christian should understand that wherever we may find truth, it is the Lord's.[31]

This legacy may be traced across the centuries and in most every culture, for wherever the gospel has been received, the academy and Christian learning have followed. This legacy can be traced through Erasmus, Luther, Calvin, Knox, Melancthon, and Comenius to the founding of major institutions in this country.[32]

For example, when commenting on the place of the humanities, John Calvin reflected: "If we regard the Spirit of God as the sole fountain of truth, we shall neither reject the truth itself, nor despise it wherever it shall appear, unless we wish to dishonor the Spirit of God. For by holding the gifts of the Spirit in slight esteem, we condemn and reproach the Spirit Himself."[33]

Calvin's contemporaries, Luther and Erasmus, though with different emphases, underscored Calvin's convictions. Illustratively, Erasmus maintained: "All studies, philosophy, rhetoric, {and literature} are followed for this one object, that we know Christ and honor Him. This is the end of all learning and eloquence."[34] The commitment of Erasmus and Calvin to a program of studies so single-mindedly Christ-centered places them among the forerunners of the integration of faith with all living and learning. Their sense of wholeness in studies and teaching, in art and science, in ethics and etiquette, in politics and government, provides a striking model for us.

Today's Christian colleges and universities must seek to become heirs of this great legacy, moving toward becoming Great Commandment schools by seeking to understand and cherish God's revelation and holy creation in our discipline-related explorations.

The Great Commandment: Applications

Being a Great Commandment institution means more than the integration of faith and *learning*; it involves the integration of faith and *living*. Jesus tells us to apply our love for God with heart, mind, and soul by loving others. Divine love issues in interpersonal love. Such application has reference to work and school, home and church, politics and play. It impacts the most elemental aspects of our daily lives—

for all thinking must be accompanied by action—thinking and acting Christianly.

This means we will seek to serve one another by demonstrating the love of God to students, colleagues, and others who have contact with us. We must show love and respect for those whom we serve. We must attempt to work for their highest good. As Francis Schaeffer said, "If we do not show love to each other the world has a right to question whether Christianity is true."[35]

The implications of a commitment to the Great Commandment call for us to be student-friendly in our educational delivery systems and service-oriented in our dealing with faculty, staff, alumni, and other constituencies. At the heart of this commitment is the visible demonstration of valuing one another. We want to model the love and forgiveness of Christ.

Conclusion

What is required of us at this time is a commonly held vision—but not just vision. We need vision shaped by commonly held values—values established on the Word of God, leading to a firm commitment to Christ and his kingdom—values consistent with the worship of God and the love of learning.

We must constantly remind ourselves that we are not called just to be great private institutions of higher learning but to be distinctively Christian colleges and universities. To start with the wrong goal is to run the wrong race.

Not long ago the sports world reported a story of a world-class female runner who was invited to compete in a road race in Connecticut. On the morning of the race, she drove from New York City, following the directions—or so she thought—given to her over the telephone. She got lost, stopped at a gas station, and asked for help. She knew that the race started in the parking lot of a shopping mall. The station attendant also knew of such a race scheduled just up the road and directed her there.

When she arrived, she was relieved to see in the parking lot a modest number of runners preparing to compete—not as many as she had anticipated. She also learned that it was an easier race than she'd been led to expect. She hurried to the registration desk, announced herself, and was surprised by the race official's excitement at having so renowned an athlete show up for the race. No, they had no record of her entry, but if she'd hurry and put on her number she could make it before the race started. She ran the race and won easily, finishing minutes ahead of the first male runner in second place.

Only after the race—when there was no envelope containing her sizable prize and performance money—did she confirm that the event she had run was not the race she'd been invited to. That race was being held several miles farther up the road in another town. She'd gone to the wrong starting line, run the wrong course, and missed her chance to win a valuable prize.[36] We all must run the right race. As the author of Hebrews exhorts us, we are to run with perseverance the race marked out for us with our eyes focused on Jesus (Heb. 12:1–2).

We thus need a vision established on the values of the priority of worship and service in all aspects of life. We must seek to develop a generation of students who can be agents of reconciliation to a fractious church in a hurting and broken world—resulting in reconciliation to God as well as to one another. Let us together run the race as we set forth the vision of building great Christian liberal arts universities established on the values of a commitment to the coherence of knowledge and God-revealed truth, flowing from our submission to the lordship of Christ, and exemplifying the Great Commandment in all we do.[37] I believe that a great commitment to the Great Commandment, its implications, and applications will bring about a great university, which can only be accomplished by God's grace and for his glory.

This address was given during the inauguration events of David S. Dockery as fifteenth president of Union University.

Chapter 2

A VISION FOR A
CHRISTIAN BAPTIST UNIVERSITY

JAMES T. DRAPER, JR.

During the harrowing years of the Civil War, the College of William and Mary emptied its buildings to supply young soldiers to the cause. In the early 1860s, no students sat in its classrooms, no professors lectured at its lecterns, no books circulated from its libraries, and no graduates were handed its diplomas. Indeed, the buildings fell into disrepair. The soaking rains dripped through unmaintained roofs, and the winter snow blew into its unrepaired buildings. The campus became like an academic ghost town. Gone were the happy voices of inquiring students; empty were the shaded walkways between the historic buildings. It looked as if it would never open its doors again.

Yet, every day of the war, President Ewing left his home and went to the college chapel. There he would take the rope in hand and ring the college bell loudly, defiantly, and belligerently in the face of the destruction that maimed the campus around him. The sound of that lonely bell echoed through empty buildings and across the abandoned countryside. It was the sound of confession and of hope—that the college would someday open again.

The South of the Civil War now rests 130 years and more behind us. Yet that act of faith and hope still rings across the tumultuous decades from so long ago. I want to take the rope of Baptist education in hand and ring another bell, a bell that peals out the message desperately needed in the American educational establishment: *a school may be Christian, Baptist, and confessional while maintaining the highest standards of intellectual pursuit.* This is a bell that must be rung.

Years ago a Catholic educator made the statement that Notre Dame was the greatest Catholic university in the nation. A cynical secularist made the comment, "A Catholic university is a contradiction in terms."

We would say today an "oxymoron." The cynic meant by his sarcastic statement that a school could not be intellectually respectable and have any relationship to a Christian confession.

This raises the question, Is it possible to be a university and be Baptist? Is it possible to be confessional and at the same time be professional as an academician, an administrator, an educator?

The bell I would ring at this solemn occasion peals out the same ringing answer: Yes! Yes! Yes! The great educational institutions of America have been rooted exclusively in the soil of Christianity. Harvard, Yale, Princeton, Brown, and the others all began because of the stimulus of Christian educational enterprise. They, in various degrees, fell away from that enterprise because the scandal of the cross falls over the educational enterprise as it does every enterprise entered into by Christians. There is no escaping the scandal of the cross in any arena of life, including the educational.

Paul wrote to the Corinthians, "We preach Christ crucified, to the Jews a stumbling block and to the Greeks foolishness . . ." (1 Cor. 1:23 NJKV). To those who sought empirical evidence, the cross was a scandal. To those who sought only intellectual sophistry, the cross was foolishness. To the educational establishment outside Christianity, this is the same today. The thought that the center of all truth is a dying Man on a cross two thousand years ago is an absolute scandal to the modern educational establishment.

How will we then react to the scandal of the cross? We can evade the scandal or we can embrace the scandal. As Christian educators, we embrace the scandal as the ultimate truth under which all other truths arrange themselves, even as servants bow before a king.

We Can Evade the Scandal of the Cross in Education

James Tunstead Burtchaell, author of *The Dying of the Light*, has done an amazing study of the more than two hundred denominational colleges and universities in the United States that have left their denominational roots and declared themselves independent of denominational control and trusteeship.[1] They used as a centerpiece of the study, as typical of all the rest, the departure of Vanderbilt University from its ties to the Southern Methodist Church. Little by little, the chancellors of Vanderbilt separated the school from Methodism.

According to Burtchaell, at first the leadership spoke of a generic commitment to an undefined Christianity. The next chancellor of the school tried to make it look more Methodist than it had ever looked before. Yet as soon as the generation of Methodists who opposed the separation passed from the scene, the school declared itself independent of any confessional stance. Burtchaell concluded that, as is typical in such situations, the third chancellor led the school to become a bastion of opposition to the very confessional message that its founders had embraced.

This sad story has been repeated with variations across the nation in the defection of denominational schools from the churches that birthed them, supported them, entrusted their students to them, and believed in them. Southern Baptists in their state colleges and universities have been no strangers to this defection.

Faithful Christians who left fortunes to those schools, endowed those schools, built buildings for those schools, and went to their graves believing those schools would forever be Christian schools have been betrayed by a generation that was embarrassed by the scandal of the cross!

We cannot evade or avoid the scandal of the cross in Christian higher education. We believe that the ultimate Truth of the universe centers in the incarnation, virgin birth, sinless life, substitutionary, vicarious death, and the triumphant resurrection of the Lord Jesus Christ. All truth is subservient to that Truth.

When academia enters into the presence of Jesus Christ, every discipline bows before him. The literature professor places every volume at his feet; the mathematician lays each equation on the altar before him; the biologist looks up from her microscope, and the astronomer looks away from his telescope to bow in the presence of the One who created both the macrocosm and the microcosm, everything great and everything small. From the single-celled paramecium under the microscope to the galaxy in the telescope, we acknowledge that Jesus Christ is the personal force holding all truth together.

Christian college presidents must never forget this. All the forces of the contemporary American academy fly in the face of this Christian commitment. To be forever skeptical, detached, analytical, doubtful, searching, cynical, and open is the watchword. To confess ultimate truth in the person of Jesus Christ is a scandal in the academy.

The challenge facing Christian college leaders is to lead their respective schools in such a way that whatever changes come in physics, there is no change in the primacy of Jesus Christ; whatever mutations there be in biology, there is no mutation in the lordship of

Jesus Christ; whatever declensions there may be in Latin and Greek, there is no declension in loyalty to the One who is Truth incarnate. We must not evade the scandal of the cross.

Burtchaell, in his famous study, noted that schools begin to leave their denominational roots when the denomination becomes a minority among the students and the faculty. This, too, is a scandal in the modern educational establishment. The cry is always for pluralism, diversity, inclusiveness without limit. Let us recognize this firmly: *for a school to serve Baptists, the school must be Baptist; across the evangelical world, for a school to serve Christians, the school must be Christian.*

Someone will object that there is no such thing as Christian chemistry, Christian geology, or Christian mathematics. It is true that H_2O is water for a Christian or a Muslim. But there most definitely is such a thing as a Christian teaching chemistry, a Christian teaching geology, and a Christian teaching mathematics. There can be a university of devoted Christians; moreover there can be a distinctively Christian university.

The late great T. B. Maston, a native of Tennessee, made a terrific distinction. He stated that *Christian* must always be a noun, never demoted to an adjective. For example, we read a great deal about Christian politicians, Christian coaches, or Christian schools. *Christian* should never be demoted to merely an adjective. There are political Christians, athletic Christians, and educational Christians, but the main word, the substantive word, is always *Christian.*

Let this university be not only a Christian university but also a university of Christians. That puts the weight, the substance where it belongs. In the patristic era, Tertullian cried out, "What hath Jerusalem to do with Athens?" He was decrying the influence of Greek intellectual idealism on the Christian message. Tertullian wanted to divorce the intellectual tradition from the Christian. *That is not the need of the present hour.*

Jerusalem must always be the priority, but Athens can serve Jerusalem; the intellectual must bow down before the ultimate. In the university of Baptist Christians, there is the singular great opportunity for Athens to be in the proper perspective to Jerusalem, the philosopher in the right relationship to the cross, the intellectual in the right relationship to the Truth.

We Can Embrace the Scandal of the Cross in Education

Far from rejecting the scandal of the cross in Christian education, we should embrace the scandal of the cross. The cross is the only adequate viewpoint from which to integrate the educational process. The Christian worldview is the ultimate worldview for the educator. Consider for a moment the inadequacy of other worldviews for the educational process. The atheistic view has never built a great university. Have you ever read, heard, or even thought of an atheistic university? To say it is absurd. Atheism never once built a great educational institution. Why? Atheism always leads to despair. There is no motive for the search, no impulse for the discovery in atheism. It cuts the nerve of endeavor and always leads to its philosophical twin, nihilism—the belief in nothing. Oxford and Cambridge were founded by Christians, not atheists. Harvard, Yale, Princeton, University of Chicago, and every other leading university in this nation were not founded by atheists.

You ask, "What of the state schools of the nation?" A curious thing has happened. In the earlier part of this century, the state universities recognized and welcomed the Christian spokesperson. Read the biography of George W. Truett. During his forty-seven-year ministry as pastor of the First Baptist Church of Dallas, there was scarcely a state university in the South that was not addressed by Dr. Truett. Only in postwar America have the theologian and pastor been banned from the campus of the state university. Implicit in all education is a foundational theistic belief.

Or consider the inadequacy of the other world religions for education. How many universities have been founded by Hindus and Muslims? Islam cannot claim an educational advantage. The fatalism that attaches to the Islamic faith cuts the nerve of educational endeavor. Let the smart be smart and the dumb be dumb; Allah wills it. By the tens of thousands, Muslims come to the universities of America that were born out of the Christian tradition. It is no accident that the impulse for education grew out of the Western Judeo-Christian educational tradition, not out of the passive fatalism and determinism of Islam. The cross has led the way in education, not the crescent.

Hinduism and the philosophies of eastern mysticism did not give birth to the educational movement. Eastern philosophy makes no distinction between the individual soul and the creation itself. In the pantheism of Hinduism and its allies, there is no world separate from the self to study. All is god, and god is all. Not a single discovery that has lifted the weight of the human race came out of that philosophy. Only in the Christian tradition that sees the creation as separate from the self, that sees humans as different from the rest of creation, has the opportunity for science and discovery arisen.

To put it bluntly, Pasteur would never have discovered microbes if he had seen no distinction between himself and a microbe. He would have looked into a mirror instead of a microscope. Only in the Christian tradition, which sees man in dominion over creation, have the discoveries in chemistry, physics, biology, genetics, medicine, and space travel taken place. What I am saying is a matter of history, not speculation. Only in those nations touched by and formed by the Christian tradition has education and its attendant discoveries won the day.

Why is this so? Truth exists in dialectic. In chemistry, the positive and negative charge make the atom. In mathematics, the positive and the negative number make the equation. In composition, the subject and the verb make the sentence. In philosophy, the thesis and the antithesis make the synthesis. In law, with its Socratic system, the question and the answer form the discipline. I could continue throughout every educational discipline. Human learning is shot through with the reality of the dialectic, the two sides, the positive and the negative poles of a magnet, the pull of gravitational force, and the push of centrifugal force. Why is this pattern so ingrained in truth in all its forms?

There is an answer. Jesus Christ is the demonstration. He is the God-Man. He lived by dying. He reigned by serving. He received glory by accepting humiliation. He offered a poverty that enriches, a mourning that comforts, a giving that receives, a stooping that rises, a hunger that fills, and a yoke that frees us. It is in that dialectic that you find truth. And Jesus is in the center of that dialectic. The Son of God becomes the Son of man; the King of the universe is judged by Pontius Pilate, and the Prince of Peace becomes the center of humanity's greatest controversy.

That is the basis for the University of Christians. In that university, you seek truth because you have already found it in Jesus Christ. In that university, you have freedom of thought because you have already submitted every thought captive to Jesus Christ as the ultimate truth. In that university, you study complexity because you have already found simplicity in Jesus Christ. In that university, you gain wisdom because you have embraced the foolishness of the cross. It is in embracing the scandal of the cross that you find the dignity of learning.

The greatest minds of the Western world have always confessed how little they actually know. So it will be with the scholar who is a Christian. One moment in the life beyond, and you will find that your most profound thought was like the thought of a child, your most significant discovery was like a little boy discovering an ant hill and knowing nothing of the mountains beyond it, like a little girl looking at a puddle of water and not knowing of the ocean.

Embrace the scandal of the cross. Herschel Hobbs, the Baptist theologian recently gone home to be with the Lord, noted that the cross is a plus sign. Whatever the academic discipline, the cross adds to that discipline. In one inaugural ceremony, the late and great president of the Foreign Mission Board of the Southern Baptist Convention, Baker James Cauthen, turned to the new president, and frail in body but lion-like in utterance, thundered the charge, "Lash the Board to the cross."

The same is true of the university. Embrace the scandal. Anchor every discipline to the cross of Christ. All truth is his truth. In that day when every knee shall bow and every tongue confess that Jesus Christ is Lord; every diploma will be thrown at his feet; every graduation will have been a preliminary to his coronation, and all knowledge shall focus on the Lord of all.

When the late and most famous theologian of this century, Karl Barth, visited the United States, a reporter asked him to state the most profound truth he knew. Expecting some incomprehensible truth that only a Continental scholar could even imagine, the reporter was shocked. Barth answered him, "Jesus loves me this I know, for the Bible tells me so." May that be our greatest wisdom as we lead great Christian universities to embrace the scandal of the cross.

This address was given as part of the inaugural events for David S. Dockery as fifteenth president of Union University.

Chapter 3

PRESERVING DISTINCTIVELY CHRISTIAN HIGHER EDUCATION

ROBERT B. SLOAN, JR.

It is good to be here with you—to be on this beautiful campus, to be with a sister institution, to be a part of such a significant conference on the future of Christian higher education, and to have this opportunity to participate in this event, which is a combination of worship and intellectual reflection.

The topic I have been given, the title of which is "Preserving Distinctively Christian Higher Education in the Twenty-First Century," is a topic that is near and dear to my heart because it is something that concerns me very deeply as the president of a Baptist, Christian institution. It is a topic that no doubt concerns the guests who are on your campus for this conference and certainly as well those constituencies who in the past created and in the present continue to support the cause of Christian higher education. George Marsden, in his book, *The Soul of the American University,* has chronicled the sad decline of Christian higher education.[1] It is a decline that really is, in many ways, staggering in its proportions. Consider the fact that about the time of the Civil War, some 95 percent of all college students in America attended private institutions, and the overwhelming bulk of those were Christian in their composition, mission, and makeup. By 1950, the ratio was about 50–50 private and public in the U.S. Today the relative proportions are something like 90–10 with respect to the numbers of college students who attend public institutions versus private institutions. Indeed, regarding that 10 percent in private universities, it is still another question to ask to what extent those private institutions maintain (if they ever had them) their historic commitments to the Christian faith. Thus, the questions we are addressing at this conference are of great relevance and indeed some urgency for institutions and their constituencies, which desire to remain faithful to their task of offering Christian higher education.

How do we then preserve "Distinctively Christian Higher Education in the Twenty-First Century"? I think I will approach this topic by subdividing the topic into two questions. One is the question, What is distinctively Christian higher education?[2] and the other is, What is a chief, or major, means for preserving it?

Christian higher education is one of those categories that people find very difficult to define. If you have ever been at a symposium such as this, or have ever addressed this question of definition in a seminar or classroom, you know how complicated and confusing the topic can quickly become. What do we mean when we refer to Christian higher education? With no doubt some oversimplification, I believe we can refer to at least six different ways in which the notion of Christian higher education has been employed. In describing these views, I want to offer what I believe to be the most comprehensive and most important definition for our purposes. One last introductory word: the frames of reference I will suggest are not exclusive; indeed, these domains often merge with, correlate to, and/or are subsumed by subsequent frames of reference.

1. When people refer to Christian higher education or when they refer to a Christian university, Christian school, or Christian institution, they sometimes are simply making reference to the *history and tradition* of that institution. It is, in fact, the case that some institutions today, which would not accept for themselves the most comprehensive definition that I will in the end give to Christian higher education, do nonetheless still refer to themselves in some sense as embodiments, or representatives, of Christian higher education. They do so simply because their history—their traditions, perhaps their founding documents, perhaps the intentions of their founders, perhaps the earliest dimensions of their history—acknowledges and affirms the Christian impulses that gave rise to their institution.

2. Sometimes when people refer to a Christian institution it may simply be a reference to the *composition of the governing Board.* Often it is the case—as at our institution and probably yours as well—that the governing board (whether they are called directors, trustees, or regents) must meet a religious qualification for membership. It is therefore possible to refer to a Christian institution by in some sense referring to this particular reli-

gious criterion with respect to the membership of the governing body.

3. Another frame of reference for Christian higher education is the *relationship the institution has to an ecclesiastical body*. To refer to a Christian school might for many people simply be a reference to a school that has some very close relationship to an ecclesiastical body or to some Christian denomination. There are, of course, schools whereby this relationship is extremely close. One thinks perhaps of Brigham Young University, where there is an enormous overlap between the governance of the university and the leadership of the Church of Jesus Christ of Latter Day Saints. Other church-related schools have much looser ties. At Baylor, for example, we speak of our "affiliation" with the Baptist General Convention of Texas, since the BGCT does not "own and operate" the university but does elect 25 percent of our regents.

There are a number of ways that this relationship to some ecclesiastical body gets fleshed out. Sometimes it has to do, as I have suggested already, with a significant overlap between church leadership and the school's leadership; sometimes it has to do with financial ownership. There are some institutions where it is very clear, or at least it is clearly argued, that a given denomination owns the institution. I know that in Texas this is a particularly difficult legal question, simply because of Texas law. Can one 501(c)(3) own another 501(c)(3)? The answer according to Texas law is, in fact, no, but therein lies another story or two.

4. We often refer to a Christian institution—and this is, I think, as a habit of speech, one of the most commonly heard ways that people refer to Christian education or Christian institutions—by reference to what is called the *atmosphere* or the *environment* of the institution. That is, sometimes people simply say: "Well, it is the *way* we do what we do. It is our *attitude* in terms of how we do what we do." It may be embodied in the values that we hold. Perhaps it is embodied in the way we relate to one another, the way we treat students, the way we handle discipline problems, or the way we have certain curfew rules or certain dress codes. In sum, this view focuses upon the moral-relational dimensions of the university as a community but does not necessarily include other issues related to the

worldview and/or the intellectual content of Christianity as a basis or resource for understanding and conveying the academic dimensions of the university experience. In certain contexts where these issues are relevant, the very word *academics* is indeed sometimes so defined as to exclude religious intellectual content.

5. Another way to think of a Christian institution is in terms of its Christian or religious *activities*. I suppose this reference point could be the social definition of a Christian institution. A Christian institution or a church-related institution may well have chapel services. It will have religious organizations on campus. It may well have some form of a Religious Emphasis Week or maybe an annual or semesterly revival. It allows and permits these extracurricular activities of a Christian nature. It might even encourage them. Is that what we mean when we say we are a Christian institution?

6. A sixth frame of reference or way of referring to Christian higher education has to do with the *curriculum*. Namely, there are certain clearly identified subject areas that point to our Christian identity. In our case, with some few exceptions, we have two required religion courses. Typically, our students take a three-hour Old Testament survey course and a three-hour New Testament survey course, though the requirement can be met in other ways. Whatever the details, we have within the framework of our required curriculum some sort of requirement which could argue that we are in this sense a Christian institution.

What I would like to argue is that all these frames of reference are legitimate. They are valid points of reference with respect to Christian higher education. Nonetheless, I would maintain that something that could be called distinctively Christian higher education requires more than this. Thus far, the first six frames of reference would allow, though not necessarily require, what Douglas Sloan refers to as the two-sphere theory of truth.[3]

The two-sphere theory of truth, I think, is one of the great intellectual myths of the twentieth century. It supports the notion that you can separate academics and faith. It argues that you can separate (or I'll use other terminology) faith and learning. It presumes that the real work of the university is something that all universities do, and these

Christian schools somehow do something else. The implicit argument is that maybe they do not do it very well.

In fact, Leslie Waggener, a professor from the University of Texas at the end of the nineteenth century and the very beginning of the twentieth century, delivered a series of lectures in various public venues in the state of Texas arguing that real education involves the ability with complete objectivity and neutrality to pursue the truth.[4] He argued that the religious schools (like Baylor) had done a good service to the state of Texas by originally establishing schools but that it was very clear that religious schools, Christian schools, could not have an objective, neutral point of view. He maintained that Christian schools had certain biases and precommitments and were committed to the core convictions of the Christian faith. Therefore, by definition, Christian schools could not possibly hope to pursue the goals of a true university.

Naturally, some Baylor administrators and others felt obliged to answer that charge. I will not bore you with the answer except to say that it had something to do with the character of the human being. The president of Baylor at the time, Samuel Palmer Brooks, among others, argued that the real character of humanity demands a kind of education that corresponds to the way people really are. To paraphrase Brooks' response, he argued that as long as human beings have some religious dimension, or as he said, "as long as man remains an essentially religious being," there ought to be some form of education that corresponds to the kind of people we are. If you will allow me to elaborate his argument, it seems to me very artificial for there to be any kind of education that synthetically, or artificially, brackets off the various pursuits of truth.

It is true that in university life, under the cultural and intellectual aegis of the scientific revolution, the Enlightenment, the industrial revolution, and now the computer revolution, we have created disciplines and subdisciplines, which by their very nature have attempted to control as many mysterious and subjective factors as possible, so that we can focus on other dimensions of our research. However, we forget that it is entirely artificial to pursue truth only in that way. Bracketing off mystery, and ultimately God, can only be, if ever, a temporary and methodological exercise. In fact, as long as we never forget that the creation is as complex as it is, as long as we remember that nature, societies, and human beings are as complex (and mysterious!) as they are, then surely we need institutions, which in terms of both method and content, are open to the pursuit of truth in all of its multifaceted splen-

dor. The relationship between spirit (God is spirit) and matter is neither a new nor an irrelevant question.

Thus, I would argue that Christian education is something more
than the six frames of reference cited above. It is more than merely the
atmosphere of our institutions, our history, our founding documents,
or our relationship to ecclesiastical bodies. It is more than chapel or
even Bible and theology courses. Christian education comes ultimately into every classroom. It involves our worldview; it involves how we
think and how we live. It involves not only how we teach and how we
live, but it also involves what we teach. It involves the very substance
of our intellectual pursuits.

Of course, there are objections to this view. As always, the rather
obvious observation and series of questions immediately follow this
line: "Well, that cannot possibly be true. I understand how that works
in the religion class or even somewhat in a literature class. In those
areas you could have Christian interests and pursuits, but is there a
Christian mathematics? Is there a Christian biology? a Christian chemistry?" To be sure, given our artificial separation into disciplines and
boundaries, it is oftentimes difficult to see the connection. There are
many things we do in common as scholars, whether Christians or non-
Christians. The fact is, however, or it seems to me at any rate, that there
is a legitimate sphere of inquiry where mathematicians or physicists,
chemists or biologists, literature professors or sociologists, the theologians or historians can and should ask larger questions about the presuppositions of our disciplines, about order and the existence of order,
and about transcendence and meaning. All of our disciplines, it seems
to me—though for some it is "farther back" than for others—can
engage these macroquestions of transcendence, meaning, knowledge,
and the ways of knowing.

Of course, the objections are many. Often the question is, Well, if
there is Christian biology, tell me what it would be. David Solomon of
Notre Dame calls this type of objection the "Heap Fallacy."[5] It is the
attempt to say something does not exist simply because you cannot
declare in detail precisely what the character and nature of it is. What
is a heap? Can you tell me what a heap of sand is? How many grains
are there in a heap? You do not know? Then there is not a heap. But
just because you cannot precisely tell me how many grains there are in
a heap does not mean the heap is not there. This fallacy is an attempt
to confuse by pressing for the details. No one should suggest that the

answers to such worldview questions are easy, but we should object whenever the question is disallowed.

Sometimes the political objection is raised. Are you sure you really want religion intruding in the classroom? Remember Galileo? Remember the church's habit of oppressing freedom and free thinking? Sad to say, but that is the truth. It is the case that religious institutions have, at times, been afraid of the truth. There is no doubt that ecclesiastical institutions have placed handcuffs on thinkers and researchers, and scientists and others have suffered in the past from an overweening concern by ecclesiastical entities.

Is it really something intrinsic to religious identity that religious authorities have suppressed and oppressed, or is it simply something that is part of human nature? Let me put it another way. Is it not also the case that secular forces, irreligious and nonreligious, have likewise placed handcuffs on people and have likewise attempted through political means to suppress the pursuit of truth? It is an objection that has a certain amount of historical merit, but it has no necessary merit to say, "Are you not afraid that religion will suppress the search for truth?" Yes, it could be, and I am also afraid that irreligious people and secular authorities suppress truth. I am afraid of the fact, as you see very commonly today, that there are increasingly more and more arenas in which you are not permitted to ask certain questions.

At Baylor I have witnessed any number of occasions where faculty members who have taught in state institutions have come to our institution and have made the remarkable assertion that there is more freedom on our campus to ask questions, to have discussions with students, and to pursue certain research projects than they found at their state institutions. How is it possible—consider the absurdity of it for a moment—that we could ever have something called a university or school, whereby a child, a student, a teacher, or any other honest inquirer could be told, "I am sorry, we do not discuss that here"?

How about the deepest questions of meaning and transcendence, of faith, of life's purpose, or questions like who is Jesus Christ, or who was Gautama Buddha? What is the significance of the religion of Islam, not only sociologically, but what are its philosophical and theological roots? What are the implications of the now current clash of cultures in terms of Christian worldviews and the religion of Islam, and how have their associated societies played themselves out in terms of various human freedoms, democracy, and cultural attainments? What are the implications of the varying worldviews?[6] What about my own desires as an individual to have peace with God, to know God, to live in relationship with people around me, and to have a meaningful marriage and a happy family? Are these not real questions that impinge deeply on the profoundest depths and dimensions of a person's existence? Should we have schools and institutions that say, "I am sorry; we do not talk about things like that here?" Between one institution that is not afraid to ask any question, including religious questions, and another institution that says, "We do not ask religious questions here," which has a greater freedom? Where is there greater openness?

At Christian schools we must believe that there is an underlying unity of truth.[7] We must refuse to separate religion and life. We must refuse to separate the question of meaning from the total academic pursuit of the truth. We must speak about the whole universe, with all of its social and natural orders, in relationship to the total person. Christian higher education is nothing less than the attempt through the individual and communal activities of thinking, teaching, researching, discussing, performing, and living to understand the totality of life, history, and the universe in relationship to the lordship of the crucified and risen Jesus Christ.

Ephesians 1 has the longest sentence in the Greek New Testament. It runs from verse 1 through verse 14. However, it has as its climactic statement, in verse 10, this notion that the entire cosmos, things in heaven and things on earth, will be summed up in Christ. Ephesians speaks powerfully about reconciliation and its counterpoint, brokenness. It talks about broken relationships between Jew and Gentile, about brokenness within the church and how, through Christ, both groups were brought together in the new creation. Ultimately, this brokenness in the cosmos, which involves thrones and principalities, rulers and dominions, and the visible and invisible spheres, will one day be, and in a sense already has been, finally and fully reconciled in and through Jesus Christ.

Now that is a theological proposition that creates a mandate, or at least a frame of reference, for the operation of Christian schools and Christian higher education. No question, it seems to me, should be off-limits in a Christian school. We should reject the dominant myths of the twentieth century that argue and/or assume that academic pursuits can somehow be easily bracketed from questions of meaning and transcendence. We must reject these twentieth-century intellectual myths that suggest that religion is merely subjective and emotional, that values are purely social convictions and/or individual options. Once you accept the proposition that the one true and living God has entered human history to redeem, reveal, and ultimately to recreate the heavens and the earth through Jesus Christ, you cannot seek the safety of hiding behind a neatly bracketed-off academic discipline. The Christian academic enterprise is somehow to understand this world in which we live, including ourselves and all that the word _world_ means, socially, naturally, psychologically, and spiritually, within the framework of our commitment to the lordship of the crucified and risen Jesus Christ.

My title demands that I press on to the second question posed in the introduction. How do we preserve these values? How do we preserve Christian higher education? There are many answers to these questions. No doubt there are methods that would correspond to all the seven frames of reference I have given in terms of history, founding documents, relationship to ecclesiastical bodies, and so on. And James Burtchaell is rightly very concerned that Christian institutions maintain relationships with ecclesiastical bodies.[8] I agree. Nonetheless, if I were to offer only one (there are many) proposition for how to preserve distinctively Christian higher education, or how to preserve the character of a distinctively Christian institution, I would maintain that it is through the faculty of that institution.

The faculty members of an institution carry the intellectual freight. The faculty members carry the traditions of learning, which they have received and seek to bring forward. Do not misunderstand me; the composition of the student body is very significant, and it is in the unique relationship between faculty member and student that the work of the university takes place. Nonetheless, however much we may rightly speak today of the "community of scholars," which includes faculty and students working side by side in collaborative research and thought, the fact remains that positing (rightly) faculty and students as social equals does not obliterate the distinctions between faculty and students. A greater accountability and leadership is required of faculty by virtue of their broader and deeper intellectual and disciplinary experience. Thus, to preserve distinctively Christian higher education, there must be at any Christian institution a critical mass of faculty members who are committed to the proposition of Christian higher education. It is precisely at the point of faculty selection that the two-sphere theory, which Douglas Sloan referred to, emerges in practical application. We all know what happens. You put an ad in _The Chronicle,_ and you say you are an affiliated Christian institution of some sort, and then you get the resumés. Here, the process gets difficult because the tug-of-war between "religious" qualifications and "academic" qualifications are, at best, often separated; at worst, they are treated like a zero sum game. It is very important for the institution—or search committee—to ask, "What are we looking for?" I am convinced that institutions often make one of two errors, and they both depend upon the mortifying assumption that somehow "academics" and "religion" can be bracketed off from each other.

On the one hand, you can simply look for good Christians, people who are sincere in their confession and have Christian values in terms of morals and behavior. After finding those people that, by all the signs of Christian grace, exemplify the fruit of the Spirit and so on, you say, "By the way, can any of you teach Spanish? Is there anybody here who could teach geology for us?" Or, on the other hand, you could make the equal and opposite error. You could look for all the best Spanish teachers in the world, if that is the position you are trying to fill, and then you could say, "By the way, now that we have got this list pared down, do any of you have any interest in religion?"

Both of these approaches constitute serious mistakes because there is a total complex of qualifications with respect to what it means to be a Christian faculty member; and it is this optimizing, realistic complex of artificially discrete domains that is the object of your search. Richard John Neuhaus[9] spoke at my inauguration in a symposium on Christian higher education a couple of years ago. What he and Gertrude Himmelfarb, who was also present, had to say was reprinted in *First Things* a few months thereafter, in early 1996. I encourage you to read these articles if you have not. Neuhaus, in his succinct and brilliant presentation, offered a number of theses, but I am thinking now of the first, which asserted the proposition that "there is no such thing as a university pure and simple."

What he meant by that thesis, among other things, is that we often assume in practice that we know what a "real" university is. The hidden implication is that religious schools involve some sort of "add-on," or worse, something that is rather eccentric or different. Such a popular assumption is very mistaken, for every university has a perspective, a character, and a set of values that drive it. This situation is true for every university. The question is not, Do you have values, perspective, and a point of view? but, What are the values, the perspective, the points of view?

I would offer a corollary to Neuhaus' thesis that there is no such thing as a university pure and simple. My corollary is, "There is no such thing as a professor pure and simple." There is no such thing as someone who is "academically qualified" to teach at a Christian school, of whom, as something of a traditional afterthought, we will ask, "By the way, do you go to church?" or, "Do you have anything against religion?" Just as life is complex, just as the personality is complex, just as every student is so complex that he or she requires the right to be taught from a full-orbed perspective with respect to the totality of truth and has the right to ask any kind of question that he or she, as a religious being and as a human being, can bring forth, so it is the case that universities and professors are complex and distinctive. They are not all the same. Professors have perspectives and points of view. To refer to an individual's "academic qualifications," as if such issues did not interact with other issues related to values, origin, and ideology, is naive. Indeed, part of the total constellation of what it means to be "academically qualified to teach at a Christian institution of higher learning" involves our commitment to the lordship of the crucified and risen Jesus Christ.

Do not mistake my call for a common commitment to the sovereign status of the crucified and risen Jesus Christ to be a call for homogeneity at every point. There ought to be a lot of diversity on all of our campuses. I think there are reasons for diversity within a Christian school, which involve both our own understanding of the composition of the church and of the new creation. In Ephesians 2, very diverse peoples are being brought together in Christ. Unlike 2 Corinthians 4, the "new self" in Ephesians 2 is not the individual Christian created new; it is the church that is the new person, the new creation, the new self. I think it pervades all that we confess biblically—our belief about the new heaven, the new earth, and the new creation—that there is no more Jew nor Gentile, bond nor free, male nor female; we are one in Christ. That oneness is still being realized, however—indeed it is an eschatological oneness that allows us here and now to turn away from our tribal prejudices and not to fear the diversities we all embody. I think there is also, perhaps, ample reason to think that ethnic, social, geographic, and economic diversity (though there probably ought to be more hard-nosed empirical study of this point) may well be a significant dimension to the learning experience itself, since learning invariably involves a "rub," that is, some level of conflict that demands discussion, if not resolution. Indeed, I would say there is another reason we cannot embrace simplistic homogeneity, that is, while "multicul-turalism" might be an ideological option, the existence of ethnic, reli-gious, and racial pluralism is a fact, a fact with which we must honest-ly deal.

In conclusion, I would say that there is still something called dis-tinctively Christian higher education, and it reaches even, and espe-cially, into the classroom, into how we think, how we perform artisti-cally, what and how we discuss, research, and teach. And, again, it is the faculty members who carry the primary load of discovering, pre-senting, articulating, synthesizing, and applying the Christian intellec-tual traditions. Therefore, to the end of preserving distinctively Christian higher education in the twenty-first century, there is no more significant enterprise for the Christian institution than the cultivation, development, and continuing enrichment of a Christian faculty.

This address was given during the Conference on the Future of Christian Higher Education at Union Univeristy.

Chapter 4

ENVISIONING THE FUTURE
OF THE CHRISTIAN UNIVERSITY

KAREN A. LONGMAN

"Thanks be to God, who always leads us in triumphal procession in Christ and through us spreads everywhere the fragrance of the knowledge of him. For we are to God the aroma of Christ among those who are being saved and those who are perishing" (2 Cor. 2:14). As we envision the future of Christian higher education, this verse from 2 Corinthians reflects my vision of reclaiming the mind of Christ in the academy, becoming places where our best scholars find freedom and fulfillment in equipping tens of thousands of students each year to be "the fragrance of Christ," making a difference for him in our world.

The Future of Christian Higher Education is our general theme. There are a lot of ways to take a cut at that topic:

- We could look at the *pressures* facing higher education in general, and private higher education in particular, and spin out ideas about our own sector. When we think about the pressures we face, what would be at the top of your list?

- *What about changing demographics?* In the 1960s, 50 percent of America's college students were attending private institutions. Thirty years later, in the early 1990s, that percentage had dropped to 17 percent. And almost 40 percent of those students were of nontraditional age. The bottom line? Private higher education is never going back to what *we* knew it to be.

- *What about rising costs?* How soon will we max out what families are willing to pay, even if they do see college as an investment? How do we respond to the fact that since 1981 tuition costs have risen at *triple* the median household income? That's 234 percent as compared to 82 percent. And here's a new wrinkle for Christian colleges: What will be the impact of a million newly energized Promise Keepers hearing Coach McCartney telling them to be out of debt by the year 2000? Are they going to choose to pay for a private college education?

- *What about the implications of technology?* Why *are* costs in higher education rising so fast? Some Christian colleges are putting millions of dollars into technology, which the students are *now expecting!* What does it mean that last year in the U.S., for the first time, more *computers* were sold than television sets? What does it mean that 50 million people are now using the Web? What are the implications of ten thousand college courses being offered on-line today?

- *What about the relevance of our "brand" of education?* There's a new phenomenon in higher education: "just in time" learning. People aren't interested in sitting in classes for four or five years studying Spanish and physics—academic disciplines they may think they'll never use. We try to make the case for a liberal arts approach to education. But *Change* magazine reported last spring that hardly anybody understands the idea of the "liberal arts." Only 27 percent of the parents and 14 percent of high school students were familiar with the concept. People think they need skills to find jobs or to keep the jobs they have. Last year 39 million people were involved in educational programs related to their work.

These are big pressures, and there are a lot more: federal funding, "administrative bloat," accountability, affirmative action, tenure, retention, and leadership. Any one of these could be the topic for an entire volume. But that's not the direction I've been asked to take. Instead, I have the pleasant assignment of dreaming about the future of the Christian university.

Abraham Kuyper, the Dutch theologian, gave us a vision of reclaiming *every* square inch, every "thumbprint" of God's creation, for the kingdom. Christian colleges ought to be the "holy of holies" for that action in the arena of higher education. What *could* our sector of private higher education—realistically—bring to an academy and a world that is falling apart around us?

The first thing that popped into my mind when I began thinking about this essay was a man, respected by people across Christian higher education and loved by many. That man is Arthur Holmes, who recently retired after teaching and chairing the philosophy department at Wheaton College for almost fifty years.

Dr. Holmes is one of the "master teachers" who helps us each summer with the CCCU's new faculty workshop. On the last evening of that five-day program, Arthur gives his testimonial. Why did a first-rate scholar like this, who could have taught in any number of settings, decide to invest his life in Christian higher education?

Arthur paints a picture for these new faculty, beginning with a chapel talk he presented at Wheaton College just a few years after Martin Luther King, Jr, gave his famous "I Have a Dream" speech. Dreams that energize people and capture their imaginations. Arthur entitled that chapel talk, "I, Too, Have a Dream." He told those students—and now tells these new faculty—"I dreamed out loud of _a hundred_ of our philosophy graduates going on to the _best_ graduate schools in the country, going from there to teach, strategically located in Christian universities as well as Christian colleges, shaping the course of Christian thought and influencing the course of history."

In that chapel address, Arthur extended the dream to talk of those who go into other callings and professions, those from other majors and other Christian colleges. He dreamed that dream and gave those students his vision for what the philosophy department at Wheaton College could offer to the world. He couldn't be everywhere, but he could multiply himself in the lives of others. Some of those students picked up on that vision, began to call it the "Holmes' Hundred," and were excited to watch it unfold and to be a part of it.

I've asked Arthur from time to time whether that goal of one hundred was reached. He says he didn't want to commit David's sin of "counting the people." But I know that several years ago he was nominated as professor of the year for the State of Illinois (the CASE award), and the number of Wheaton College graduates with Ph.D's in philosophy and teaching in colleges and universities around the world was nearing ninety.

If you know Arthur Holmes, you know that his life does bear the "fragrance of Christ"—a man who loves the Lord with his heart, soul, and _mind_. It's that kind of person, that kind of dream, multiplied in other faculty and in other disciplines, student development staffs, and campus ministries, that is going to change our world for Christ.

Thinking about the dream that God gave to Arthur Holmes, I want to ask, What could we be? What does God want us to be? What might we offer if we catch a vision that takes us beyond our current realities? To do that, I want to think about this business of "dreaming" from the perspective of our students. That's a novel idea, isn't it? To think about the students we serve.

What kinds of students *are* coming to our campuses? The ninety-four member institutions of the Council are reaching 175,000 students every year. These are academically solid students. They have *higher* high school GPAs than students who enter private colleges in general or those in the national norms generated by Sandy Astin's research at UCLA.[1]

Why do they come? Several years ago we worked on a project that interviewed sixteen hundred students at various stages of the "admissions funnel": four hundred prospects from the ACT pool; four hundred "inquirers" who had never followed that up by applying to any CCCU institution; four hundred "applicants" who did not matriculate; and four hundred students who began their freshman year as matriculants on our campuses. We wanted to know what college-bound students thought about this thing called a "Christian liberal arts education"—what factors caused them to pursue it or caused them to opt out.

What we found was that one particular question in the interview cleanly divided those in the prospect pool who matriculated and those who did not. What was that one question? *On average, how many times are you in church in a given week?* "More than once a week" was the response given by 87 percent of the matriculants. Dr. Jack Maguire, the theoretical physicist who oversaw the project, told us later that in all of his years of research he had never seen *one question* so clearly define the pool of students we should be going after. And what happened when the following question was added? *Is a Christian atmosphere on campus important to you?* A full 96 percent of those who would move from the college-bound prospect pool to the matriculant pool on our campuses answered "yes" to both questions.

Here's another dimension: that same research project asked students in all four pools what they considered to be the most important aspects of campus life as they made decisions about which college to attend. Across the board, the quality of faculty was ranked first by the students who were interviewed.

What does all this have to do with envisioning our future? Students who pursue a Christian liberal arts education care about "the life of the mind" *and* "the life of the spirit." Campuses like ours are the best place for these two to merge. When we finished that project, Jack Maguire talked with us about trends in American culture and the distinctives of our colleges. His sense, as a Roman Catholic, was that these colleges had the potential to create a collective identity, something like the mystique of the Jesuit colleges, that would click into people's minds when they heard the term _Christian college._

The Jesuit schools are not the only institutions of higher learning that have a unique identity. Individual colleges have also kept themselves on the map of higher education by sharpening their distinctives. When you hear Hillsdale College or Middlebury College, what comes to mind? These are private institutions that students select because they know they'll get a solid liberal arts education with a distinctive perspective. How could Christian colleges, like the Jesuits, like Middlebury, better position themselves to offer something truly distinctive?

I think the key lies in the phrase often used by Christ-centered colleges and universities: "communities of Christian scholarship." The brighter our distinctiveness shines as thoughtful _Christian_ institutions, the more we'll have to offer to a world that is searching for truth and spiritual vitality. I hasten to add that there's great hope for this. Based on the data being gathered from the CCCU's Collaborative Assessment Project, the "spiritual indicators" for our faculty are pretty impressive. Some 99.4 percent say they have a personal, meaningful relationship with God; 96.6 percent say that their day-to-day life is affected by their relationship with God; 98.1 percent say that they encourage students to consider new insights related to their faith. Students, too, are highly engaged spiritually (see table at the end of this chapter).

But we also need to focus on the word _communities._ I heard George Barna speak a few weeks ago about the different perceptions of various generations: boomers, busters, builders, and seniors. Today's college-age students, he said, are motivated by two things: (1) relationships and connectedness, and (2) investing themselves in pressing causes they believe in. Our campuses need to be places where students develop meaningful relationships and experience community, especially given the fragmented nature of life in general.

Finally, we need to take seriously the word _scholarship._ We have the potential to help students understand what it means to love the Lord with all of their _minds;_ to reclaim the idea of having the mind of Christ across every academic discipline and in every area of life.

Let's consider five dreams that I think are doable and could make Christian higher education shine more brightly in the mosaic of American higher education.

Helping Students Succeed

What if Christian colleges became known as places committed to helping every incoming student succeed? By that I mean to succeed in achieving what we say a Christian liberal arts education is all about. David Winter, president of Westmont College, has emphasized in recent years how important it is that education be understood as much more than the transfer of knowledge or information "content." That's a part of education, yes. But he outlines three other areas where Christian colleges have the potential to shine. In addition to content, one of those areas is character development. Another is the development of "competencies." The fourth is in creating global "citizens." It's in the combination of these four areas that Christian liberal arts colleges have a powerful package to offer incoming students.

What if Christian colleges, as part of that package, became known as places that seek to ensure that every entering student graduates, having experienced success in these four areas? When I was in graduate school at the University of Michigan, I chose as my major professor a man who had a reputation for toughness but also for getting students through the dissertation process. I knew I'd probably work harder because his standards were high, but I also knew that if he agreed to serve as my committee chair he would make sure that I would *finish* (and that's worth a lot in a doctoral program).

There's a statistic that concerns me about higher education. The fact is that only 46 percent of those students who begin a college education actually finish, anywhere, ever. Christian colleges are doing slightly worse than the national average. Obviously, some of those students *shouldn't* finish; in fact, they shouldn't have started. But the majority start with great enthusiasm, optimistic about what a college education can contribute to their future.

My major professor in graduate school had a reputation for helping students succeed. How could a *college* work at tapping the enthusiasm and the optimism of incoming students to help them move from their first day on campus toward graduation so they'll be prepared to go out and make a significant contribution in our world?

Here's the question from the other perspective: _What's the toll on the human spirit_ and the lost contribution of talent to our world and the kingdom from that 54 percent who don't make it, who drop out, who feel like they never fit in the college environment? These are people who go through life having given up, perhaps feeling like failures, in one of the most significant undertakings of life. Yet, retention experts tell us that most of them aren't quitting because they can't do the work. They're usually quitting because classes are boring or because they feel that nobody cares; they aren't motivated; they say the educational experience isn't worth their investment.

Let's dream about an alternative to this scenario. This fall we began a Collaborative "Quality/Retention" Project. One of the consultants to this project is Dr. Chip Anderson, a psychologist at UCLA who, as a Christian, believes that Christian liberal arts campuses should have the strongest retention rates in the country because these can be places where students are encouraged and helped to come "alive"—_intellectually, emotionally, spiritually, and relationally_.

This desire to "be alive," to experience life fully in all of its dimensions, can be one of the great motivators for the college experience. Dr. Anderson talks about four traditional approaches to retention, then develops what he calls a _spiritual_ approach. He writes: "A spiritual approach to student retention purposely addresses the most basic and most powerful motivation of all: The drive to be alive and to experience a sense of personal aliveness. Aliveness is experienced as: enthusiasm, being inspired, optimism, growth, development, increased courage, increased hope, and a feeling of joy and gratitude for being connected to something that transcends. . . ."[2]

His thesis is that people get involved with counterproductive behavior, like the binge drinking that has killed students at MIT and LSU this fall, because they are looking for ways to experience "life." So one aspect of the CCCU's Quality/Retention Project is to help our campuses consider this "spiritual approach" to retention, in which students, as part of being in a "community of Christian scholarship," are surrounded by people who are also involved in this pilgrimage of seeking to be fully alive, intellectually, emotionally, relationally, and spiritually.

As I thought about this, I was reminded about a similar vision that was painted for our chief academic officers last spring by Dr. Dallas Willard, a professor of philosophy at USC. He was working on the topic of joy and described the role of faculty in Christian colleges as helping our students become better "lovers"—to love the Lord with all of our minds. "Full joy comes from loving a lot," Dr. Willard said.[3] He referred to a talk that he had given to the School of Education at USC in which he said that the most important thing about education was to help people to learn to love the right things. And then he developed that concept by talking about "Learning to love numbers and equations, and continents and demographics, and art history." Students get excited about learning and knowing and creating because they're around faculty who are alive intellectually. "If you want to get a mind that is alive and growing and never going to stop, instill in students *love* and the joy that comes from loving," Dr. Willard concluded.

Think about the potential of Christian liberal arts colleges to be distinctive in the education they're offering—to help students feel like they're coming alive intellectually, relationally, emotionally and spiritually. Chip Anderson asks:

- What student would want to leave a college environment that is alive with vibrant, growing, developing people?
- What student would want to leave a campus where people take a keen personal interest in the student and in how to help that student become more fully alive?
- What student would want to leave a college in which faculty and administrators are alive and are committed to creating enlivening experiences for students?

Affirming Giftedness

What if Christian colleges were known as places that intentionally focused on helping students figure out how they are gifted, on what their strengths are, on what they could contribute to the world? If any sector of higher education ought to resonate with that idea, it should be Christian liberal arts institutions. That could be one of our hallmarks.

I think of the man who is now director of pediatric neurosurgery at Johns Hopkins Hospital, a wonderful African-American named Dr. Benjamin Carson. He was the main speaker at this past year's National Prayer Breakfast in Washington, D.C. He began his talk this way:

> I always wanted to be a missionary doctor. I harbored that dream
> from the time I was eight years old until I was thirteen, at which time,
> having grown up in dire poverty, I decided I'd rather be rich. So at
> that point, missionary doctor was out, and I decided I wanted to be a

psychiatrist. On television they seemed like very rich people. They live in big fancy mansions, drive Jaguars, have big plush offices, and all they have to do is talk to crazy people. It seemed like I was doing that anyway, so I said, "This should work out quite well," and started reading *Psychology Today*. I was the local shrink. I majored in psychology in college, did advanced psych when I went to medical school.

Then I discovered that I wasn't going to be a psychiatrist and had to stop and ask myself, "What are you really good at?" I discovered I had a lot of eye-hand coordination, the ability to think in three dimensions. I was a very careful person, never knocked things over and said "oops," and I enjoyed the brain. So I put all that together, and that's how I came up with neurosurgery.

When I think about what *could* set Christian colleges apart from the pack, I think about the enormous impact it would make on higher education and on the world if all students at Christian colleges went through a battery of tests and spent the freshman year in a situation where faculty advisors and student development staffs helped them identify their areas of giftedness . . . and then moved them toward an academic major that fits who they are. The whole area of academic advising, by the way, is the area most in need of bolstering, according to recent research we have done.

Parenthetically, this idea of identifying gifts and strengths seems to be especially important for female students on Christian college campuses. And it is important to note that 60 percent of the students on our CCCU campuses are female, whereas only 30 percent of the faculty are. The tables at the end of this chapter reflect data from the CCCU's Collaborative Assessment Project, which began with baseline data on 10,500 of our incoming freshmen in the fall of 1994. While our incoming female students have, on average, considerably stronger academic records than our male students, they are much less likely to rate themselves as above average in several key areas, including intellectual self-confidence, mathematical ability, and social self-confidence.

Last winter several of us spent a day with Don Clifton, founder of SRI (Selection Research, Inc.), the group that bought Gallup. SRI has worked with more than one thousand client organizations to help them identify what makes people "the best" in different professions. By interviewing those who are at the top of their fields, certain patterns emerge. Good ice hockey players, for example, literally watch the puck move in slow motion because their eye "locks in" fifty times a second. Most of us have eyes that would lock in on a puck about twelve times a second. So, when Wayne Gretzky was asked to describe his strategy for success, he said, "I skate to where the puck is going to be." That's a great principle for life, but most of us don't have the eye for it!

Similarly, Don Clifton would say that the best teachers tend to have certain traits in common. They're always thinking about the interests of individual students, for example. So, if an elementary school teacher visits Disneyland, that teacher is thinking about the student who loves dinosaurs or trains and is watching for opportunities to pick up things that would stimulate and encourage those interests. The theory, and it seems to work, is that key interview questions can be developed that help to identify people who are naturally gifted to be "the best" in given fields. Don Clifton wrote the book *Soar with Your Strengths*. He says that our world would be a lot better off if we spent more energy identifying and affirming the unique giftedness that every individual has, freeing each person to make a contribution.[4]

If any sector of higher education ought to be receptive to the idea that every individual has been gifted by God and is equipped to make a unique contribution to our world, it should be Christian colleges. I think of Berea College and College of the Ozarks, colleges that have a reputation in higher education for giving each student work experience in lieu of paying tuition. Wouldn't it be something if Christian colleges as a movement had a reputation for taking the students who walk in our doors and, within a year, doing significant work to help them identify their strengths and move toward an appropriate major?

Opening Up the World

What if Christian colleges were known as places that opened up the world for our incoming students? Based on what I'm hearing from our campuses, I wonder if we could be moving toward the day when every student coming into a Christian liberal arts campus will know that they'll be involved with at least one significant cross-cultural experience during their college years. Goshen College, a Mennonite school in Indiana, has been doing this for years. Students choose to attend Goshen because of that distinctive.

Why is it so important to give our students exposure to the world? I think about what we're learning from the CCCU's assessment project as we track what happens to students during the four years of a traditional, undergraduate education. Most of our students (about 75 percent), coming in as freshmen, could be identified as "foreclosed"—that's one of four "identity formation" statuses in the work of psychologist James Marcia. They can't really articulate _why_ they believe what they say they believe; they don't really "own" their own beliefs.

If graduates of our colleges are going to go out into the world with the kind of full-orbed faith that prepares them for the complexities of life, they need to move from this "foreclosed" status toward what Marcia calls "identity achievement."[5] And Marcia would say that the way this usually happens is for individuals to go through some kind of a "crisis"—a period in which something causes them to think deeply about how they view life—coming through it to _own_ their beliefs more personally and deeply. The hard reality is that students typically don't move from "foreclosure" toward "identity achievement" simply by growing four years older within the confines of their comfort zones.

Sharon Parks, who spent twenty years at Harvard and is best known for her book _The Critical Years,_ which looks at the college experience, has recently coauthored a new book called _Common Fire._[6] She and her coauthors looked at the stories of more than one hundred people who have invested their lives in working for the common good. One of the defining characteristics of these people was that they had an experience of what she called "emphatic bonding" with someone who is different—something had moved them outside of their comfort zones and forced them to realize that the world was bigger than they'd known it to be.

Similarly, a psychologist at Houghton College, John Van Wicklin, and his colleagues have been involved in tracking students from their freshman through senior years, trying to figure out what helps move students from "foreclosure" to "identity achievement." Looking at about 100 seniors, these researchers reported similar findings. Of those seniors who had not traveled outside the United States or Canada, 53 percent left our campuses still in a "foreclosed" status—even after four years of a liberal arts education. These students could articulate what they believed but didn't really seem to know why, nor did they "own" that belief system in a way that would carry them through the complexities of life. On the other hand, only 11 percent of the seniors who had spent four months or more in another country were still "foreclosed." The rest had moved on toward identity achievement.[7]

In fact, getting students into a setting that causes them to experience "the other"—whether it is working in the inner city or going overseas—for as little as one month appears substantially to affect the total impact of a Christian liberal arts education.

Today's college students need to realize that the world does not revolve around them. Wouldn't it put Christian higher education on the map if these schools, individually and collectively, were intentional about giving every student a cross-cultural experience? This is happening in the most amazing places! Goshen College, in the cornfields of Indiana, has made this experience one of its hallmarks. Several schools have modified their language requirements into a "Global Awareness" or a "Cross-cultural Studies" requirement. That's the case at Cedarville College (OH), Messiah College (PA), and Northwestern College (MN). Eastern Mennonite University in Virginia has a required cross-cultural experience for all students, either a semester abroad or a three-week experience in May. According to Beryl H. Brubaker, their vice president for enrollment management, "Evaluations indicate that these experiences, especially the semester-long ones, are the most significant learning experiences students have during their entire university experience."

Tapping the Best of Technology for the Kingdom

What if Christian colleges collaborated to offer higher education from a biblical perspective for believers around the world? When we think about the impact of film and television on modern life, one of the tragedies is that the church largely marginalized itself when the television industry was emerging and consequently has been marginalized from it. Isn't it telling that the first book that came off the printing press in the fifteenth century was the Bible? Now "fast forward" to the twentieth century.

When film was becoming a significant medium, a firm called Gospel Films (based in Michigan) literally had to buy film projectors in bulk and sell them at no markup to the churches in order to get believers to use that new cutting-edge technology! Within the last three years, Gospel Films has invested more than a million dollars to develop a significant presence in cyberspace for the evangelical world, offering web sites *free* to more than a hundred organizations—groups like InterVarsity, Youth for Christ, Navigators, and the CCCU. It's called GospelCom, and it offers a virtual "shopping mall" of Christian resources to explore. It's a model of the body of Christ cooperating with modern technology to get its message out to a needy world.

What about distance learning? By fall 1998, 90 percent of those institutions with ten thousand students or more will be offering at least some distance learning courses. But, as a Department of Education report states, "Small colleges are latecomers to the distance education movement."

The CCCU has a global vision statement: "Quality higher education from a biblical worldview for those who seek it." The fact is that many people simply can't afford a residential liberal arts college experience, or circumstances in their lives don't allow it. Our campuses, in total, now serve about 175,000 students. Yet there are hundreds of thousands of students, earnest about their faith, studying on other campuses in the United States. When George Gallup tells us that 35 percent of the American population describe themselves as "born again," we know that there are millions of other adults who could be interested in college-level instruction from a Christian perspective if that were a visible, viable option.

Last July our board authorized the formation of a "Distance Learning Institute." Two weeks ago that group hosted the first consultation in Chicago, involving about sixty people from fifty different colleges, to talk about what Christian higher education could do collectively to have a significant presence in what's being offered.

Any time a group of schools works at something as complex as distance learning, there are going to be big issues. What about quality standards? Who grants credit? How are the finances managed? There are a lot of different models out there. But the message we're hearing is that Christian higher education needs to "dream big" about this together. With almost all of our campuses reporting in on a survey last month, 77 percent said they _felt strongly_ that it was important for the CCCU to provide leadership in distance-learning collaboration.

What might emerge? The Western Governors University, initiated in 1995, is certainly making a splash in higher education—a "virtual university." Another model exists in California, where students can take a limited number of courses electronically but then must choose one of the California institutions to plug in those credits and earn a degree.

What could we dream about?

- Some of the best Christian scholars from around the world offering seminars for faculty development at Christian colleges in this country and abroad

- Electronically transporting in speakers as resource people for modules that could be incorporated into existing courses
- The best of education at Christian colleges in this country available for emerging Christian colleges overseas
- Continuing education for the 1.3 million alumni of our institutions
- Training for Christian teachers in K-12 schools

Think what it could mean for the kingdom if the best that our colleges offer were made available to churches around the world? We must get moving on this—others already are. The possibilities are mind-boggling.

Nurturing Exceptional Faculty

What if Christian colleges, collectively, became known as the focal point for the best of thoughtful Christian scholarship? Many people could speak eloquently for a "dream" of restoring the original vision of Christian higher education, where the best of theological education was not viewed as the domain of the seminaries and the best of scholarly work was not seen as the domain of the large research universities. Mark Noll lays out this history in *The Scandal of the Evangelical Mind.* Those who attended the 1997 conference at Wheaton College heard him talk about how much he'd been encouraged by new initiatives to foster Christian scholarship—the Pew-funded "Evangelical Scholarship Initiative on Renewing the Christian Mind," the Lilly-funded projects coming out of Valparaiso University, the CCCU's work with faculty development, and the maturing of the professional networks of Christian scholars.

A lot of work remains to be done, both better to equip faculties across the *breadth* of Christian higher education—helping them catch a vision for what it means to teach from a distinctively Christian worldview—and to offer a *depth* program of faculty scholarships for the bright stars that exist on every Christian college campus. We could dream of a day when the world would look at the church, as represented by the Christian colleges, and say, "See how they love one another . . . *and* love the fullness of life," including the life of the mind.

Students coming to Christian colleges are as good as, or better than, their peers that attend other private colleges. The quality of faculty is their top priority in choosing a college. We have some *really* bright students on every one of our campuses. In terms of giftedness and giving them a dream, couldn't we be more intentional about reaching these "best and brightest" with a vision for investing their lives in Christian scholarship?

On a survey last spring of our chief academic officers, half said they've had trouble finding qualified faculty candidates. That doesn't need to be the case. I understand that Brigham Young University has a system of tracking Mormons who are pursuing graduate studies and Mormon scholars around the world. Couldn't our denominations and colleges, or Christian higher education as a movement, do the same for our graduates?

Similarly, we know the names of thousands of graduate students through InterVarsity and Campus Crusade for Christ. Are there ways to link these students with mentors, perhaps offering teaching assistantships, both within and beyond Christian higher education? Why shouldn't we be more intentional about "growing our own"?

Arthur Holmes has given us a model. We need to clone his "dream" in different departments and across Christian higher education. We have the "fragrance of Christ" in faculty whose vision and commitment is multiplied in the lives of students who themselves go out to invest in the lives of others.

These are some big dreams as we think about what could make Christian higher education distinctive, worth paying for, worth investing in. Let us envision a future of equipping the students of the next generation with the "mind of Christ" and sending them out into various areas of service around the world. To me, that's exciting.

This address was given during the Conference on the Future of Christian Higher Education at Union University.

CCCU

"Taking Values Seriously:
Assessing the Mission of Church-Related Higher Education"
1995 Faculty Survey

Regarding Spiritual Values/Concerns	Rating	% Students	% Faculty
Personal, meaningful relationship with God	Strongly Agree/Agree	95.3	99.4
Open to consider new insights in rny faith	Strongly Agree/Agree	91.3	97.2
Day-to-day life affected by relationship with God	Strongly Agree/Agree	91.9	96.6
I encourage students in their relationships with God	Strongly Agree/Agree	n/a	95.7
I encourage students to consider new insights in their faith	Strongly Agree/Agree	n/a	98.1

Reference: N= 2,191 Faculty
44 CCCU Colleges & Universities

CCCU

CCCU Female Freshmen
(In Contrast to Males) are
MORE APT to:

More Apt To:	Females	Males
Have had an A or A+ high school average	24%	15%
Play a musical instrument	60%	49%
Discuss religion	60%	50%
Have frequent personal devotions	42%	32%
Strongly agree that her relationship with God improves her sense of well-being	72%	62%

Reference: Fall 1994 CIRP Survey
N = 10,521 Students

CCCU

CCCU Female Freshmen
Are Less Apt to Rate Self
ABOVE AVERAGE in:

Less Apt to Rate Self Above Average in:	Females	Males
Mathematical Ability	35%	47%
Physical Appearance	30%	45%
Physical Health	43%	67%
Popularity	27%	41%
Intellectual Self-confidence	47%	61%
Social Self-confidence	41%	50%

Reference: Fall 1994 CIRP Survey
N = 10,521

Chapter 5

LEARNING AND THE LORDSHIP OF JESUS CHRIST

TIMOTHY GEORGE

It was the best of times; it was the worst of times. It was the age of wisdom; it was the age of foolishness. It was the epoch of belief; it was the epoch of incredulity. It was the season of light; it was the season of darkness. It was the spring of hope; it was the winter of despair. We had everything before us; we had nothing before us. We were all going direct to heaven; we were all going direct the other way. In short, the period was so far like the present period that some of its noisiest authorities insisted on its being received for good or for evil in the superlative degree of comparison only.

Those famous lines from Charles Dickens's novel, *A Tale of Two Cities*, describe the mood of the world, or at least the world that we used to call Western civilization, on the eve of the French Revolution. It was the best of times, for it was an age of exuberance and optimism, of enlightenment and progress; "ever onward and upward" was the motto of the day. Guided by Voltaire, Rousseau, and Kant, the world had shaken off the shackles of the past and was ready to embrace a new dawning age. It was the best of times. But it was also the worst of times. An age of skepticism and doubt, of violence and war, a "darkling plain" of ominous foreboding, as Matthew Arnold put it, a world that witnessed at once the death throes of the Middle Ages and the birth pangs of the modern world. It was an amazing era that began with the storming of the Bastille in 1789 and ended exactly two hundred years later with the fall of the Berlin Wall in 1989. Now at the far end of that epoch, which we call, for lack of a better term, modernity, you, the class of 1997, stand at the brink of another historic intersection in the human drama. For you, too, it is the best of times.

The Cold War is over. Inflation is down. The economy is booming. Today's Nashville *Tennessean* reports that the level of unemployment in this state is hovering at a near record low. *The New York Times* reports that this year's graduating seniors are more likely to find a job in the field they want than at any time in the last two decades. But while it may be easier to make a living, it may be harder than ever to make a life.

For this is also the worst of times. An age of racism and terrorism, not only in faraway Beirut and Belfast, but also in the heartland of America. A culture with an insatiable appetite for scandal and sexual deviation of every kind, where Jenny Jones and Geraldo and the lawyers of O. J. are better known than our senators and representatives and justices of the Supreme Court. In the midst of this culture of death, we have seemingly no way to stop, or even slow down very much, the holocaust of abortion on demand. "How shall we then live?" asked Francis Schaeffer in the 1970s. It is a good question for the 1990s too.

Twenty-five years ago I sat in a civic arena, much like this one, in Chattanooga, Tennessee, listening to a commencement address of which I can now remember neither the speaker nor a single word he said. That may be my fate twenty-five years from now for some of you who listen tonight. I hope not. That was a big occasion in my life because I was the first person in my family ever to receive a college education. That is true for some of you too. But far fewer of you, I suspect, than with the class of 1972. Some of my classmates would be shot down from helicopters in Vietnam. Others would join the bloody protests against that war in the streets of our nation. In 1972, the echo of rifle bullets in Dallas and Memphis still rang in our ears. In high school we all read George Orwell's *1984,* but back then 1984 still loomed far distant on the horizon, and the year 2000, well, that seemed like an apocalyptic eternity away. And yet tonight, here we are. Here you are on final approach to the third millennium. That fatal year 2000 will be here before some of you finish paying off your car or complete your graduate studies or get your first promotion or have your first baby. And what will it bring for you and for the world in which God has placed you and called you to serve?

Already prophecies and strategies of retreat abound everywhere. Some are wildly optimistic about a golden age of universal peace and cosmic harmony that will dawn, they say, around 2000. To this end, the

Millennium Society has reserved the luxury ship _Queen Elizabeth II,_ which is set to sail from New York Harbor on December 31, 1999, with a complement of the world's most inspiring people aboard. Billy Graham, Pope John Paul II, Bruce Springsteen, Shirley Maclaine, and Michael Jackson have all been invited, among others. You need to check the mail to see if your invitation has arrived! Just as the _Mayflower_ brought the Pilgrims to our shores, so this ship will carry the spiritual icons of another new age, so they say. Meanwhile, down in Adelphi, Texas, Richard Koninger is getting ready for another kind of millennium. He has rented a fleet of blimps to float in the skies while down below earthquakes and volcanoes and tidal waves make a catastrophic shift in the earth's axis in the year 2000. Where will you, the class of 1997, be? Will you face the future with naive, wild-eyed optimism, with exuberant self-confidence and cockiness: "I am the master of my fate: I am the captain of my soul". Or will you be paralyzed with fear and dread, overcome with anxiety and despair? Do you make your reservation on the QE2 or with the Texas blimps?

On this commencement evening I want to suggest a third way: that you move forward from this service tonight neither with optimism nor despair but with something altogether different—hope. The kind of hope that is based on the lordship of Jesus Christ over all of life: past, present, and future. The kind of hope that will empower you not just to make a living but to make a life, a life marked by gratitude and service. In a few moments President Dockery will ask you to stand, and he'll say words something like this: "Upon the recommendation of the faculty and by the authority of the board of trustees, I confer upon you the degrees you have earned." Why do we do this? Sure, this is a part of academic ritual. It goes back to the Middle Ages just like these funny costumes we wear. But it has a meaning far deeper than that.

Tonight you are not just a graduate of Union University. You are being _graduated from_ Union University. That is the correct term. Something is being done to you tonight. You are being invested in what we used to call "the learned company of scholars." We used to use expressions like that—"a gentleman and a scholar," "a lady and a scholar." But more than that, you are being commissioned by this university to model the graces of the Christian life in whatever calling or vocation you are led to pursue.

Henry Dunster was the first president of Harvard College. He said, "The primary purpose of the founding of Harvard was to lay Christ in the bottom as the only foundation of all sound knowledge and learning." Thus, on the college seal of Harvard dating from 1650 are inscribed the three Latin words *In gloriam Christi*—"unto the glory of Christ." Tonight you are being graduated from a university which holds to that same ideal, which acknowledges Jesus Christ as the Lord of biology as well as of theology, which affirms the priority of the Ten Commandments over the theories of John Dewey, and which refuses to bifurcate reality into that damnable divorce of sacred and secular. Tonight you take your part in a community of learning, which confesses with the New Testament that all things were created by Jesus Christ and for Jesus Christ.

The great Dutch statesman and theologian Abraham Kuyper said one hundred years ago: "There is not one single inch of this universe about which Jesus Christ does not say, 'This belongs to me!'" Jesus Christ is the Alpha and the Omega, Creator and Consummator of history, of all human history; and one day our time will come to an end. One day this age will screech to a halt. And we must all appear before him to give an account of what we have done with the gifts and the lives he has entrusted to us. Because that is true, all who know him and serve him and love him can live in this "best of times/worst of times" world of ours with confidence, not despair. Hard pressed on every side we may be, but not crushed. Perplexed sometimes we are, but not in despair. Persecuted on occasion, yes, but not abandoned. Struck down even, yet never, never destroyed! Thus we can agree with James Russell Lowell in saying:

> Truth forever on the scaffold. Wrong forever on the throne
> Yet that scaffold sways the future, and, behind the dim unknown,
> Standeth God within the shadow, keeping watch above his own.

So on this last day of May 1997, on final approach, you are about to be graduated into that honorable company of learned scholars. May you dream high, reach far, and accomplish much for God and for good. And may it all be done as the seal of Harvard College says, *In gloriam Christi*, "unto the glory of Jesus Christ."

This address was given at the Spring 1997 graduation at Union University.

Chapter 6

I Saw Gooley Fly

KENNETH G. ELZINGA

If you have had a class in economics, you know how economists make use of assumptions. In the theory of perfect competition, we assume sellers face infinitely elastic demand curves. In consumer demand theory, we assume buyer rationality.

So perhaps you will forgive me if I make two assumptions in this chapel talk. The first assumption is that while some of you are delighted you are at Union University—this is exactly where you want to be—some of you think you are missing something by being here. You think if you were at a secular university, like the one I serve, you would have access to whatever it is you think you are missing here. The second assumption is that while many of you are followers of Jesus, some of you are not—or you are moving away from faith in Christ.

If I'm wrong on these assumptions, you may tune me out. I won't mind if you read a book or put your head down and take a nap. But if I'm right, then I want to tell you about Herb Gooley.

Herb Gooley is the subject of a short story I read when I was a new Christian. He is a young man, kind of nerdish, kind of awkward, who goes off to school. This is a school where lots of people have an interest in flying. The faculty teach classes on aerodynamics. Students take courses on flying where they read books and articles on the subject; they write essays on flying and talk about how important flying is. In the evenings, students have bull sessions about what their professors taught them about the theory of flying. What was different about Herb Gooley was that he learned to fly: that is, he could fly personally, all by himself. As a fellow student reported: He'd be walking along with you and suddenly he's airborne. Nothing spectacular. I mean it was all very quiet. His rise was almost vertical, and he flew along at about fifteen or twenty miles per hour. No other student at the school, or teacher for that matter, flew around personally, the way Herb Gooley did. They talked about flying, studied flying; they just didn't get around to flying themselves.[1]

I think it is very important for Union University to be a kind of flight school—not just one that talks about flying, writes about flying, or discusses flying, but one that flies. I would like Union University to be the best flight school in this part of the country. And I say this not so you can be proud when you list your degree on your resumé. I want Union University to be a great flight school because our culture desperately needs this to happen. I shall return to Herb Gooley.

Right now, I want to speak to those students who fit my first assumption, students who think they are missing out on something—they may not be sure exactly what—by being at a distinctly and unabashedly Christian school like this one. If you have never wondered, *Did I make a mistake coming to Union University?* you can put your minds on screen-saver mode.

I want to take a very different angle on this question than your parents might. I know parents who want their children to go to a Christian school because they think their children are less likely to get involved in drugs, to get AIDS, to fall in love with a non-Christian. Well, it's a long list, but the list goes right down to less likely to end up wearing a ring in their lip. I don't want to make light of these parental concerns, but my remarks will go in a different direction.

I meet students at Christian schools who think they are missing out on something. My reaction is that you are getting something added. In economics lingo, your "choice set" is larger. What is far more likely to happen to you here—than at a school like mine—is that you will be exposed to an integrated curriculum: courses that integrate the Christian faith with each discipline.

Now what does that mean?

It does not mean that when you study the elasticity of demand in a microeconomics principles class the formula is different here than it would be at my institution. At my school, we use the concept of elasticity to study the incidence of excise taxation. You do that here too. But here you are also free to consider the issue of taxation in a broader perspective. When the question of income distribution in a free-enterprise economy is being discussed, it is fair game here to puzzle over the question: What do the Old Testament teachings about leaving extra grain for the poor to glean mean for an industrialized economy? When you study the term *structure of interest rates* in a money and banking class, you are free to raise questions about what the Bible teaches concerning debt and the charging of interest.

It may surprise you, and it may seem a paradox, but you have a freedom to pursue questions and topics in your classrooms that do not generally get pursued in secular institutions. And if you raise questions that have a Christian slant on them, they will be taken seriously. They might be taken seriously at my institution as well; but they also might be taken derisively or simply considered inappropriate.

Some Christian students at state schools who want to explore the integration of their faith with their studies do so off campus at Christian study centers, or they wait until graduation and take a year at a seminary or a place like Regent University. You don't have to wait.

I shall briefly mention a corollary to this freedom. Your professors are free to do things in the classroom that professors at state schools are not able to do. Your teachers are free to explore topics that I'd best not explore, because the taxpayers of the Commonwealth of Virginia have not hired me to expound my faith in the Lord Jesus and because I have not been hired to integrate my discipline of economics with the teachings of the Christian faith.

I can pray for my students. But I don't have the freedom to pray with them in class. You might think that is a ho-hum deal. But that's because of the economic law of diminishing marginal utility; you might be jaded by the practice here. I'm not. When I go to a Christian school, I am like a kid in a toy shop as I enjoy the freedom to pray with a class.

Are you missing something here? I'll rephrase the question: What would you be missing if you weren't here?

Let me insert a footnote to my remarks at this point. I find myself in a peculiar position giving this talk. I teach and do research at a secular university—one of the most secular institutions of higher learning in the United States. Christian students at the University of Virginia battled the administration at my school recently in a court case that went all the way to the Supreme Court (and the students won) to do something you would take for granted here. I count it a blessing to be on the faculty at Virginia because that is where I believe God has placed me. But I regularly surprise parents and high school students who are considering UVA by suggesting that they consider a Christian school if they are or want to become followers of Jesus Christ—if they really want to be people who fly.

Now I want to say a few words to students at Union University who are right where you want to be—you are delighted with your choice. I probably will never have an opportunity to speak with you again, so I shall be as candid as I can be in a few words.

If I am correct that we live in a culture that is more and more hostile to the things of Christ, and if I am correct that secular institutions more and more will raise the barriers against teachings that are explicitly Christian, then institutions such as this—schools that can be salt and light in the culture—become more important, don't they? In economics lingo, the marginal productivity of your education goes up. In business school lingo, the value added of your education increases.

I see that very clearly from my vantage point at a secular institution. But I wonder if you do?

Here's my concern. I'll put it in the form of a question. Because you are somewhat insulated from the cultural forces that are hostile to the things of Christ, are you integrating faith and learning so that you someday can be salt and light in the world?

You have the opportunity to be everything Christ would have you be. That's why schools like this were formed. Don't be casual about it. I hope you see the difference between having an opportunity and running with it as opposed to blowing this freedom by being comfortable in Zion.

Scripture asks you to take every thought captive to the Lord Jesus Christ (2 Cor. 10:5). That should be your motto if you want to optimize your time here. Put that verse on your computer screen or over your desk. Here's another benchmark verse for you: Scripture asks that whatsoever you do, in word or in deed, do as unto the Lord (Col. 3:23). That means in classrooms, the labs, the library, and bull sessions in your dorm rooms—everywhere. These are very high standards for being a student in college; they are higher standards than non-Christian students are called to.

Now let me say something to you about the faculty at Union University. Those who teach you are called to the same standards. They are to take every thought captive to Christ; whatsoever they do, in word and in deed, it is to be done as unto the Lord.

Here is an implication of the faculty's calling that you may not have considered before: if your teachers are called to take every thought captive to the Lord Jesus Christ, you have a right, indeed I would say an obligation, to encourage and expect your teachers to be aspiring to these standards. You have a right to expect your teachers to be thinking Christianly about what they are teaching you and to impart and explore this with you. This puts the bar very high. These too are higher standards than non-Christian faculty are called to. But they won't reach these standards unless they mix it up with students who share the same calling.

You see, when I teach economics at a secular institution, I mimic what the discipline of economics teaches. I work hard at that. I want my students to be well trained in modern economic analysis. But that is all I am expected to do. I don't have to go an extra mile in the classroom and in effect say: let's try to take this body of economic analysis and put it through the grid of Scripture. I don't get to say: let's take this economic proposition and stack it up against what God's Word says. And let me add, there are Christian students at my institution who long for a classroom experience where that would happen.

Did you know that those who administer this university are called to the same standards as you and the faculty? Your president, your deans, your trustees; whatsoever they do, whether it be in word or in deed, is to be done not to augment their own credentials or power, but it is to be done for the Lord.

To be a member of the governing board at my university is a coveted position. The governor of Virginia makes these appointments. It is both a political plum and statewide honor. It has to be different here. I'd express it this way: the Lord Jesus makes divine appointments of the people who administer this place—and they must be men and women who soberly but joyfully serve in this capacity.

I was not a Christian as an undergraduate, and so I covet the freedom you have to try to take every thought captive to Christ. My vision for those of you who are glad you are here, who understand this is where God has positioned you for your education, is that you would raise the bar of expectations—you would realize that God has put you in a place of Christian nurture and development so that you will be more prepared to be salt and light in a culture largely without the gospel—whether you enter the world of business, the arts, communications, homemaking, social work, government, education, or the church.

Now how does this happen? According to Christian precepts, it is a subtle mixture of things. It is by your earnestly seeking it. It is by God's grace. It is by the chemistry that takes place between you and your teachers and other students who want this to happen. It is by your board and administration providing an enabling environment. And it is by your recognition of how much you need to be trained to be salt and light in an anti-Christian milieu.

The hot topic in the culture of my university, and most state schools today, is diversity. It is sometimes given the name *multiculturalism*. There is a Christian doctrine of diversity. It is a wonderful doctrine: that the church of Jesus Christ will consist of people from every tribe and nation. This doctrine teaches that the gospel of Jesus Christ does not apply only to the literal children of Abraham but rather that "everyone who calls on the name of the Lord will be saved" (Acts 2:21 from Joel 2:32).

But the concept of diversity, as it exists in its secular rendering, is hostile to the Christian faith. It applauds religious expressions of various sorts—except biblical Christianity.

Now why is that? Because the Christian faith makes a claim of exclusivity. And that's seen as the opposite of diversity. Exclusivity is seen as the opposite of multiculturalism.

Into this secular philosophy that applauds diversity comes Christianity. Here is a faith where we sing songs like, "One name, under heaven, whereby we must be saved." Along comes Christianity; here is a faith with a Book it claims is God's Word, a Book that sits above all other books, a Book in which we read of Jesus saying, "I am the way, the truth, and the life. No one comes to the Father except through Me" (John 14:6 NKJV).

In a culture of diversity, this exclusivity is a scandal. It is the main scandal of the gospel. Every Christian student at my institution knows this.

To a lot of the people Christian students encounter at my institution, it would be pleasant for them simply to say: "My religion is Christianity. It is a wonderful religion to me. It meets my needs. But of course it is only one of several ways to God. All the different ways are very good. If you'd like to know about the way I follow, I'll tell you. But I don't think it is any better than the religion you now embrace. You'll have to decide what's best for you."

For you to be salt and light in today's culture, you need to be learning how to move into a culture that thinks this way. Your generation is called to present the grace and mercy of Jesus Christ to a culture that views God's plan of salvation as unseemly.

I recently heard a talk by Bill Hybels, in which he discussed Christianity's biggest competitor. Now you might be prone to think that the biggest competitor to Christianity is atheism. Or agnosticism. Or maybe you think it is Islam, or Hinduism, or New Age, or Buddhism. Hybels would argue it is Moralism. It's a rival to Christianity that says: "I'm good enough. I'm not really so bad, at least compared to the other people I see or read about. I'm pretty good really. I'm pretty honest. I'm certainly no ax murderer or serial killer." For these people, the cross of Christ sounds like nonsense. They are asking, "Why should Jesus die for me?" And they are claiming, "I can take care of myself."

This view is very common at the University of Virginia. "I don't need Christ because I'm already a pretty moral person. Hey, if God grades on a curve, I'm in. No problem."

It is only very recently in the Western world that people have come generally to believe they are moral and upright before God just as they are and that God's standards of holiness are so permissive and low that a C- is a passing grade. But that is today's culture.

Union University should be preparing you to be salt and light in such a culture. And it won't happen unless you are learning to take every thought captive to Christ.

There are, of course, dozens of other areas where Union University should be training you—as you endeavor to take every thought captive to Christ, as you endeavor to do everything as unto the Lord.

At the start of my talk, I made a second assumption: that there are unbelievers in this audience, people who are turning away from the Christian faith—or maybe students who are living a lie, that is, they have never really become followers of Jesus Christ, but nobody really knows this about them. Perhaps that assumption is mistaken, but I'm going to proceed as if it is accurate.

Every year at my institution there are students who come out of a church background or were active in high school with Young Life or FCA, and during high school they thought Christianity was important to them. It certainly seemed that way at the time. Then they get to Virginia. And something happens. It may not be what you would think. They never renounce the Lord Jesus. They don't proclaim they are now unbelievers. They just drift away from Jesus Christ. And the striking thing is that they don't even recognize the drift when it begins. Only later in the school year, it might dawn on them that they don't care about the Lord anymore. These students never slammed a door; they just kind of strolled out of the room.

If you can relate to that, I can relate to you, and I would like to say something to you. Contrary to what you might think, Union University should be an ideal place for you. If the Christian faith is true, then

Union University should welcome your unbelief the same way Jesus welcomed the doubts of Thomas.

Unless your unbelief is so rock hard that you have come to hate the things of Christ, I suggest you stay right here and relish being a doubter at a place that should have enough confidence in Jesus' being the Way, the Truth, and the Life, to allow you to test that amazing proposition in the crucible of the classroom with faculty and in the crucible of living with other students who are followers of Jesus.

I say that not only in the hope that you will come to saving faith in Christ but also in the hope that you will be a very useful challenge to the faculty and your classmates. Union University benefits from student doubters. You can be a test of Christians' ability to do what Peter asks of them: "Being ready to make a defense to everyone who asks you to give an account for the hope that is in you, yet with gentleness and reverence" (1 Pet. 3:15 NASB).

One of my nephews went to a Christian college, not as a Christian, but as an honest inquirer, to test for himself whether putting his faith in Christ was credible. God claimed his heart and mind and soul while he was a student at Gordon College. I would like to believe that the same kind of tough-minded but accepting experience would have happened to him here.

I'm new to Union University. As you can tell from my Herb Gooley metaphor, I think of this institution as a flight school. I hope it is a place that can explain the truths about flying to those who aren't sure they even believe in the concept of flight. The propositional truths about aerodynamics are remarkable. So are the propositional truths about the triune God. And these truths, in God's inspired Word, merit our study. The Bible is our flight manual. But Jesus did not ask his followers simply to believe in written theories and propositions about him. He wants followers, people who expect to fly. By that I mean students who aren't simply asking what they can do with the education they receive, but students who will ask what their time in college will do to them.[2] Are you just going to read about flying, or are you actually going to fly? I would like you to think about the following question. Will they ever talk about you around here like they do at another school about Herb Gooley?

This address was given during the lectures on the integration of faith and learning sponsored by the Pew Charitable Trusts.

Chapter 7

WHAT BUSINESS NEEDS FROM THE CHRISTIAN UNIVERSITY

NORM SONJU

I applaud this conference for probing into issues that are important for Christian education and for the future of our country. All of us love the many opportunities that we still have in our country, but we must be alert so that we do not become complacent and fall prey to the myth that says our country will remain strong forever.

As a Christian leader in the world of professional basketball for twenty years, and ten years prior to that in the corporate world, I have been given a unique platform to share my convictions. Time and time again I have had opportunities to share truths and principles that were important to me. However, I found that most people did not want to take the time to delve too deeply into issues. Most were unaware of decisions that were being implemented that could have a direct impact on their futures.

My sense is that we have a quasi-uninformed population, busy in the marketplace "earning a living," but not necessarily as concerned with "how to live." However, those who are active seem to have a vendetta for their causes. Things have changed from when I was in school. Then, disagreements and open debate of various issues were encouraged. Now, opposing ideas are oftentimes suppressed, ridiculed, and squashed. No prisoners are taken, but a mean-spirited atmosphere prevails.

I negotiated all of my player contracts going back to my days with the Buffalo Braves in the mid-seventies. I used to kid while negotiating with agents that most of their philosophies seemed to be, "What's mine is mine, and what's yours is negotiable." Yet the iconoclastic elite of today seem to say, "What's mine is mine, and what's yours better be the same as mine, or I will crush you!"

Carl F. H. Henry, in his book *Twilight of a Great Civilization*,[1] calls this mentality "a new barbarism." He goes on to say that this barbarism has embraced a new pagan mentality, which rejects the legacy of the West and instead embraces a new pagan mentality where there is "no fixed truth."

Those attitudes, no matter how bizarre, which are spawned on the college campus in one decade become the norm in the marketplace within the next two or three decades. That is why I believe that college professors have a greater influence on our country's future than any other profession. Each of you has a tremendous responsibility to your students. As Christian leaders, I applaud your efforts to remain true to God's Word and to the mission of turning out bright, focused young people who can make a difference in our world.

The influence of a professor is astounding. Professors in our country influence the next generation of doctors, accountants, politicians, and business leaders. In addition, half of the world's future leaders get some of their education in our country. The ripple effect from the influence of the college professor is incredible.

The professor can make an indelible mark on an impressionable young student. That influence can be either for good or for bad. In the early 1950s, a science professor at a small midwestern college greatly influenced a young man by the name of Robert Noyce. When interviewed many years later Noyce said that his college professor's influence on him had been "infectious." Robert Noyce is credited with being the cofounder of the integrated circuit, which is so vital for our modern computers. His influence on society has been awesome. He is legendary in Silicon Valley, though his professor, Grant Gale of Grinnell College, is relatively unknown. Yet it was Gale who was the inspiration behind the legend.

A decade later, another professor at a well-known east coast university challenged his students to "turn on . . . tune in . . . drop out." His influence was also profound, but unfortunately it helped spawn the devastating drug culture in our country. Though I have never met either of these professors, I have been dramatically impacted by both. The computer has helped me to achieve a level of efficiency far beyond anything I could have ever imagined. Meanwhile, Timothy Leary's vicarious influence probably has done more damage to the franchise that I founded back in 1980, the Dallas Mavericks, than any opponent we ever faced on the court. The best player we ever had could not gain victory over drugs and alcohol and wasted what could have been a brilliant career. When he played, we won more than 65 percent of our games. When he was on our team but messed up because of drugs or alcohol, we won less than 40 percent of our games. He impacted every player, every coach, every staff member, as well as all of our fans. Yes, the influence of a single professor can have an effect that is exponential.

There are some ill-conceived myths that were spawned on the college campus years ago, which have profound influence on society today. Unfortunately, these myths now permeate every aspect of society. As leaders of Christian universities and colleges, I would like to challenge you to buckle up your foundational belts and to instill truths into what you teach, so that your students can face their world with confidence rather than confusion.

I have hired thousands of employees throughout my corporate business career and still others during my tenure as president and general manager of NBA franchises. I loved it when employees had assurance in who they were and in what they wanted to accomplish. I enjoyed it when they knew right from wrong, had serving hearts, and knew how to work hard.

Unfortunately, that generally was not the norm. Many employees lacked confidence in most everything, had no defined goals or sense of absolute truth, did not have a clue about service, and were shocked at the demands of work. Their focus was on money, prestige, position, and status. Their learning curve was oftentimes much greater and took longer than it should have to make them viable contributors. Why is that so? I think it is because of some myths that are prevalent in a secular society. Gary Bauer, director of the Family Research Council, talked about an address that Chuck Colson, former Nixon aide, gave in Chicago some time ago. In that address Colson identified some of the myths that had been born on the college campus some time ago and today affect society negatively. These need to be identified and countered by the Christian colleges, so that you can help your students to be prepared to face these issues in the years to come.

Myth #1: _Humans are good and innocent and not responsible for any wrongdoing!_ This is a sick myth. Unfortunately, many young people have bought into it, and it affects every part of society. This myth is often perpetuated after riots, when some TV commentators blame everyone or everything other than the rioters for the damage done. After the Rodney King verdict, they blamed "society in general" and "all of us" and shifted the blame and responsibility from those who had done the rioting to society as a whole.

At that time there was much pent-up aggression and emotion on the part of many. However, after the Chicago Bulls won their first NBA title in 1991, everyone in Chicago should have been happy. Chicago had defeated Los Angeles four games to one. Yet there were riots in Chicago as well. Why? Because those who chose to tear up their city did so! The victory over the Lakers did not incense anyone. The aftermath of the game was simply an excuse to do what some wanted to do all along, and that was to cause havoc in their city. My challenge to you Christian college leaders is to instill in your students that *every person is responsible for his or her actions*. Not taking responsibility for one's actions is an unimpressive trait. It takes a strong person to say, "I am responsible; I was wrong." It shows no strength whatsoever to blame one's actions on others or on one's circumstances.

It is clear in the Bible that we are not good and innocent. "For all have sinned, and come short of the glory of God" (Rom. 3:23 KJV); the best we have to offer is like a filthy rag (Isa. 64:6); and "There is none righteous, no, not one" (Rom. 3:10).

No, humans are not good and innocent but rather sinful and in need of a Savior. The Bible says that we are responsible for our actions. This secular myth produces a weakened society. The truth of God's Word produces confidence!

Myth #2: *There are no absolutes; all moral values are relative.* This myth is very prevalent today and got its start in our country from men like Sigmund Freud and John Dewey, among others. They greatly influenced society during the early part of this century. They believed that humans were autonomous and did not have a need for a higher authority.

Unfortunately, this myth has become the norm for many today. To them the Bible is irrelevant, and each person is to determine what is right for himself. For Freud it was through psychology and by "knowing oneself." For Dewey it was through an educational system that he created, which was naturalistic and anti-supernatural. Today the results are very much like those during the time of the judges in the Bible, when "everyone did as he saw fit" (Judg. 21:25). A philosophy without the foundation of God's Word breeds insecurity and a lack of confidence and results in a weakened society.

Ideas always have consequences. Bad ideas can be devastating to society and can eventually bring about its destruction. Saying that there are no absolutes and dismissing the Bible as irrelevant are bad ideas. Jesus said, "Heaven and earth will pass away, but My words shall not pass away" (Matt. 24:35 NASB).

My challenge to you Christian college leaders is to guard against becoming "biased neutral" toward religion. It is so easy to start to compromise. Sometimes it might be to appease someone special. It could be to attract some talented person to join your faculty. It takes just a little softening here and a little easing up there, and in no time you will start to see a watered-down, weak, and ineffectual student body and school.

It is very easy to think that it simply could not happen at your college, but let me assure you that no liberal has ever founded a college. Liberals simply take them over. It's been stated that of the first 119 colleges started in our country, 104 were founded by Christians who wanted to equip students with the truth of God's Word. Yet you know that many of those schools are anti-Christian today.

Keeping your focus on his truth will be an ongoing challenge because there will always be someone who will pose questions like: "Why can't I? What's wrong with . . . ? Who says so?" Unfortunately, those are the wrong questions. The emphasis needs to be on, What do we need to do to strengthen our school?

Those who buy into this myth that there are no absolutes also like to rewrite and change history. At times they tend to redefine terms to make them more palatable. Killing babies becomes "choice." Abhorrent practices become "alternative lifestyles." These new terms may sound more appealing but will not change the facts.

People can kid themselves all they want. They can change the spelling, redefine the term, and can even get a majority to vote for it; however, it will not change the truth of God's Word one iota. His Word is unchangeable! His Word is inviolate! My recommendation to you leaders is for you to do everything possible to instill these truths into your students. They will build strength into their lives and will help enable them to face the challenges of this age.

Nothing instills confidence more than knowing that absolute truth is found in God's Holy Word. You can embrace it, or you can deny it. However, you do not want to be "biased neutral" toward his Word. It takes nothing to be a "biased neutral" person. Remember, even a dead fish floats downstream! Be willing to take your stand with vigor!

Myth #3: *The cult of radical individualism is superior to everything else.* This philosophy dismisses the church, the community, and the family unit as irrelevant. It instead produces a focus on materialism rather than on service and hard work. It generates an emphasis on I, me, and mine versus team and family values. It produces people who do not feel a need to honor their commitments if things do not work out quite right for them. Their word is meaningful only if everything turns out well.

The result of this philosophy has been an epidemic of bankruptcies, flippancy toward marriage, and an abandonment of family. We need to instill the importance of honoring one's commitments. We need to instill in our students the importance of building strong families. No civilization can survive indefinitely if the family unit is destroyed. Most civilizations crashed when the family unit was weakened. The demise of both the Greek and Roman Empires are examples.

Michael Novak, a modern writer, says it best: "One unforgettable law has been learned through all disasters and injustices of the last thousand years: If things go well with the family, life is worth living; when the family falters, life falls apart."

We need to instill community responsibility. None of us are "islands unto ourselves." We need others to succeed. During the sixties, the Boston Celtics were the best team in the NBA but never had the league's high scorer. They knew that a team was more important than one star. That philosophy needs to be instilled in our young people today. They need to learn to respect others no matter what their differences and to get things done through teamwork and cooperation.

Though many in my generation have failed miserably in this regard, we must continue to instill those values that will help students buck the fallout that comes from this warped myth. Values do matter!

Myth #4: *Government can provide utopia.* It is a sad commentary on society, but many enter the post-college world thinking of government as some kindly grandfather who cares for them from birth to the grave.

This attitude takes away the incentive to be productive, resourceful, and responsible. It creates a dependence on government and puts government into areas it was never intended to be involved in.

What society needs are energetic people desirous of making things better, not a generation of takers wanting to go along for the ride. All of you remember the presidential debates some years ago when a young pony-tailed person in the audience asked the candidates what "they were going to do for me." Though this scene, showing a capable young man, seemed pathetic to many of us, it is unfortunately becoming more the norm than the exception today.

Government is important. It needs to do several things and do them well. However, it does not need to be involved in every area of our lives. We need to instill in our students that they need to take responsibility for themselves. We need to create an atmosphere in which we encourage students to become doers and contributors, not just receivers.

We also need to challenge our students to get involved so that they can make a positive difference in society someday. We desperately need political leaders who recognize that character and values are important. There is no better place to instill these attitudes than on the Christian college campus. I want to challenge each of you to encourage your students to become leaders wherever they go, including the political arena.

It is a dangerous myth to believe that government can provide utopia. However, it is also wrong not to recognize that many do believe this today. Keeping the focus on doing rather than receiving will help your students greatly.

I would like to leave you with one final truth from God's holy Word. It is found in Paul's letter to the Colossians. "Whatever you do, do your work heartily, as for the Lord rather than for men. . . . It is the Lord Christ whom you serve!" (3:23–24b NASB).

When you keep your focus on that truth, you will want to do everything possible to provide your students with the necessary tools to equip them to become effective and faithful in their world. The myths of a secular society are very potent. However, all the more so is God's Word and the absolute truth that is found in it. The wonderful thing is the assurance of knowing that his Word is available to each of us today!

This address was sponsored by the McAfee School of Business Administration at Union University in an event for the business community during the Conference on the Future of Christian Higher Education at Union University.

Chapter 8

THE ROLE
OF PROFESSIONAL EDUCATION
IN CHRISTIAN HIGHER EDUCATION

DAVID S. DOCKERY

One of our local newspapers recently ran a series of articles and editorials focusing on the rise of crime in western Tennessee. Each author addressed the crime issue solely from the standpoint and perspective of economic deprivation. I read and reread the articles, thinking I was missing something. One approach was anthropological, another sociological, another economic—each dealing with systemic issues, which I don't doubt for a moment exist. But missing from the articles was any sense of human responsibility. Crime was discussed without raising the issue of morality. I couldn't believe it. Then it dawned upon me that there were diverse worldviews at work between those authors and me, the reader.

A Chinese proverb says, "If you want to know what water is, don't ask the fish." Water is the sum and substance of the world in which the fish is immersed. The fish may not reflect on its own environment until suddenly it is thrust onto dry land and struggles for its life. Then it realizes water provided its sustenance.

Immersed in our environment, we have failed to take seriously the ramifications of a secular worldview. Daniel Yankelovich, sociologist and social watchdog, defines *culture* as an effort to provide a coherent set of answers to the existential situations that confront human beings in the passage of their lives. A genuine cultural revolution is one that makes a decisive break with the shared meaning of the past. The break particularly affects those meanings that relate to the deepest questions of the purpose and nature of human life.[1]

Particularly in the last three decades, we find ourselves the hapless possessors of a culture unhinged from its Creator's mooring. The foundations of life are being seriously challenged.

One of the most symbolic structures of our time is the Wexner Art Center on the campus of Ohio State University. It is a fascinating building that has no pattern. Staircases go nowhere. Pillars support nothing. The architect designed the building to reflect life as he saw it. It signifies confusion, chaos, and the lack of absolute truth. Life from this vantage point is mindless and senseless, going nowhere.

Yet even in this postmodern architectural feat, the foundation of the building is quite traditional. You can't do to the foundation what was done with the hallways and stairways without the building crumbling. You can't do with the foundation what can be done with the infrastructure without serious implications. You can get away with random thoughts that sound good in defense of a worldview that ultimately doesn't make sense. However, when you begin to tamper with the foundations, you begin to see serious effects. Today our cultural foundations are in jeopardy. They no longer provide coherence for our contemporary culture.

Ravi Zacharias has said that there are four indispensable dimensions to our life that have been significantly impacted by enlightenment and postenlightenment worldviews, representing the zeitgeist of our times. These are the loss of eternity, the loss of morality, the loss of accountability, and the loss of charity. He says: "Ours is an age where ethics has become obsolete. It is superseded by science, deleted by philosophy, dismissed as emotive by psychology. It is drowned in compassion, evaporates into aesthetics, and retreats before relativism. The usual moral distinctions between good and bad are simply drowned in a maudlin emotion in which we feel more sympathy for the murderer than the murdered, for the adulterer than the betrayed, and in which we have actually begun to believe the real guilty party, the one who somehow caused it all, is the victim and not the perpetrator of the crime."[2]

By losing eternity, we have redefined existence. By losing morality, we've destroyed essence. By losing accountability, we've eradicated conscience. By losing the dimension of charity, we have lost the idea of benevolence.

I'm sure you are asking what all this has to do with higher education. I would respond "everything," precisely because the loss of eternity, the loss of morality, the loss of accountability, and the loss of charity strike us every day in areas of health care, business, economics, and education. I believe that now may well be the moment of opportunity to strengthen, expand, and emphasize the range of educational opportunities and options.

Why Christian higher education? you might ask. Aren't others providing similar career preparation? The answer is yes _and_ no. Yes, they are providing similar programs, but the uniqueness of a thoroughgoing Christian approach to higher education is its commitment not only to content but also to value-added education, to character development, competencies, and a Christian worldview that challenges the predominant secular way of seeing life and work. So what must we do?

First, as Chuck Colson has exhorted institutions of the Council of Christian Colleges and Universities, we must train the mind by inculcating truth and developing graduates who will go out and infiltrate the world with what some call a "backyard apologetic." We want professors, staff, and students who are competent in their professions, caring in their relationships, but who also confess and, if necessary, contend for the truth of God that is foundational for life and living.

This once was the goal of every college in America. It is no longer the case. Prior to the nineteenth century, every college started in this country—with the exception of the University of Pennsylvania—was a Christian college committed to revealed truth. It all changed in the nineteenth century with the rise of secularization and specialization, creating Kantian dualisms of every kind—a separation of head knowledge from heart knowledge, faith from knowledge, revealed truth from observed truth, and careers from vocation.

What happened was a loss of worldview in the academy. There was a failure to see that every discipline and every specialization could be and should be approached from the vantage point of a Christian worldview.

Those involved in Christian higher education must be intentional about integrating faith and learning in every discipline—not as a cliche, or public relations watchword, but as a foundational reality. We must be intentional about a commitment to truth, for by him and for him are all things held together.

Science and health care programs must be seen from a Christian vantage point. Science is measuring what is; it is observed truth. But observed truth need not conflict with revealed truth. They are complementary. We could really have no science without recognizing that God has created an orderly universe. If it's not orderly, nothing applies. For as Abraham Kuyper, the great Dutch thinker and statesmen, said in his Stone Lectures given at Princeton in 1898: "God created the world and cares for his entire creation, and by his saving grace he brings regeneration and justification to his own, but by his common grace he sustains the creation he has made and he calls us to be participants in that common grace, to be agents of it—as he cares about its expression in every single aspect of life."

Such a worldview is also at the root of mathematics, which is foundational to business, accounting, and economics. This does not mean there is a Christian mathematics or Christian multiplication tables. No, what is affirmed is that there is Christian truth and order at the root that makes it possible to make mathematical calculations.

A Christian worldview shapes our view of education, pedagogy, and the social sciences, for all must answer the question: What is it that motivates humans? This is at the root when we talk about the nature of men and women. There are several implications of these truths.

First, faculty and students at Christian colleges and universities should be better teachers and learners because our motivation for learning is different. We want to learn more about God and his world, his purpose, and his activities as they impact our areas of focus. The purpose of learning is different. It is shaped by values different from just wanting to get a good job, as important as that is.

Second, education that integrates faith and learning can help restore the loss of morality and accountability. It can help us be better people, better citizens, better employees. It gives us standards and ideals for which we can aim in order to be better people because it is an education concerned not only with content but also with character. Then we can know what is right and do what is right. So a Christian worldview not only impacts and shapes the mind but the will as well.

Education shaped by a Christian worldview can better prepare someone for his or her *vocation*. This is not vocational education, but it helps us see that our own unique vocation is a calling from God, a holy thing from God.

The goals of Christian education are: to enable men and women to be prepared for their chosen vocation in such a way that they can be salt and light in the marketplace; to help students become servant leaders and change agents in our world; and to help us be prepared for work and to see it from God's perspective in a way that will bring glory to him—preparation for vocation—not just job training or careers, but work, calling, *vocatio*. The Bible tells us that in the state of innocence, humans, as the apex of creation, were given work to perform as part of their normal existence (Gen. 2:2). This is contrary to much modern thinking that adopts the skewed attitude that work is something evil to be avoided if at all possible—again, a difference in worldview.

Certainly Genesis 3 tells us that sin has corrupted and degraded work. It specifically states that because of sin work will change its character to become the cause of humankind's ultimate physical disintegration. Thus, work at times in Scripture embodies the idea of weariness, trouble, and sorrow, especially in Ecclesiastes.

Yet in some sense, the Genesis story tells us that humanity has been graciously invited by God to get in on the work. A rabbinic paraphrase indicates in effect that God said, "I've enjoyed so much creating this garden that I want you to come in and help me tend it."

Yet work, that gracious gift from God, is transformed because of human sin. Adam and Eve are cursed to spend all their days fighting with the once-benevolent world, fighting in work, and kicked out of the garden.

Most of us spend many of our waking hours at work. Thus we are right to seek meaningful work and to prepare ourselves for it as well as we possibly can.

The Christian tradition has affirmed that all work is divinely ordained. Martin Luther attacked medieval monasticism by saying one need not be a monk or a nun to serve God. Thus, the servant, the plowman, and the maid, he claimed, all do their work for the glory of God.

Luther's thought on work is not so much a glorification of human activity, however. It is rather a celebration of the continuing creativity of God. Luther's emphasis wasn't on jobs, but on vocation, calling (from the Latin *vocatio*). We are called by God not just in our jobs but in everything we do to glorify God in all things. Our vocation, then, is not so much work as it is worship. We do on Monday at the office what we do in church on Sunday—glorify God.

What does this mean for students? It means they can glorify God by studying hard. Students have been called to the vocation of student. They have gifts and graces that come from God for study and for carrying out God's call on their lives. Study is not just for the self but so that one can better contribute to others through study. So we urge students to study. That's their current vocation.

As we prepare students to be better employees, we recognize that work can be carried out as service unto the Lord. Our work, our vocation, is a blessing from the Lord.

As we prepare to be business leaders, ministers, managers, missionaries, nurses, teachers, artists, or scientists, we recognize that Jesus is Lord of all. Thus, there is no partiality in his sight.

In summary, the implications of a Christian worldview are fivefold. We are committed to the preparation of students in all areas of life because:

1. Work is essential and is a gift from God (Gen. 2:15).
2. Work is to be pursued with excellence for it is done for his glory (2 Thess. 3:6; 1 Cor. 10:31).
3. All honest professions are honorable: Adam was a gardener, Abraham a rancher, Joseph an administrator, Deborah a judge, David a shepherd, Lydia a businesswoman, and Paul a tentmaker.
4. We recognize that the gifts and abilities we have for our vocation come from God (Rom. 12:6; Dan. 2:21).
5. We recognize that prosperity and promotions come from God (Deut. 8:18; Ps. 75:6).

The apostle calls us to work as unto the Lord with excellence as our standard (Col. 3:23–24). We are responsible to plan and prepare well, to utilize and mobilize the resources, the capacity, the intellect, the drive, the ambitions, and all that God has given us, use them to the fullest, and perform them with the highest degree of excellence. Or, as the wise preacher said almost three thousand years ago: "Whatever your hand finds to do, do it with all your might." And we would add with the apostle Paul—do it all for the glory of God! *Soli Deo Gloria.*

This was the 1997 Fall Convocation Address at the dedication of Union University's extension campus in Germantown, Tennessee.

Chapter 9

THE CHRISTIAN UNIVERSITY
IN A DIVIDED SOCIETY

STAN D. GAEDE

The topic for this chapter is, "The Christian University in a Divided Society." Central to that topic, I believe, is the issue of diversity. As such, I want to address three questions: First, why is anything having to do with diversity such a difficult subject to talk about in our society? Second, what should we be doing about diversity on our campuses? And third, what shouldn't we be doing? That is, what are the dangers inherent in being a Christian college or university, at this moment, in a diverse and divided society?

Using Diversity

Let me begin by saying, quite bluntly, that there are few subjects as difficult to discuss as diversity. Perhaps none. The topic of diversity has the potential to divide us along every conceivable line—political, theological, sexual—you name it; the possibility of alienation over this one concept is ever present. For that reason, many good and decent people who like civility and peace ignore it altogether (unless they know they are in a safe place with others who agree with them). It creates just too much potential for a blowup; too much potential for pain, grief, or worse.

Why is that? Why do we find anything having to do with diversity so difficult to discuss? Well, there are many reasons, I think, but I will reduce them to two. First, we use the term loosely—to cover a multitude of sins—rarely specifying what we mean by diversity. And that's a problem.

For example, it is not uncommon for people to say that they are strong proponents, or opponents, of diversity. Since it is the former

81

who typically speak out in the academy, let's pick on them for a moment. What does it means to be "for diversity." On the surface, that's a very strange idea, isn't it? It's a little like saying that one is "for addition." What does that mean? Are you against subtraction? Are you for addition under all circumstances? the addition of pollution? the addition of color? the addition of good? the addition of evil? The problem is, the word is a modifier at best; it has meaning only in the context of other words or ideas.

And such is the case with diversity. All of us, I suspect, are for certain kinds of diversity and against others. We all want diversity when we sit down at table: The more variety of foods before us, the more we drool. A feast implies diversity. We typically enjoy diversity in the realm of aesthetics as well. A beautiful field of flowers is beautiful precisely because it is a contrast in colors. If the colors weren't diverse, the field wouldn't be beautiful.

But notice even there how difficult that term is. A few months ago, my wife and I were in Minneapolis where I was speaking and attending a conference. At one point, we were looking out over the landscape of Minnesota, and I declared, "This place is . . . well, boring. Everything is just one shade of green." We then began comparing it to the colors one finds in Santa Barbara or New England, two places where we have lived, and both of which seemed more aesthetically diverse than Minnesota in June.

What were we doing in making this comparison? Our background and experiences had defined for us what aesthetic diversity was and what it wasn't. And my guess is that any good Minnesotan would have told us: "You aren't seeing what I'm seeing; I see diversity everywhere— in the shades of green, in the contrast to the sky or the fields, in contrast to the way it looked a few months ago when it was covered with snow!" And of course, the Minnesotan is correct. There is diversity from a certain perspective . . . and little diversity from another.

Now, here's the point: If the term *diversity* is difficult, even when you narrow it down to the flora and fauna of Minnesota, then it is infinitely more difficult when you are talking about people. Infinitely. Let's take sex for just a moment. Clearly, diversity is built into our appreciation of, or attraction to, the opposite sex. That is, part of what we find attractive about the "other" is that the "other" is different from us, physically to be sure, but in other ways as well. But that's not the whole story, is it? Because we are also attracted to people who are like us in some ways. Aren't you often struck by the fact that many couples seem to be so much alike, not only in taste or humor, but even in looks at times? So we don't simply like diversity in the sexual domain; we like some kinds of diversity and some kinds of uniformity.

This desire for both diversity and uniformity, by the way, is why the homosexuality debate in our culture seems to me to be so confused and difficult. Those who put themselves on the side of "gay rights" will argue that it's just a matter of appreciating diversity. They say we ought to understand that people are different, accept that fact, and even rejoice in it. But people on the other side argue that the homosexual community is denying fundamental elements of diversity that are built into human nature, namely, the differences between men and women and their need for one another to bear children and perpetuate the race. In my opinion, both of these arguments move us away from clear thinking, not toward it, because both are simply using diversity for their own purposes. If we want to communicate on this matter, we will need to define our terms very clearly, but few seem willing to do that these days.

This sensitive topic of homosexuality, as it relates to diversity, brings us to the second reason we find diversity such a difficult concept to discuss: It is at the center of some of the deepest controversies of our age. Indeed, it is part and parcel of our current struggle to understand not only what is true and false but also how one might even go about finding truth.

Let us return to the homosexuality debate for a moment. I would contend that it is not really a debate about diversity at all but a debate about worldview. More precisely, when we engage in the homosexuality debate, we are contesting moral visions in our culture these days—not only which moral vision ought to give direction but also how our various moral visions ought to conceive of sexuality in general and homosexuality in particular.

The flap over the decision of the Southern Baptist Convention to boycott Disney for its "gay friendly" policies is a wonderful illustration. Did you read the editorials or look at the caricatures? Fascinating. At least in the papers I read, one sees very little about the central issues: Disney's policy on homosexuality and the precise objections of the Southern Baptists. Rather, one sees cartoons, like the one that pictures Mickey Mouse, locked up in stockades, with two glum looking seventeenth-century Puritans looking on, and the words "Southern Baptists" emblazoned on their clothing.

Now this is very interesting. At one level—I would call this the level of communication—this is an absurd caricature, since it is equating a rather anemic request not to purchase a product from a particular company with a legal arrangement in which governments persecute nonconformists. The differences could not be more stark. But it does make sense if one understands that this debate is not about the comparison of historical events but about "the good"—that which we define as good, right, and true. Since we have so little agreement on what good is, the same cartoons are absurd to one community and perfectly understandable to another.

Now I say all of this only to make a very important point: When we raise the issue of diversity, we are using a term that is many things to many people. It has been employed in so many ways, for so many political and moral ends, that it is rarely a vehicle for good communication and often the basis of division and conflict. Indeed, it is such a loaded and fuzzy term that I would abandon it altogether were it not for two reasons. First, it is part of our literature at most Christian institutions. Over the last five years, we have used the term extensively; it's in our documents, goals, and standards. We can't just back away from the term at this point without rewriting a large portion of our literature.

Secondly, I don't think backing away from the term is the best approach anyway, especially for a college or university that desires to engage the culture, as we intend for our institutions to do. We are not isolationists. Our objective is not simply to develop pristine communities that people admire for their cleanliness and charm. And thus, while confusing and loaded terms may make life a bit more complicated for us, they are also an opportunity for engagement with the culture, for rethinking our own moral vision, and—I would contend—for redemption. And redemption has a very nice ring to it, don't you think?

In the midst of all this confusion, how should we think about diversity? What do we mean by it? To what are we committed? And the place to begin is to recognize that even among ourselves we have very different views of diversity, and we have such differences for good reason. In other words, let's admit right from the start that we have different reactions to the term *diversity*. For some of us, it's a positive term; for others, it's a worrisome term. But I want to suggest that we have these different reactions not because some of us are stupid and others wise, not because some of us are deeply moral while others are not. Rather, I suspect that in many cases it is actually our common commitment to Jesus Christ that is the source of both reactions, along with our various encounters with this particular culture. Let me explain.

A few years ago, I was asked by a group of graduate students at an Ivy League university to speak on the topic of political correctness and multiculturalism. I did so with some hesitation because of the loaded nature of those terms but also with the sense that I had no choice; I had spoken to this group before on a number of occasions and always enjoyed it. I decided that I couldn't turn the group down this time just because the topic was a difficult one. I won't bore you with the details of that evening, but I will report the result. I started my talk at about 7:30 in the evening and left the campus sometime well after midnight. My talk was less than an hour long. I stayed until after midnight because the students would not let the topic go. They were in deep, deep angst over the issue of multiculturalism. And bright, caring students that they were, they were not about to let the evening end until they had figured out the reason for their angst.

And what was the reason? Well, on the one hand, as Christians they felt deeply committed to a cross-cultural perspective on ministry, to the oneness of humanity, and to the concept of justice for all people. They were themselves a multicultural group, with Anglos in the minority and a wonderful tapestry of color all around. And yet, as they encountered multiculturalism on their campus, there was something that worried them, that made them uneasy, and in fact seemed quite wrong. And it was not so much the conclusions of those who advocated multiculturalism that bothered them as their reasons for their conclusions. It was the epistemological rooting of the concept that gave them pause. For multiculturalism, like diversity, can be planted in very different kinds of soil. And the soil for much of the discussion in academia—by those both for and against these concepts, by the way—was and is a kind of moral relativism or, better yet, a moral subjectivism that is quite distant from a biblical view of the human condition.

The logic goes something like this: Truth is a conundrum at best, a complete unknown more than likely. Those who think they possess the truth are thus the greatest danger because they think they have something they don't. They create all kinds of havoc—starting wars, perpetrating injustice, and infringing on the rights of others. Like the rest of us, they need to understand that everyone comes at life from their own perspective, and that perspective is entirely conditioned by one's culture, life experiences, and so on. What we have, then, are just different perspectives, not truth. Multiculturalism enables us to appreciate that fact—to appreciate the multiperspectival nature of thought—and, for that reason, to be sensitive and accepting of those whose perspective is different from our own. Thus, multiculturalism is good, and confidence in any particular truth claim is bad. End of argument.

As you reflect on that argument, I would suggest that you—like my group of graduate students—ought to find yourself deeply conflicted. On the one hand, something quite right is being said: We do have different experiences, and those differences influence how we look at life. Moreover, understanding those differences—living in different cultures, for instance—greatly broadens our view of the world and gives us a much deeper, much richer view of life. It will also make us much slower to judge others, no doubt, because we will better understand both our own limited knowledge of certain things and the complexity and nuances of life. In other words, a multicultural experience can lead to greater understanding, and that understanding can enable us to be more compassionate, sensitive human beings. All of that seems undeniably true.

But notice that last word: truth. Making a truth claim about multiculturalism, such as I have done, gives us a huge ontological problem, unless we assume that there is some truth out there on which we are gaining perspective. Indeed, let me say bluntly: The relativistic argument I used for multiculturalism a few minutes ago is pretty much nonsense. It is popular and even has intuitive appeal because we live in a highly subjective age, and we are used to lots of nonsense, even in the academy (perhaps especially in the academy). But here's the problem: What good are multiple perspectives on something that does not exist? If there is no truth out there that we can know in some form, then why bother to acquire many different perspectives on it?

There is an answer, by the way, and it is likely to go something like this: Gaining multiple perspectives at least undermines our dogmatism. Its value is that it very quickly teaches us that our particular truth claims are just that, particular and relative, and not worthy of great confidence. As such, we will at least become a bit more humble.

I would agree. But notice, again, that we are becoming more humble about nothing unless we believe that there is some truth out there about which we need greater cognitive humility. Let's face it, if the relativist is right, multiculturalism is a complete waste of time. Its only value is to break up our quaint but anachronistic notions of truth. After that, it offers us no reason whatever to learn about other cultures and people. For what is there to learn? And what is to be gained? Little more than further evidence for nihilism.

I hope this discussion of truth doesn't sound too obtuse, because I think this is important. It says two things to me. First, we must reject the relativistic rooting of multiculturalism because, if for no other reason, it completely undermines its own value and, I would contend, undermines the liberal arts project as a whole. Of course, as Christians, we do have other reasons to reject it, not the least of which is that we are followers of One who claims to be the Truth, a claim that is rooted in a tradition of God as revealer and truth teller. We are, for better and for worse, a people of truth. And we cannot abandon that commitment for the sake of the spirit of the age.

Secondly, we don't need to abandon our commitment to truth. Indeed, I would argue that multiculturalism makes so much more sense and is worthy of appreciation precisely because we are a people of truth, and want to know the truth, and love the truth, and be faithful to its call on our lives. And one of its calls on my life, I would say, is to make sure that my understanding of the truth is not culture bound, not rooted in parochialism, and certainly not unaware of the differences that make up the human family.

Our commitment to truth, then, calls us to explore—eagerly explore—the variety and diversity of God's creation, with the aim *not* of undermining the truth, but of broadening it—of understanding our Creator, his world, and ourselves more fully. I think that will lead to a measure of cognitive humility and will make us more aware of our limitations and finitude. True humility comes not from embracing intellectual chaos but from embracing the One who is the source of our understanding in the first place. For it is only as we can rest confidently in him that we will have the security to say, "I don't understand," when we don't understand. And that, it often turns out, is the beginning of wisdom.

Applying Diversity

What does all this mean for us at Christian colleges and universities? What are the implications for this project we call Christian higher education?

First, and most basically, we do not simply want diversity at our institutions; we want diversity that flows out of our self-definition. That is, we are colleges and universities of a particular ilk. We are followers of Jesus Christ. Thus we are called to embrace certain kinds of diversity and not others.

Sometimes it will be easy for us to know which is which; sometimes it will not. But it is precisely in those areas of the unknown that education takes place—our own and our students. Thus, we don't avoid those areas; in fact, we seek them out. But as we do, we keep our voices low, knowing that we are entering areas of exploration. So, how do we discover and embrace appropriate kinds of diversity?

First, our approach to diversity must be mission driven. If it isn't, we will be in deep trouble. Either we will find ourselves embracing a relativistic conception of diversity or reacting against it with some kind of mindless uniformity. Neither are appropriate at a Christian institution, and we must avoid both.

Second, if we approach this issue in a mission-driven fashion, we will discover that there are some forms of diversity that are more important for us to pursue at this moment in time than others. You can't do everything at once. For that reason, each of us will need to think strategically about the issue of diversity in the light of our mission and to decide which issues to pursue first and how to pursue them.

For example, I think a priority for many of us in the days ahead is to bring about a better balance of men and women on our campuses—on the faculty, administration, and staff. Why do I pick this one first? Well, there are a number of reasons, but let me mention only two. First, and perhaps at the most basic level, I think it is simply a matter of serving our students well and providing them with the very best education possible.

Most of us have more women than men in our student bodies; that's a fact. And, in my opinion, that's not something to bemoan but to appreciate. Indeed, in many cases, the reason we have more female than male students is because we place the emphasis, first and foremost, on academic quality. Because of this academic focus and because we have more women than men applying, we wind up with a larger number of women in the student body.

In some ways, I think the same principle applies when we are looking for faculty. We are first of all not looking for men or women but people of quality: quality scholars, quality teachers, quality persons of good character and deep faith. But we must also have a faculty that is well suited for the student body. And that means, I believe, a healthy mix of women and men. We do not want an overly imbalanced student body, faculty, or administration. And we seek this balance, not because it is (or isn't) politically correct. We seek it because it's good for the college as a whole and especially good for our students. We seek it, in other words, for educational reasons.

Drawing conclusions in this arena is always dicey. But we do know a few things. For example, we know that female students who attend our colleges tend to be a bit brighter than the male students (based on standard measurements). What is striking is that the research consistently shows that female students have much less self-confidence as scholars, both when they come in as first-year students and when they leave as seniors. In other words, they are better prepared to be successful scholars, but they don't act that way, either before they get in or after they arrive. As a result, their scholarly aspirations are deflated; fewer expect to go on to graduate school after they leave, and fewer take pride in scholarly accomplishments while enrolled.

We also know that pedagogy is not gender neutral. And while individuals vary and it would be a mistake to stereotype the learning styles of men or women, it is also the case that patterns do exist, and these patterns tend to affect the classroom. For example, and I'm sure this won't be a surprise to any of you, female students, as a rule, tend to interact differently than males. They will hesitate a bit more when they speak; they will begin, pause, and begin again when they start sentences and use qualifiers such as, "Now, don't you think such and such?" and, "Wouldn't it be better to do so and so?"

Male students, on the other hand, tend to point more, make gestures when they speak, act and talk assertively, move very quickly from analysis to conclusion, and make their judgments with much more finality and emphasis. This behavior has been described as "report" talk by some, and it exists in contrast to "rapport" talk, which is more likely to be used by women.

The point of this is not to say that one way of interacting is right and the other is wrong but simply to note that these differences exist and can very much affect the classroom. For example, what if one values report talk more than rapport talk in the classroom, or vice versa? How will that affect the learning environment? How will it influence who gets called on during discussions? Which students think their contributions are valued? What kinds of testing methods are being used? What kind of papers are assigned, and how they are graded?

All of this suggests to me not that we ought to try to be all things to all people but that we need a good mix of folks in the classroom and out of it, so that the variety among our students is somewhat matched by the variety in our faculty. Otherwise, I think we will find ourselves either not serving our students well or trying like crazy to serve them well and looking pretty stupid in the process.

I remember our daughter's experience in a psychology class at Bowdoin College, for example, in which her professor tried to vary her teaching style—not only from time to time, but from sentence to sentence—repeating everything four different times in four different ways so that everyone with every conceivable learning style could understand her. And what was my daughter's response? Well, she thought it was pretty dumb and accomplished very little, besides being extremely repetitive. And I think she was right. We can't be all things to all people. What we want from our faculty is "them": them doing what they do best in the way they do it best in order to get the best out of their students. The answer to the fact of diversity in our student body is not each of us dancing forty different dances a day, trying to satisfy our students. Rather, the answer is diversity on the faculty itself, so that each of us doing our best provides nice diversity for diverse students so they can also do their best. Does that make sense?

My point, then, is that I think we are going to do a better job of educating both our male and female students if they find themselves in and out of the classroom interacting with both male and female faculty and staff.

I'm somewhat more hesitant to mention the second compelling reason for my conclusions than the first because this is based on anecdotal evidence and seems much less secure than the first. Nevertheless, I believe it, so I'll mention it. It seems to me that a faculty and administration made up of a good balance of men and women simply works better than one that is not so composed. And I mean not simply in the classroom but everywhere: in committees, faculty meetings, debates, whatever. We do a better job together than apart.

I remember, by the way, when this idea first hit me with force. It was twenty years ago. I was at another Christian college and on a committee that had recommended and, in fact, helped institute a change in one of our dorms. The change was the conversion of an all-male dorm into a coed residence hall (or Christian version thereof). We, of course, being barbarians at heart, were worried that coed dorms would lead to sex, parties, or worse: It might lead to dancing! But you know what really happened? Well, it transformed what had been an all-male, somewhat rowdy dorm into one of the most civilized residence halls on campus. Instead of sex and parties, we got men and women treating one another like brothers and sisters and becoming better students in the process.

Now, I don't want to make too much of this, and I don't want to imply that there aren't times when all-female or all-male events are appropriate. Of course there are. But over the long run, in the long haul, I think we work better together than apart. And I think that is true for students, faculty, and administrators as well. We will treat each other better, we will consider more and better options, and we will come to better conclusions if we are peopled by both men and women.

The point of this is not so much to recommend a particular policy for all our campuses but to say quite starkly: We need to think both carefully and strategically about diversity on our campuses. We can't pursue it willy-nilly. We can't pursue it because it's always a "good" (it isn't). Rather, the diversity we pursue must be mission driven.

Resisting Diversity

What shouldn't we be doing? I have pointed out a form of diversity that does seem worth pursuing. So what isn't? What are the dangers inherent in being a Christian college or university at this moment in a diverse society?

Here I need to shift our thinking just a bit because you are probably expecting me to discuss certain forms of diversity that are politically correct and therefore culturally suspect. That is the way most of us tend to think these days, regardless of what end of the political spectrum we find ourselves on. But it is precisely because we are so aware of this motive that I think it poses the least danger for us at this particular moment in time. The great danger, in my opinion, comes not from the external political environment but from assumptions and values that already permeate our campuses. And they are, to be precise, the assumptions of the guild and the consumer.

First, the guild. I am firmly convinced that one of the most problematic forms of diversity we face is that which comes to us from the disciplines themselves, whether located in the humanities, the natural or social sciences, or the professions. And, to be honest with you, the problem is not so much the guild itself but the environment in which the guild operates. I'll be blunt: The modern academy has lost any consensus on that which is true, right, good, or beautiful. That's another way of saying that the ontological and epistemological foundation for the pursuit of truth has pretty much crumbled, leaving a worldview vacuum of yawning proportions.

Into this vacuum has entered the guild—the professions—communities of scholars who identify with one another primarily because they share a *particular* area of study, a particular degree, or went to a particular school. I emphasize the word *particular* because the focus keeps getting narrower and narrower. We were once called philosophers; then we became biologists and economists and psychologists; then we developed subspecialties within our disciplines. Now most of us have broken off into camps of people within our subspecialties who share our particular bent or orientation. We each have our own journals, our own projects. And we don't much care about those who work outside our little domain. Indeed, we may not even understand what the fellow down the hall is doing, even though he or she shares the same title or discipline. What we care about is us, our project, and the questions and issues inherent therein.

Now don't get me wrong. There is nothing wrong with specialization—except when it occurs in a philosophical vacuum, which is precisely the current situation. Then, instead of the particular enlightening the general, the particular enlightens only itself. What this has led to in the modern university is the non-university, or the di-versity, a place that is not even remotely uniform in vision, purpose, or effect. That this is a bizarre state of affairs seems, on the surface, fairly obvious. Yet we continue happily to send our children to be educated at such institutions, and, of course, these are the places where all of us have earned our Ph.D.s and learned our trade. From such places, in other words, come our faculty.

We must now ask the following questions. To whom are our faculty members loyal? And for whom are they doing their work? Is it for their students? for the cause of truth? for the cause of Christ? In other words, are they deeply rooted in the mission of the school or deeply rooted in the particular questions of their guild? If the answer is the latter, then your curriculum is guaranteed to become increasingly diverse, your faculty increasingly fragmented, and your students increasingly in love with themselves, pursuing their own careers, their own self-interests, and their own agendas. In other words, your public relations material will increasingly resemble a clanging gong or a tinkling cymbal.

So, threat number one is the guild. But threat number two is the consumer. And if it is the faculty whose purpose and mission are threatened by the guild; it is the president and provost who are most likely to be undone by the consumer.

I had a conversation a few years ago with a student at another institution, which will remain nameless. This student was bitterly complaining about some policy the faculty of his college had passed and to which he responded, "No student likes and no student ought to endure! Don't the faculty know," he said, "that this college is the student body? If they don't pay more attention to what we need, this college is going to go down the drain!"

Bold words, I thought to myself, especially for a nineteen-year-old only beginning his sophomore year. But they are also chilling words, particularly if you are an administrator trying to run a college on a shoestring, with little endowment, little history, in a brutally competitive market. And the temptation—indeed, the reality—is that many administrators who find themselves faced with such pressures feel nearly compelled to respond to the wishes of the consumer, offering whatever major will sell, whatever program is in vogue, whatever curriculum will bring in the students. And the end result is more diversity—diversity not driven by the mission of the college, but diversity driven by the need to stay in business and to succeed according to the dictates of the market.

Now before all the faculty members respond with "amen," let me suggest that though this consumer model is primarily a pressure felt by provosts and presidents, it also works its way into the curriculum. Faculty, let me ask you, what has happened to the grade-point average in your classes over the last decade? Have your students gotten brighter? Or have they gotten what they want?

I'm being very bold here, I know, and surely overexaggerating. But provosts like me—and presidents and faculty alike—must remember in these days that while we are in a market, truth is not for sale. Who of us would raise our children on a consumer model? What we want for our children is for them to grow up in the truth (the good, the right, and the true)—to learn it, to love it, to be held accountable for it; so that they might become the people they ought to become. And isn't that what we want for our students as well?

You see, the real test of our teaching is not so much what our students think about it at the time it is delivered but what they will think about it when they lose a job, a career, a child or spouse, or face their own mortality. Those are the moments when our teaching is put to the test. We will either prepare them for those moments with the truth or we won't.

Let us covenant together in these days to root our colleges and universities in the truth of Jesus Christ. Let us define *diversity* in the light of that truth. Let us pursue diversity for the sake of that truth. And then, I guarantee, it will be good.

This address was delivered at the Conference on the Future of Christian Higher Education at Union University.

Chapter 10

THE POSTMODERN CHALLENGE: THE CHRISTIAN MIND AND HEART IN A POSTMODERN AGE

MILLARD J. ERICKSON

Certain issues seem always to be with us. The reason is not that they cannot be answered but that the answers given in one age are not adequate for another age. They have to be constantly readdressed. One of these issues is the relationship between truth and the meaning or purpose of life. Can we find a rational, defensible basis for our hope for the present and the future, or must it simply be an unsupported wish? In a Christian context, this is the question of faith and reason.

Some, to be sure, answer this question not only with a negative but with an emphatic negative. They contend that meaning and purpose must have some rational basis, but because the latter does not exist, neither does the former. The problem, however, is broader than this. For we face today an environment in which the idea that any objective truth exists, any truth that is true for everyone, is being seriously questioned. I refer to the phenomenon commonly termed "postmodernism." Although there are rather widely differing understandings of what postmodernism is, there is significant agreement that it is real and that it is increasingly coming upon us. It may be helpful, in this connection, to listen to the words of Martin Luther, reminding us that the specific point of challenge to the Christian faith at any given time is where we must be most vigilant: "And it is of no avail that someone says, 'I will gladly confess Christ and his word in every part, except that I would like to be silent on one or two that my despots will not tolerate, such as the two forms of the sacrament, or something of the sort.' For whoever denies Christ in one part or word, has thereby denied the very same Christ who would be denied in all parts, since there is only one Christ, complete and unique in all his words."[1]

In one sense, postmodernity is simply that which follows the modern period. That definition would make it much like the identification of Aristotle's *Metaphysics,* as that which came after the *Physics.* But if we use this chronological criterion, we encounter a strange problem. For by definition "the modern" is what is now, or new, and there really could not be a postmodern, only a different modern. Even the temporal identification of postmodernism is a mixed matter, that it is that ideology which follows temporally upon the ideology of the period that has been designated "modern," in contrast with the "premodern."

By now, some of my readers are probably already rolling their eyes, wondering when this abstruse discussion will end. May I shift the focus somewhat and thereby hopefully bring the discussion into a sharper view? Let me do so by passing on to you a parable, given me three years ago by a music teacher. This is a parable in the form of a question in a music test, as it might be asked at different points in history. Some of you may be familiar with the horrible, you-may-be-a-redneck-if questions. I was first introduced to these by a young man from Jacksonville, Florida, who was a student in my class at Southern Seminary in January 1995. I remember a couple of them that went like this: "If your cousin just bought a new house and you have to go over and help him take the wheels off, you may be a redneck, or if your wife goes to work wearing an orange vest, you may be a redneck." Now, what I am suggesting is that if you select a certain one of these questions and even give a certain answer to it, you may be a postmodernist. Here is a particular test question in music, as it might be asked at different decade intervals. I have adapted this for use in my theology class, using the doctrine of immanence, but here I will present it in its original form, as a music test.

1930. Define *rhythm.*

1960. The movement of music in time, including tempo and meter, is called _____.

1990. The movement of music in time, including tempo and meter, is called:
   A. melody
   B. harmony
   C. rhythm
   D. interval

2000. The movement of music in time, commonly called rhythm, makes you feel:
   A. I don't understand the question.
   B. I think this is an unfair question.

    C. I don't know what the word *rhythm* means.

    D. It doesn't matter how I feel, as long as it is my own authentic feeling.

This test may help to establish the issues for us with a degree of urgency. Let me now sketch a bit more sharply the nature of postmodernism. It can be best understood in terms of its contrast with the modern period. The modern period was characterized by an optimism, in several respects, not the least of which was confidence in human reason and in the ultimate rationality of the universe. It believed that a pattern of rationality and order was present within reality and that the human mind was capable of discovering and understanding it. The modern period shared this common conviction with the premodern period. What it rejected from the premodern period was any transcendent basis for this rationality. Nothing, whether a Christian God or a Platonic realm of forms or ideas, nothing that lay outside of or behind the perceivable natural order was considered to have any reality, or at least any reality that could be known, and it certainly was not considered to have any influence upon what happened within the human experience of the natural order. This knowledge that was believed to be attainable was to be objective. One could free oneself from the conditioning particularities of one's situation in time and space and know things as they really are. The most extreme form of this modernism was the Enlightenment, which exalted human reason and the human individual. It rejected any supernatural, which made it naturalistic. It also rejected any authority above humanity, which made it anthropocentric.

    There are actually several varieties of modernism. These varieties can be clustered into two general types, a more moderate and a more extreme form—which I term *soft modernism* and *hard modernism*, respectively. Soft modernism shares with its forerunner, premodernism, belief in the rationality of the universe and in the human ability to know and understand the truth. Both believe that inclusive explanations of reality, or in other words, integrative metaphysical schemes or worldviews, can be constructed. Hard modernism goes beyond soft modernism, however, by excluding anything else. Hard modernism maintains that reality is limited to what can be experienced, thus excluding supernaturalism of any kind. Knowledge is restricted to what can be known through reason and experience, excluding any sort of intuition or anything of the sort. What is not logical is not considered real.

    Corresponding to these two types of modernism are two varieties of postmodernism, which, interestingly enough, I also would label as "hard" and "soft." Soft postmodernism rejects merely those extremes of modernism found in hard modernism: the dogmatic naturalism and antisupernaturalism; the reductionistic view of reason, which reduces psychology to biology, biology to chemistry, and chemistry to physics. It rejects the limitation of knowledge to sense experience and the meaningful use of language to those statements for which we can identify sense perceptions that would verify or falsify them. It rejects the restriction of the understanding of human personality to stimulus-response conditioning. It rejects the type of naive objectivity that denies the effect of historical and cultural situations. In other words, it rejects logical positivism, behaviorism, and all other artificially scientistic approaches to reality. Hard postmodernism, on the other hand, best represented by deconstruction, goes beyond soft postmodernism to reject the idea of any sort of objectivity and rationality. It maintains that all theories are simply worked out to justify and empower those who hold them, rather than being based upon facts. It not only rejects the limitation of the meaning of language to empirical reference; it rejects the idea that language has any sort of objective or extralinguistic reference at all. It moves from relativism to pluralism in truth. Not only is all knowing and all speaking done from a particular perspective, but each perspective is equally true or valuable. The meaning of a statement is not objectively to be found in the meaning intended by the speaker or writer. Rather, the meaning of a statement is what the hearer or reader finds in it. "What it means to me" is its meaning, even if that is quite different from what the speaker or writer intends the meaning to be.

I would propose, as a Christian and a theologian, that there is much for Christians to be encouraged about in soft postmodernism. It opens the door for Christians to contend for the truth of the Christian faith, in contrast to a secular world that formerly excluded anything of faith of this type. What may not be so apparent is the threat that hard postmodernism poses to the cause of Christianity. Let me suggest several reasons I believe Christianity has a significant stake in the kind of objective truth that hard postmodernism rejects.

First, *I believe Christianity has a significant stake in the kind of objective truth that hard postmodernism rejects because the Christian doctrine of God is at stake.* One of the things that stands out as unusual about the picture of God as revealed in the Scripture is the absoluteness of this God. Here is an intolerant, exclusive God. Whereas some of the other gods of the religions surrounding Israel were apparently able to coexist with other gods, that is not true of the God of Abraham, Isaac, and Jacob, of Moses, Isaiah, Jesus, and Paul. This is a God who is jealous of the love and devotion of his people, who expects total commitment and worship from them. Because he is the only true God, he will not share any portion of the commitment of his people with any claimant to deity, who, of course, cannot really be that. He is the universal God, not just the god of one place or one group of people. He has created everything that is, has given life to every human being, has made every human being in his own image and likeness and for fellowship with him. He has given his Son as the only sacrifice for the sins of the world, and he will ultimately judge everyone who must appear before his judgment seat. Because he has created everything, a rationality pervades the creation. Because he is in control of all of history, there is a grand narrative. Because he is the supreme being, his word is the truth, and his will is the right for all persons, everywhere, and at all times.

As Christians, we must therefore recognize that the very heart of our faith is at stake. We must contest with all of our being the radical postmodernism that might grant the truth of Christianity, but also of views which contradict it, or would make it simply one type of truth for some persons at some times and places.

Second, _I believe Christianity has a significant stake in the kind of objective truth that hard postmodernism rejects because basic human rationality is at stake._ Extreme or hard postmodernism, especially in the form of deconstruction, ultimately undermines basic human rationality. What we used to call _ad hominem_ arguments become the order of the day, where an idea is not evaluated on its merits but in terms of the supposed motivations of the persons presenting it. Further, in extreme postmodernism, the law of contradiction breaks down. A proposition and its contradictory can both coexist. What really happens, however, is that if both propositions are considered true, then neither is, at least not in the customary sense of the word.

I would argue, however, that this contention cannot be sustained, or at least it cannot be commended to others for belief. Belief in the objectivity of truth and in the validity of the laws of logic is not restricted to the modern period or to the premodern and the modern periods, but it is a part of the human person. Theologically, I would say that this belief derives from the fact that all humans are made in the image of God, but that is not what is at stake here. These beliefs are also inherent in the hard postmodernist. The evidence can be seen from an examination of what the postmodernist is doing and saying.

When the postmodernist discusses the issues of the modern and the postmodern paradigms, what paradigm is he using to conduct that discussion? If it is the postmodern, then the statement, "Postmodernism is true," is true. But if this is the case, then the statement, "Postmodernism is not true," is also true.

To put it somewhat differently, the statement, "Modernism is true," is also true. It is something like a T-shirt I purchased at an American Philosophical Association meeting a few years ago. I occasionally wear it to class under a dress shirt and jacket and reveal it to my students. The APA logo and these words appear on the front: "The sentence on the back of this shirt is true." On the back of the shirt appear the words, "The sentence on the front of this shirt is false." After modeling the shirt for my students, I ask them what they think of my shirt. Do they like it? Do they believe it?

It would appear to me that the postmodernists may be wearing T-shirts like mine. When they present their arguments, are they contending that their view is simply one of many, and that the contradictories of their contentions are also true? Is the meaning of their statements whatever the hearer takes that meaning to be, or are they contending that the meaning is what they intend to assert? Are they contending that the deconstruction of other views is really correct and true and ought to be believed by others than themselves, or is this only a case being made to justify themselves? In other words, must not deconstruction also be deconstructed, or submitted to a hermeneutic of suspicion, just like any other view? If not, why is it entitled to such an exemption, and why is no other view so entitled?

Let me illustrate. Stanford philosopher John Searle wrote a ten-page critical review of Derrida's thought in *Glyph*.[2] Derrida wrote a ninety-two page response and rebuttal, in which he contended that Searle had misunderstood and misrepresented Derrida's intended meaning.[3] But how can this be? This is not a postmodern or deconstructive response. This is a terribly pre-postmodern type of statement. I would assert that every effort to present postmodernism for acceptance by others presupposes a rationality of the type found in premodernism and modernism. That is because there is a fundamental rationality to the universe, and human discourse presupposes it.

Third, *I believe Christianity has a significant stake in the kind of objective truth that hard postmodernism rejects because human freedom is at stake.* There is, of course, a very real possibility that hard postmodernists are sincere and consistent. If, in fact, they are sincere, they are not presenting their ideas as objectively true assertions to be accepted by others. Rather, they are simply presenting their ideas to accomplish their ends. In other words, they simply want their cause to prevail and will enforce it by whatever means are necessary, not by logical persuasion. And what is the means by which they accomplish their ends? In the academic setting, it is done by restricting the expression of any viewpoint other than the correct one. This may be done through actual repression and intimidation of those who hold differing views. It may be done through simply not giving the other options expression. I think of a student of mine at Southwestern, a graduate of a rather strong state university with an English degree, who told me that in his department at that school, every member of the department was a deconstructionist, with the exception of one instructor, who was not given tenure. This is not an isolated case. A university ought to be the one place where ideas are allowed to compete freely in the intellectual marketplace, but that is not always true. The only thing that is new about "political correctness," in which only the "correct" view is allowed, is that it is now publicly recognized and acknowledged. It has, however, been with us for some time. In the state university from which I graduated, something more than ten years ago, all except one of the members of the philosophy department were logical positivists; and in my minor field, psychology, every last member of the faculty in the department was a behaviorist. We have come full circle in sixty or seventy years. From the days when fundamentalist Christians succeeded in passing laws that forbade the teaching of evolution in the public schools, it is now virtually impossible to teach anything else, even as one option among many. It is contended that the consideration of any other option is teaching of religion and that such teaching violates the separation of church and state. Actually, what is involved here sounds like something quite different, the exclusion of any religion from any state-connected enterprise, which, if strictly enforced, would require rather severe alteration of the content of the lectures of some humanist professors.

When belief in objective truth is lost, or at least eroded, not all views are treated as equally true and legitimate in practice. Rather, the view held by those with the power to do so is given exclusive rights. This is what led the late senator and vice president, Hubert Humphrey, himself clearly a liberal, to complain of a "new moral authoritarianism" on the part of some intolerant liberals, and it probably lies behind Rush Limbaugh's rather carelessly applied epitaph of "Feminazi." It is also why Allan Bloom chose to entitle his significant book of a decade ago, *The Closing of the American Mind*.

I am concerned that with the loss of belief in the objectivity of truth will also come at least some restriction of the free exchange and competition of ideas. Ironically, some of those who scream "academic freedom" at the least suggestion of responsibility on their part actually encroach upon the academic freedom of students. One of the more liberal colleagues I have ever had was noted for his suppression of differing opinions, insisted that students who had taken his required course in another school must take it again for credit in our school, and even on at least one occasion, expelled a student from class for persistently disagreeing with him (in a fashion that other students in the class did not find objectionable). It is as if much were made of the freedom of these students to eat any kind of food they wished, but the menu was so controlled that certain options were never available. The free exchange of ideas in the intellectual marketplace does not stem from the belief that all of the ideas are true, which really means that none of them are. It assumes that there is such a thing as objective truth and that therefore it makes sense to attempt to determine which belief more closely approximates this.

The answer to this threat will not be a counterauthoritarianism. It will be the careful, fair, and honest presentation of all of the legitimate options on an issue, followed by, and only then, a critique of the viewpoints involved and argumentation for the instructor's conviction. This is the philosophy of education I was taught and have tried to practice. There is, to be sure, a certain risk in this philosophy. I recall a conversation with one of my students on the platform of the Chicago & Northwestern Railroad in Wheaton. Half seriously, she said to me, "I'm angry with you." Concerned that I had offended or mistreated her, I asked, "Why Betty?" "Well," she said, "I'm a biology major, and I had hoped to apply for a full-time lab assistant position in the biology department here. But because of your class, I am no longer sufficiently convinced of the error of evolution to be able to teach here. The day in apologetics class that you put the five views on the board, presented the argument for and against each one, and then argued for progressive creationism was the first time I had heard evolution presented that fairly and persuasively. In four years of biology classes, I had never been tempted to accept evolution." Some conservative listeners may fault my methodology because of that temporary defection from the creationist view. Before they do that, however, I would urge them to consider the students who have been virtually driven from Christian faith because of a dogmatic or intolerant position on it.

It is the objectivity of truth that I am concerned about, not merely the correspondence theory of truth, for those two are not necessarily identical. Indeed, listen to a definition of truth from a philosopher who will remain anonymous for the moment: "Truth, as any dictionary will tell you, is a property of certain of our ideas. It means their 'agreement,' as falsity means their disagreement, with 'reality.'" Now, who do you suppose wrote that? Those words are from William James, in *Pragmatism's Conception of Truth*.[4] The pragmatism of an earlier day, not that of today's neopragmatist, Richard Rorty, believed that there really was one idea that objectively worked better than another.

As Christians, and particularly as a Christian university, we need to do several things:

1. We must recognize those valid insights of postmodernism, especially soft postmodernism, and utilize them. Certainly, the Christian celebrates soft postmodernism's rejection of the narrowness of hard modernism in the Enlightenment model. There are insights that cannot be denied, and we need not do so and return to a premodern way of thinking. I recently received a letter from a laywoman who was concerned that my utilization of the idea of the human unconscious committed me to the whole view of human sexuality, aggression, repression, etc., that Sigmund Freud taught. I think the discovery of the human unconscious to be an approximately correct understanding, and something that need not be rejected, as is also true of quantum mechanics, non-Euclidean geometries, Einstein's theories of general and special relativity, and many other concepts.

2. In our conversations, we must recognize that postmoderns are postmodern and begin where they are. If they are more oriented to narrative, then we may legitimately begin with a narrative approach. I am referring to the communicative role of narrative, its ability to convey truth, rather than the hermeneutical role, the idea that narrative is the key to the interpretation of the Scripture, or the heuristic role, the idea that the telling of stories, including our own, is the means to discovering truth.

3. We must insist on the discussion of the meta- or theoretical issues in any discipline. This is the discussion of the very foundation of assertions, or the basis of discussion. For example, we must ask what paradigm is being employed when we discuss paradigm change and what language game we are playing when we discuss language games. I believe we will find that one of two things happens. Either the dis-

cussant will lapse into some sort of authoritarian stance (as was shown earlier), or the discussant will have to come to grips with the inevitability of the objectivity of truth.

4. We resist the common tendency to what C. S. Lewis and others have termed "chronological snobbery," or what I choose to call, more broadly, "chronocentrism." This is the conception that any idea that is more recent is superior to one that is older. As Thomas Oden has pointed out, annoying though it may be, we need to ask people whether they are using "new" as synonymous with "good," and "change" as synonymous for "improvement" or "progress."[5]

5. We need to avoid binding our thinking too closely to present-day expressions. One reason I prefer the term *chronocentrism* to some alternatives is that it points up the tendency to regard the present view, not simply as superior to the past but as final. We need to bear in mind, however, that postmodernism will also pass and will be replaced by something that we might term, despite its clumsiness, "postpostmodernism." Some postmodernists act as if this is unthinkable. We may expect this postmodern period to last even a shorter time than the modern period for at least two reasons. First, change is now taking place much more rapidly, and the rate of change is accelerating. Second, this movement, with its self-defeating view of truth, meaning, and language, contains the seeds of its own destruction. Indeed, it may be that postmodernism is, in some respects, already beginning to decline, even as it is gaining strength in some other respects. Harold Bloom, for example, of the Yale school of literary criticism, has, in his recent remarks, begun to sound more like Allan Bloom.

I am particularly concerned that we take this final guideline seriously. Evangelicals have typically been among the last to react to a new idea and sometimes adopt or adapt it after the broader culture has already abandoned it. I note some evangelicals today who, in their desire to be postmodern, are propounding what sound in evangelical circles novel and creative ideas but are actually warmed-over versions of ideas held a generation earlier in more liberal circles, and in some cases, now abandoned there. I do not want us always to be running after the train. I want us to be waiting at the next station when it pulls in. We need to take postmodernism seriously and to develop a post-postmodernism to present to disillusioned postmodernists when they recognize the failure of their view.

This address was delivered during the inaugural events for David S. Dockery as the fifteenth president at Union University.

Chapter 11

SUSTAINING CHRISTIAN INTELLECTUAL COMMITMENTS: LESSONS FROM THE RECENT PAST

JOEL A. CARPENTER

It seems a little odd that the editors would ask a historian to think about the future of Christian higher education. The historian's view is like that from the rear seat of my station wagon. It is great for seeing where we have been, but it is not well positioned for scanning the horizon up ahead. In my very short tenure as a college officer, I have learned that there are plenty of seers and prognosticators for the future of higher education. They constitute a small industry, in fact, and in these uncertain times they command some rather hefty fees. Historians come cheaper. So here is my perspective, and I'm happy it's part of this book.

My assigned topic was "Trends, Challenges, and Issues Facing the Christian University." I have decided that it is prudent to stick to one trend, one challenge, and one issue, all of which are interrelated. The trend is secularization; the challenge is to sustain authentically Christian universities; and the issue is how to keep our commitment to Christ-centered higher education vigorous and healthy in the years to come.

Those of us who serve evangelical colleges and universities understand the rather humble status we have. Many academies question the legitimacy of what we aim to do. In 1988, for example, a subcommittee of the American Association of University Professors proposed that the AAUP declare colleges and universities that have placed academic freedom within the bounds of religious commitment to have forfeited "the moral right to proclaim themselves as authentic seats of higher learning."[1] In response to the rather modest suggestion at the end of George Marsden's book *The Soul of the American University,* that a truly tolerant and inclusive university ought to welcome scholarship from a Christian perspective, Penn historian Bruce Kuklick snorted that the very idea was "loony."[2]

My purpose is not to dwell on our marginality, however. In many respects, Christian higher education is doing quite well today. Evangelical colleges and universities are thriving and getting noticed in national surveys for their increasing quality. Even the "outrageous idea of Christian scholarship," as Marsden's new book puts it, is receiving a hearing one might not have expected just a few years ago. Boston University sociologist Alan Wolfe, who argued in 1996 against Marsden's pleas for the inclusion of religious scholarship in secular universities, now seems to be relenting a bit. In his review last month of Marsden's second book, Wolfe suggested that perhaps a revival of religious thought could enrich the larger enterprise after all.[3] Not only the idea of Christian scholarship but the product itself is showing up increasingly in the main channels of intellectual discourse. At my home institution, three professors presently have religiously oriented works in print with Oxford University Press, and two more have books under contract with the same firm. A modest renaissance of Christian scholarship is on the rise, something which we should feel gratified to see in our time.

Still, I want to sound a more sober note concerning the long-term prospects of Christian learning and cultural achievement. The history of efforts to sustain a Christian influence in American higher education over the past century does not give us much assurance that current evangelical efforts will meet with lasting success. Three stories in particular are worth looking at: Marsden's *Soul of the American University,* which shows how the once-pervasive influence of Protestantism in America's most accomplished universities all but totally vanished; Philip Gleason's *Contending with Modernity,* which tells how Catholic higher education fostered a cultural and intellectual renaissance in the 1930s, only to see the whole enterprise crumble in the 1960s; and Douglas Sloan's *Faith and Knowledge,* an account of how in the 1950s mainline Protestants tried and eventually failed to challenge the pervasive secularism of the American academy. As we look to the future of the Christian university, it is worth at least a few glances in the rearview mirror.

The American Academy's Lost Soul

George Marsden's masterful study of Protestantism's role in shaping the modern secular research university takes a fresh look at the oft-repeated story of the secularization of American higher education. Others have pointed to the inherent tensions between divinely revealed religion and Enlightenment science, the nation's growing cultural and religious pluralism, or the influence of industrial capitalism. Marsden argues instead that the American university was begotten of the marriage of evangelical Protestantism and the ideals of the American republic. A broad-based, generic Protestantism, in league with scientific and technological advance and serving the cause of democratic liberty, was thought to be the foundation of the Republic. There was an informal religious establishment in the United States by the mid-nineteenth century that aspired to the moral transformation of American society. The old-time Protestant colleges were part of this comprehensive vision of turning the United States into a truly Christian nation and a moral example to the rest of the world.

Marsden notes that as the nation grew more internally varied, mainline Protestantism chose to stretch its religious convictions ever broader and thinner to retain its cultural leadership and centrality. In the era from 1870 to the First World War, when modern research universities emerged, they were led by liberal Protestants who stood for the principles of openness and free inquiry and embraced both science and the ethical teachings of Jesus. They assumed that science would remain an ally of faith and that morality needed a religious foundation. Their vision was the heart and soul of the Progressive era. Over time, these ideals became more broadly moral and less distinctively Christian. In the end, they were indistinguishable from generic cultural norms. Daniel Coit Gilman, the founding president of the Johns Hopkins University said, "The ultimate end of all education and scientific effort, as well as of all legislation and statesmanship—is identical with that at which Christianity aims . . . 'Peace on earth, good will to men.'"[4] It would not take long for critics to wonder whether this kind of religion had much of value to add.

In Marsden's account, therefore, secularization did not simply happen to educational institutions as they responded to broad, impersonal forces. It was _actively pursued_ by the earnest liberal Christians who built and led the emerging universities. Even their desire for cultural unity and their establishment of a unified worldview worked against them in the end. To the increasingly secular-minded inhabitants of the universities, even the broadest and least offense-giving forms of Christianity seemed sectarian and unfit for a leading role. Nevertheless, American universities remain deeply establishmentarian, Marsden argues, but now they have established nonbelief. They do not easily include and tolerate perspectives that dissent from their vision of tolerance and inclusivity.

Contending with Modernity

Philip Gleason's history of Catholic higher education in the twentieth century is a necessary companion to Marsden's book, for it explores the attempts of a vigorous and substantial religious community outside the Protestant establishment to make higher education Christian. It has some remarkable parallels to the history of conservative Protestant encounters with modernity. Gleason claims that two events of seminal importance shaped Catholic higher education in the beginning of the twentieth century. The first was the theological conflict surrounding "Americanism," which resulted in a reprimand from Pope Leo XIII in 1899 to those who called for the Catholic church to embrace America's democratic spirit and freedom of inquiry. The second was the Vatican's denunciation of "modernism" in theology and biblical criticism in 1907. Many scholars since Vatican II have emphasized the chilling effect of these proscriptions on intellectual inquiry, but Gleason insists that these events also led to a revival of neoscholastic philosophy that inspired new confidence and creative energy among Catholic intellectuals. Modern democratic culture was in crisis in the wake of World War I, they believed, and the Catholic faith had the remedy. It understood the reasons for the malaise, it had the cure, and it had a master plan for rebuilding Western civilization.

In the thought systems of Thomas Aquinas, Catholic intellectuals found a unified worldview for shaping education and providing a comprehensive vision of life. Catholicism is not merely a religion; it is a culture, said Catholic intellectuals. Catholicism has its own vision for art, economics, psychology, and ethics. It has its own history, heroes, art, and tradition. Catholic colleges and universities would not just defend the faith, then; they would be creative centers of Christian culture and tradition. Catholic cultural activity flourished in the 1930s and 1940s, as this great religious tradition and its immigrant adherents came into their own in America. By the 1950s, the Catholic intellectual tradition seemed well established and riding high. Neoscholastic philosopher Jacques Maritain was teaching at Princeton, while John Courtney Murray, the scholar of the Catholic Renaissance, was at Yale. At the same time, Catholic colleges and universities were rapidly expanding and improving. By the end of World War II, they offered postgraduate education in every major profession and academic field of inquiry and increased their share of national enrollments. Catholic educational leaders served on important government commissions, including the one that formed the National Science Foundation in 1950, while Catholic university scientists worked on a variety of government research projects, including the atomic bomb.

Catholic intellectuals soon found that success had its own perils. The bold actions of Catholic leaders to help the unions organize, support the New Deal Democratic coalition, and even more, to take action on matters of public morality, began to prompt some anti-Catholic sentiment in national cultural politics. After World War II, a major anti-Catholic backlash flared up. The most notorious instance was a diatribe by Paul Blanshard, _American Freedom and Catholic Power,_ which equated American Catholic activism with the Catholic church's alliances with right-wing forces in Spain and Latin America.[5] The Church's public stand against immorality in movies and pulp fiction and its attempt in some states to influence legislation restricting birth control really set off alarm bells.

Catholic intellectuals felt caught in this brief flare-up of "culture wars" in the late 1940s and early 1950s. On the one hand, they had been eager supporters of the call to build a Catholic culture and to "redeem all things in Christ." On the other hand, they were not champions of censorship, and they were shocked when in 1954 the Vatican cracked down on John Courtney Murray, the brilliant Jesuit philosopher, for publishing an argument that American-style separation of church and state was fully in accordance with Catholic thought. Catholic intellectuals became disgruntled with the Church's embattled posture and yearned to break out of the religious ghetto and its siege mentality. They sought to enter into the mainstream of American cultural and intellectual life. Their earlier posture of standing against the modern world and proclaiming that the Catholic faith had the answers for the current crisis of Western civilization gave way to a sense that there were many positive aspects of modernity, especially its emphasis on human freedom. A liberal movement began within American

Catholicism, which sought to engage in "vital contact with the spirit of our age."[6]

Meanwhile, Catholic university leaders were losing confidence in their ability to integrate all of their curriculum. Several major national attempts to state a distinctly Catholic vision for higher education failed. A study at the University of Notre Dame in 1961 showed that where once Catholic professors pointed to intellectual unity and integration as the standard for excellence, they were now pointing to the norms of excellence within each discipline or profession they taught. Professional competence in specialized fields was replacing a distinctively Catholic intellectual vision that encompassed all of learning and life.

Catholic educators had been confident that they could build graduate research programs and professional and technological schools without affecting the fundamental commitments of their universities. However, they found out that these programs were not value neutral. They were products of a university world that increasingly favored scientific naturalism as the way of knowing about the world and promoted a mechanistic and instrumental worldview. Thus, Catholic science, business, and engineering professors began to question the relevance of the neoscholasticism for their work. Humanists resonated with historian John Tracy Ellis' lament about American Catholicism's religious and intellectual separatism, "we have all the answers" triumphalism, and alleged preference for religious orthodoxy over professional excellence. And many philosophers and theologians had tired of neo-Thomism. They responded to Vatican II's call for a new opening up to the modern world by sweeping away entirely the old philosophical structure of Catholic higher education.

The result, Gleason argues, has been a profound identity crisis among Catholic colleges and universities. Catholic colleges have continued to improve academically, and very few have abandoned their Catholic character entirely, but they no longer share a consensus about the substance of religious beliefs, moral commitments, or academic mission. The problem, Gleason concludes, "is not that Catholic educators do not want their institutions to remain Catholic, but that they are no longer sure what remaining Catholic means."[7]

Mainline Protestantism's Last Stand

Douglas Sloan narrates the story of a major effort mounted during the 1950s by mainline Protestant theologians, university faculty members, and campus ministry leaders to reassert a Christian influence in American higher education. The neoorthodox theological movement in the 1930s and 1940s was a key catalyst behind this movement. Theologians such as H. Richard Niebuhr, Reinhold Niebuhr, and Paul Tillich had stressed that all of human culture rests on religious commitments. Much of their critical task had been to expose the faith-based presuppositions behind modern secular thought and to test their adequacy when compared to a Christian worldview. Scientific naturalism had its gods too, they insisted; it rested on some basic and unprovable assumptions about the nature of reality. Furthermore, the rise of totalitarianism and the horrors of World War II showed very clearly that Western civilization's faith in science to bring moral progress and social and political democracy was deeply flawed. The spurious value neutrality of scientism created a spiritual vacuum that was as likely to be filled by totalitarian as by democratic commitments. Modern universities had driven these ideas, and if the churches really wanted to influence Western culture with the Christian message, they had better engage the university-based intellectual scene. Warned Reinhold Niebuhr: "If the academic work of the college is basically hostile or indifferent to religion, the extracurricular religious activities can serve to maintain the religious loyalty of the minority but will accomplish little to give our whole culture a more positive religious content."[8] The most pressing Christian mission to the university, then, was not to foster personal spirituality or social action, important as both of those missions were. The most important task for Christian scholars was to be truth-seekers in every intellectual realm. Thus, every Christian in the university should be a lay theologian.

By the early 1950s, Sloan reports, mainline Protestants were developing an institutional base for a mission to higher education. The Student Christian Movement was to play a role, as were various denominational and ecumenical campus ministries, religious studies programs and departments, the National Council of Churches' Commission on Higher Education (which published the movement's main organ, *The Christian Scholar*), the Faculty Christian Fellowship (which had chapters on nearly half of the nation's campuses), and two charitable trusts, the Hazen Foundation and the Danforth Foundation, which provided major funding for studies and programs.

These efforts to reinvest religious perspectives in the universities created some important literature, featuring attempts by Christian professors in many disciplines to critique the reigning assumptions of their fields and to pose some alternative Christian understandings. These Christian critics hammered away at the "cult of objectivity" that pervaded the research university and its abdication of responsibility for how knowledge was used. They argued that in the search for an integrating cultural vision, the Christian faith had some answers concerning the ultimate meaning and purpose of life and human nature. At the same time, these Christian scholars pushed hard at the churches' anti-intellectualism. They were determined to see this intellectual mission move higher up on the churches' task list, which was dominated by other programs, even on college campuses. They were confident that they could make a difference in the life of universities and make them centers for cultural renewal and the revival of Christian faith and thought.

This whole enterprise was short-lived, Sloan reports. Several trends conspired to soften its impact and limit its life span. First, it never was able to move the student ministries toward an intellectual mission. These ministries had been activist minded from their beginnings in the Student Volunteer Movement for Foreign Missions, and they were in the process of converting their missionary and social gospel activism into solidarity with the civil rights movement, which at least had a common Christian commitment behind it, and then with the larger student radical movement, which did not. Then a second trend emerged, which abetted the student ministries in this move and undercut the Christian scholars. Mainline Protestant theology during the 1960s was moving from the neoorthodox critique of modern secularity from the standpoint of a transcendent God to a secular theology that gave up on the realm of metaphysics, faith, and the quest for meaning. Secular theologians favored "letting the world set the agenda," and embracing its pragmatic, problem-solving, and instrumentalist values. They rendered the whole quest for a Christian critical perspective on modern secularity irrelevant.

A third weakness in the mainline Protestant intellectual mission came from within the faculty itself. While the Faculty Christian Fellowship turned out fourteen hundred people for annual meetings and sent its newsletter to thirty-seven thousand, it never had more than four hundred formal members. Were Christian professors finding it difficult to wear spiritual labels in the university environment? Was the erosion of religious vitality that was nagging at many mainline congregations also affecting professors' conviction and resolve? Sloan does not venture any theories about this, but a certain softness in faculty commitment was evident from the start.

The heart of the problem for the mainline Protestant university mission, Sloan insists, was an intellectual one. The main problem Christian scholars needed to address was the role of faith, meaning, spirit, and value in a climate of opinion where scientific naturalism and knowledge-is-power pragmatism ruled. Since the turn of the century, empirical science had been touted as the dominant mode of knowing anything for certain in the modern world, the key to technological mastery over nature, and the solver of social problems as well. The founding president of the University of Chicago, biblical scholar William Rainey Harper, proclaimed the university "the Messiah of democracy, its to-be-expected deliverer."[9] But it did not take long for even the most optimistic liberal Protestants to find out that modern science was not the easiest of friends for religion. Especially during the years following the First World War, the alliance of religious idealism, progressive politics, and scientific knowledge began to unravel. The hard, valueless, mechanistic edge of the scientific worldview came to the fore, and a naturalistic philosophy—that nature is all there is, and science is the only bona fide source of knowledge—came to dominate the university scene. Mainline Protestants could not avoid this challenge any longer: What place did faith have in the house of knowledge?

Sloan presses this question relentlessly. He contends that the dominant answer mainline Protestantism gave was a sort of two-realms dualism, which says that faith and knowledge are two different categories of knowing. There is a spiritual reality that science cannot countenance. This strategy carved out a niche for faith, Sloan argues, but, in effect, it made faith marginal to the dominant intellectual power of the age. Compared to empirical science, faith seemed less real and less relevant. Much as the neoorthodox theologians and a variety of Christian university scholars following in their train might punch away at the myth of scientific objectivity, they were never very successful in building a case for ways of knowing that surround, suffuse, and transcend nature. So the Protestant theological renaissance of the mid-twentieth century failed to penetrate the cognitive center of the modern university, and the churches eventually fell back and gave up on the critical task. By the end of the 1960s, says Sloan, the "engagement of the Protestant church with American higher education had collapsed, and its forces were in rout."[10]

Lessons and Strategies for Evangelicals

I have discussed these developments at some length, but I hope I have made clear the striking parallels and similarities to contemporary evangelical academe in these past efforts to make higher education Christian. Just when *The Christian Scholar* was giving way to a secular publication named *Soundings*, the evangelical journal, *Christian Scholar's Review*, was being born. Mainline Protestants such as E. Harris Harbison, the Princeton historian, probed the presuppositions of their disciplines and defended the explanatory power of a Christian worldview in the 1950s, and now evangelical scholars such as Harry Stout, the Yale historian, have taken up the same task. The Catholic Renaissance was an extraordinary event in American religious history, and from the vantage point of Calvin College, at least, its claiming a mandate to redeem the whole of culture under the lordship of Jesus Christ sounds endearingly familiar. Less endearing, perhaps, but all too familiar, is the commitment to a "Christian America" that drove the Protestant educational establishment of the early twentieth century. It still abides in the bosoms of conservative Protestants today. Hence the divided loyalties reflected in the motto of Baylor University: "Pro Ecclesia, Pro Texana."

If these historical ghosts show so many similarities to today's evangelical Protestant academy, can we expect to follow their fate as well? Will the evangelical intellectual and cultural enterprise collapse just as suddenly as did these other Christian efforts? Historical fate is full of surprising twists and unintended consequences. Who in Catholic higher education thought that by pushing hard to develop graduate research and professional programs, they would undermine a Christian vision for the integration of faith and learning? Likewise, the liberal Protestant leaders of America's best universities at the turn of the century thought that science and religion would be forever friends. So we cannot presume to control the mark we make in history. That is in God's hands. We can only pledge to be faithful to the charge we have to serve God in the present age. But it may help to be guided by some lessons from the past.

Three Lessons

What lessons are there for us in these stories? There are many, and I would commend these books to every Christian educational leader. But let me list just three.

1. *Christian higher education needs an authentic cultural vision and mandate.* The liberal Protestant founders of the modern research universities had a noble vision. They dreamed of an America whose alabaster cities would one day gleam, "undimmed by human tears," where brotherhood (and sisterhood) would reign "from sea to shining sea." The wedding of scientific and technological knowledge with religious ideals, for the sake of the flourishing of democracy in America, was their aim. The vision fell victim, however, as Marsden shows, to the incessant growth of pluralism in America, making it impossible for Protestantism, even of the broadest sort, to make claims on all of society. And as Sloan emphasizes, it also fell victim to the instability of the relationship between religion and science. Hard-edged naturalism and knowledge-is-power pragmatism drove religion out to the margins.

    The Catholic Renaissance had a beatific cultural vision as well. It admired the Christendom of the Middle Ages, when all of culture was assigned a role in incarnating the mystical body of Christ. In their clearest thinking, however, Catholics recognized that Christendom was no more; the Church's contemporary mission was not to create a homogenous civilization, but in Jacques Maritain's lovely phrase, it was to be "scattered over the whole surface of the globe . . . [like] the host of stars strewn across the sky."[11] Catholics' vision of a Christian culture was a mandate for a countercultural movement, something the Catholic hierarchy often forgot and of which Catholic intellectuals grew weary. They yearned instead to join the main currents of contemporary life.

    The lesson for us is to guard a lively sense of the kingdom of God; to make sharp distinctions between it and the kingdoms of this world; to never grow weary of being keen witnesses to the way of righteousness, justice, peace, and of human flourishing of every kind that the Bible calls *shalom*; and to recognize that ours is a countercultural vision. It is not a return to the notion of Christendom, even in its peculiar "Christian America" form. It is not a call to join the mainstream on its own terms, either, or to let the world set the agenda. It is not a mandate to a siege mentality, or a ghettolike separatism, or a launching of culture wars. But it is a call, as the apostle Peter put it, to "always be prepared to give an answer to everyone who asks you to give the reason for the hope that you have. But do this with gentleness and respect, keeping a clear conscience, so that those who speak maliciously against your good behavior in Christ may be ashamed of their slander."[12] It is a mandate, then, to give witness to another way, one that can be realized only incompletely in this world before Christ comes to complete his redemption of all things.

2. *A "culture wars" atmosphere is not conducive to the task of the Christian scholar.* In addition to the problems with the "culture wars" approach I've implied above—a false understanding of the cultural mandate and the culture warriors' frequent neglect of the Christian way of engaging in a contest of ideas and values—a warring approach has other perils for Christian scholarship. First, it is a distraction. The life of the scholar demands perseverance and concentration. The noise of battle, where ideas are used as weapons, can distract scholars from their main work of being the critical weighers, cultivators, and imparters of ideas. It takes a near-athletic devotion to thinking, research, and careful communication to stay sharp as a teacher and scholar, and as many can tell you, time spent out on the hustings is time away from one's main task. Sooner than one might think, the intellectual weapons get rusty, the mental muscle loses its tone, and the trail grows cold in the pursuit of the truth. Second, culture wars can promote internal backlashes as dangerous as the external struggles. Scholars can become so ashamed of the excesses of their combative compatriots that they start sympathizing with ideas and perspectives of which they should be more critical. Evangelical scholars' embarrassed and loathing reactions to Randall Terry and Pat Robertson have led many to sympathize with contemporary secular ideas more than they should. A third danger is that a culture wars mentality can very quickly turn anti-intellectual. Ideas that don't have immediate payoff as ideological weapons are thought to be of no value. Hence the infamous words of Daniel Berrigan at the height of the antiwar movement. "Scholarship," he said, "is

raw sewerage."[13] The search for truth devolves into the search for ways to win, or at least to stick your opponent.

3. _The basic spiritual issue in the survival of Christian higher education is an intellectual one._ Campus ministries can do much to provide a religious home away from home, bring the blessings of personal salvation and the support of a loving fellowship, and lead students into a life of service. But unless the challenge of a naturalistic worldview is met head-on in the intellectual arena, all of this effort will be but compensatory work around the margins. Ideas matter. Ideologies and worldviews drive— and drive down—whole civilizations. Christian scholars and ministry leaders who invoke a two-realms, spiritual-scientific dualism have taken themselves out of the main struggle in the nation's intellectual arenas. The notion that a Christian college education is mainly a value-added enterprise, adding faith and values to the realm of knowledge as already determined by the secular academy, is positively destructive. The secular, naturalistic, instrumentalist values of today's knowledge industry drive faith into a small and inconsequential corner of life. There is no more critical spiritual concern for Christian college leaders than the nature of knowledge and its implications for every discipline. The fate of Catholic universities, mainline Protestantism's university missions, and even more tragically, mainline Protestant church-related colleges, make this point utterly clear.

Three Bits of Advice

So much for the lessons of history. But what, you might be asking, should Christian educational leaders do in light of these lessons?

1. _Every Christian college needs intellectual leaders who focus on questions of faith and knowledge and a Christian worldview._ Every one of our campuses needs some keepers of the Christian cultural vision, of the faith's intellectual flame. Someone, or some group of leaders, needs to have an acute sense of Christian ways of understanding knowledge and knowing and of faith's role in learning. Some must have a clear vision of the kingdom of God, a sharp sense of the Christian community's mandates to give witness to the kingdom, and a firm understanding of how the task of learning fits into God's larger economy. There must be some living sources of insight

about how the Christian faith encounters, undergirds, or critiques the basic assumptions of every academic discipline and profession. Thank God for the intellectual leadership of Arthur Holmes, for example, at Wheaton College and around the Christian college circuit. God be praised for Nicholas Wolterstorff's polymathic prowess at Christian thinking for so many years at Calvin College and now at Yale. Geniuses such as theirs may be as rare as Einstein's, but every campus needs scholars who are competent to lead and to teach other scholars in this way.

2. *Every professor must in some sense be a lay theologian, or take on an intellectual apostolate.* Even if some faculty members need to take the intellectual lead, others must be active learners. There should be no place in Christian colleges for the simple practitioner who is content to plug away at some specialty and never turn a critical, faith-enlightened eye to the presuppositions and assumptions of her own field, whether it be classics or chemistry. This assignment is a very tough one for most of us. We usually are attracted to our fields of work because of our innate talents for them and our love of the day-to-day practice of them. And it certainly is true that being a good practitioner in a field is itself a calling from God, which can be used to further his kingdom. But if I don't ask some questions about the assumptions and worldview behind my trade, how can I see the way to be faithful to him in my use of it? It is not, after all, a neutral tool. Those of us who are better equipped to be practitioners than critics and theorists need to recognize the crucial importance of such work and be conscientious consumers of it. We need to be lay theologians and philosophers, every one of us, equipped to grapple with life's basic questions as they apply to our disciplines and larger callings.

3. *Every Christian college academic officer has to make these intellectual perspectives central features of campus discourse.* Our primary task is faculty formation, or faculty development. Every fresh cohort of faculty members we hire comes to us from an intellectual and social context that is driven by values, orientations, and reward structures quite different from and often at odds with our own. How they are educated in the task of Christian scholarship and what they do to influence the outlook and orientation of the colleges you serve, will determine

the future of Christian higher education. If they are to be formed in Christian ways of thinking, teaching, and approaching scholarship, most of that formation must take place on your campus. Academic officers and departmental leaders must provide intensive work in faculty development and exert some personal leadership on campus in setting an ethos that welcomes the search for Christian intellectual perspectives. Many of the virtues of the life and work of a Christian scholar are caught as well as taught. Evangelical higher education must be decisively Christian in an intellectually compelling way, at its substantive core, in every discipline and professional program. Without this passionate commitment and the work and will to sustain it, our colleges will fail in the long run.

That much, my friends, we have learned from history.

This address was given at the Conference on the Future of Christian Higher Education at Union University.

Chapter 12

THE SPIRITUAL LIFE OF THE CHRISTIAN SCHOLAR: PRACTICING THE PRESENCE OF CHRIST

CLAUDE O. PRESSNELL, JR.

As we consider the future of Christian higher education, it is easy to overinstitutionalize our thoughts by dreaming about facilities, curricular designs, and enrollments. Though these items do demand our attention, Christian scholarship is about individuals and community. We must also devote our attention to the inner life of the scholar. Unless we attend to the spiritual life, we will never accomplish the dreams we hold for the future of Christian higher education.

For higher education to be Christian, it must be taught by those who not only identify themselves as Christians but live lives with the marks of Christianity. Christian scholarship is more than merely an intellectual assent to a biblical understanding of a particular academic discipline; it is the expression of a life that is being fully redeemed by the activity of the living Christ. "Convictions must not only be lodged in one's head but also penetrate the whole person."[1] Christian scholarship finds its effectiveness and growth in the inner spiritual reality of life in Christ.

Richard Foster writes, "The desperate need today is not for a greater number of intelligent people or gifted people, but for deep people."[2] The need for intelligent academicians goes without question, and this paper should not be used as an excuse for lazy scholarship. The Christian academy must continue to equip scholars with the intellectual prowess to confront the naturalistic infestation of the university system. However, becoming contemplative Christians will serve as a source of strength in bringing our intellects under the lordship of

121

Christ. Seventeenth-century scholar Francis de Sales reminds us, "[True devotion] not only does no injury to one's vocation or occupation but on the contrary adorns and beautifies it. Care of one's family is rendered more peaceable, love of husband and wife more sincere, service of one's prince more faithful, and every type of employment more pleasant and agreeable."[3]

The lack of attention to the inner life of the scholar is costly. C. S. Lewis reminds us of the demands of discipleship when he writes, "I [Christ] don't want so much of your time and so much of your money and so much of your work [scholarship]. I want you. I have not come to torment your natural self, but to kill it. No half-measures are any good."[4] Scholarship without devotion reduces itself to an attempt to jockey for position in the academic community rather than offering it as a form of worship to Christ. Students can quickly perceive the shallowness of those who intellectually claim to be Christians yet live lives of atheists. It behooves us to realize that our worldview is much more evident in our lifestyles than our scholarship.

Tragically, a number of faculty within our own Christian colleges and universities struggle with how to think Christianly about their disciplines.[5] We have lost the unification of knowledge under the lordship of Jesus Christ. One contributing factor to the inability to think Christianly about our lives is the inattention given to the daily pursuit of companionship with Christ. There is more value placed on the articulation of Christian doctrine than the training of the inner life. In our quest to become viable scholars, we have neglected to train our inward spiritual experience, resulting in unrealized potential for our scholarship.

How can one be expected to think Christianly when he does not have the fullness of the Christian experience to draw from? Can a business professor teach employee relations Christianly when she has never paused to contemplate the justice and mercy of God? How can a biology professor fully articulate the uniqueness of humankind in the creative order when he has spent more time meditating on Darwinian theory than the wonders of God? My point is not to diminish the need to be cognizant of competing theories but to illustrate the need to be equally rigorous in our spiritual lives as scholars.

This paper will seek to establish the need for a renewed emphasis on the spiritual life of the scholar. First, I will make a case for why attention to spirituality is necessary to the scholar. Second, through a brief and selective historical survey of Christian spirituality, I will seek to demonstrate that our intellectual heritage is tied to the nurturing of the spiritual life. Finally, I will look to the future of the Christian academy by offering some specific challenges to the individual scholar and to the Christian academic community.

Spirituality and the Christian Scholar

In his work *The Spirit of the Disciplines,*[6] Dallas Willard articulates one of the finest arguments available for the need to attend to the spiritual life. His discussion is based on the first three chapters of Genesis, the creation narrative and subsequent advent of sin.

In the creation narrative, God creates humankind in his image, the *imago Dei*. We note the God-given capacities for intelligence, work, relationship with God and others, and the ability to interact with the creative order. In Genesis 2:19–20, we see that Adam is exercising many of the physical and nonphysical attributes of his God-given design. At this point Adam is fully living in his God-intended condition.

It doesn't take long, however, before God's created order is totally defaced by sin (Gen. 3). Willard calls this "paradise lost."[7] There is not one area of the human experience, hidden or unhidden, that is not corrupted by the deadly forces of sin. The apostle Paul asserts, "For all have sinned and fall short of the glory of God" (Rom. 3:23).[8] The psalmist David testifies that:

The LORD looks down from heaven
    on the sons of men
to see if there are any who understand,
    any who seek God.
All have turned aside,
    they have together become corrupt;
there is no one who does good,
    not even one. (Ps. 14: 2–3)

The fall is complete, impacting not only all of us, but every ounce of all of us. Our entire human experience has been corrupted by the advent of sin. The rest of the Christian Scripture is, in essence, a testimony to the fallenness of humankind and the redemptive purpose of God. As James Sire states, "Human beings were created good, but through the fall the image of God became defaced, though not so ruined as not to be capable of restoration; through the work of Christ

God redeemed humanity and began the process of restoring people to goodness."9

Consequently, our need for redemption is as permeating as our fallenness. Every aspect of our beings, physical and nonphysical, need to be justified and sanctified by Christ throughout life. Any area of our beings left in a defaced condition will ultimately hinder our pursuit of holiness and, consequently, fulfillment of the Christ experience.

It is important to pause and make a clarification between what is meant by justification and sanctification. As John Calvin states in the *Institutes*, justification is "an acquittal from guilt of him who was accused, as though his innocence had been proved. Since God, therefore justifies us through the mediation of Christ, he acquits us not by the admission of our personal innocence, but by an imputation of righteousness; so that we, who are unrighteous in ourselves, are considered as righteous in Christ."10 Justification is a point-in-time action taken by God to make us right before him. For the purpose of this essay, justification of the scholar is assumed.

Sanctification, on the other hand, is a lifelong regenerative process where the entirety of the human experience is remade in the image of Christ. Once again, Calvin states, "As God the Father has reconciled us to himself in Christ, so he has exhibited to us in him a pattern to which it is his will that we should be conformed. . . . Christ, by whom we have been reconciled to God, is proposed to us as an example, whose character we should exhibit in our lives."11 The regenerative power of God in Christ allows us to regain the paradise that was lost in Genesis 3. We have the ability in Christ to reclaim right relationships, right emotions, right actions, right thinking, and so on. Sanctification must be holistic, claiming every area of our lives. Christ's life, and consequently his demand on us, calls for the complete sanctification of the human experience.

Willard goes to great lengths to drive this point home. We "must take the need for human transformation as seriously as do the modern revolutionary movements. The modern negative critique of Christianity arose in the first place because the church was not faithful to its own message—it failed to take human transformation seriously as a real, practical issue to be dealt with in realistic terms."12 Martin Luther describes the sanctification process as reenacting the christological epic. Darrell Reinke comments concerning Luther's thoughts on sanctification: "The Christian life is an imitation, one which conforms to the christological model both in external behavior and interior attitudes and self consciousness."[13]

Those involved in Christian scholarship must come to grips with the need to sanctify the intellect. In the fall, our ability to think rightly was lost. Thus Paul admonishes us to "set your minds on the things above, not on earthly things" (Col. 3:2) and, "Do not conform any longer to the pattern of this world, but be transformed by the renewing of your mind" (Rom. 12:2). In reality, most of us have spent our graduate and post-graduate experiences training our intellects in a nontheistic worldview. Conversely to what we learn in Scripture, we have been memorizing, meditating, and contemplating a thoroughly naturalistic view of reality. Therefore, our need for reclaiming the intellect to the Christian worldview perspective is ever present.

The transformation of the intellect, however, cannot be separated from the need to sanctify the rest of the human experience. Willard convincingly argues for our need to emulate Christ in our daily lives as he lived in his daily life, not simply in the sporadic moments of crisis, "living as he lived in the entirety of his life—adopting his overall lifestyle. Following 'in his steps' cannot be equated with behaving as he did when he was 'on the spot.' To live as Christ lived is to live as he did _all_ his life."[14] As important as it is, the reclaiming of the intellect must be seen only as a single element of that which must be sanctified in Christ. To work diligently to reclaim our thoughts while neglecting the rest of our being is to become spiritual nugents, grotesquely disformed, with the potential of doing more harm to the kingdom than good.

We have all seen and experienced the unbalanced Christian life, an acute intellect eloquently speaking the Christian apologetic while his family disintegrates or he treats his students with pious contempt. Or conversely, the scholar who attempts to be Christlike in action by serving the poor, loving the sick, and reaching out to the neglected but fails to see the connection between her Christian faith and her academic discipline, taking on a thoroughly naturalistic approach to learning while only interjecting a Christian proof text now and again.[15] One thing is sure: Our students and colleagues can sense the disingenuousness of our faith.

Resolution of this crisis begins with a holistic view of sanctification. "Spirituality is simply the holistic quality of human life as it was meant to be, at the center of which is our relation to God."[16] We must seek to be Christlike in the fullness of our being. Christ taught us through his life how to live in such a way as to think rightly and act justly. His life was filled with the practices of godliness, such as prayer, meditation, solitude, asceticism, fasting, worship, discipleship, and so on. Likewise, we should practice the presence of Christ. The role of the spiritual disciplines "rests upon the nature of the embodied human self—they are to mold and shape it" in the full likeness of Christ.[17]

Looking back on many of the great personalities of the Christian intellect, we see lives marked with dependence on the spiritual disciplines. Surveying our spiritual heritage does not demand our full agreement with each individual, but it does demand our attention. God can instruct us if we explore the spiritual lives and writings of those who have gone before. In the next section, we will see that our intellectual heritage is linked to Christian spirituality.

Historical Overview of Christian Spirituality

The review of Christian spirituality reveals a heavy reliance on the Catholic tradition. Due to the rise in persecution soon after the New Testament era, Christian spirituality moved to secluded groups in the wilderness. The influence of these secluded groups becomes obvious in the subsequent monastic movement. The advent of the Protestant Reformation resulted in a dearth of information about the exercise of the spiritual disciplines. Not until recently have Protestants begun to advocate the practice of the full range of the spiritual disciplines as tools for a deeper walk in Christ. What we do see, however, is that the practice of the disciplines was commonplace in the Scriptures.

Christian scholarship is to be firmly rooted in the biblical perspective of reality. Consequently, we must not fail to see the fullness of the spiritual lives played out in scriptural narratives. Too often we neglect to recognize that the Scriptures, more often than not, give us life accounts of laypersons, not clergymen. Many of the patriarchs were either herders or farmers. Many of the most notable Old Testament personalities were politicians or military leaders. In the New Testament we find fishermen, tent makers, tax collectors, and the like. Very few of the biblical heroes were actually what we would call ministers. Rather, like us, they were individuals seeking to live intimately related to God on a day-to-day basis.

What is common to their lives is an exercise of spiritual disciplines. We witness Isaac going off in solitude to meditate and pray (Gen. 24:63) and Joshua renewing his thinking by meditating on the Book of the Law (Josh. 1:8). King David, in order to make right political and military decisions, sought God in prayer, meditation, through fasting, and communally in celebration and worship (cf. Ps. 119:15, 27, 145).

Jesus himself engaged in the spiritual disciplines, including fasting, prayer, meditation, solitude, worship, discipleship, and others (cf. Matt. 4:2; Mark 1:35, Matt. 6:9–15). He lived a life that displayed to us the practical steps to an intimate relationship with God. His very participation in the spiritual disciplines demands them in our daily living (1 Pet. 2:21). "It is the intelligent, informed, unyielding resolve to live as Jesus lived in all aspects of his life, not just in the moment of specific choice or action."[18]

The spiritual disciplines were so readily exercised in the Scriptures that their use was assumed. When Paul instructs us to present our lives as "living sacrifices" and be transformed by the renewing of the mind (Rom. 12:2 KJV) he takes for granted that the reader will know what practical steps to take in order to live such a transformed life.

It was not long before the exercise of the spiritual disciplines was taken captive by extremists. There was a certain movement during the fourth and fifth centuries called the desert fathers (and mothers) who chose to banish themselves to solitude in the deserts in a quest to have a deeper fellowship with God. Bizarre stories can be found concerning their self-imposed sufferings and extreme asceticism. Although there are many writings from this era from which we can benefit, the overall effect of their abuses of the spiritual disciplines is still being felt today. There are still those who associate asceticism with the extreme experiences of the desert fathers. What is lost is not only a proper understanding of the spiritual disciplines but also the genuinely good devotional material from this era. One of their best-known writers, Antony, had a major impact on the life of Augustine.

Probably one of the greatest minds of early Christianity is in fact Augustine of Hippo (354–430). His works, such as *The City of God* and *The Confessions,* have had an impact on nearly all of the great minds of Christianity. *The Confessions* is an autobiographical sketch of his life in which he tells of his days as a philosophical wanderer. Augustine goes into great detail about his faith struggles and the influence of his Christian mother. At one point in his life, he was committed to Manicheanism, but he gave it up after witnessing the incongruities between the teachings and life actions of his instructor. Ultimately, after years of philosophical explorations, Augustine found peace in Christ. Bernhard Christensen writes concerning Augustine's conversion, "we see that his heart ultimately found rest not through human philosophy or learning, not even through the arguments of persuasive preaching, but through personal contacts with people with a living faith in Christ."[19]

The Confessions and other writings by Augustine are filled with challenges to our intellects and our hearts. Augustine openly discusses his struggles with sexual passion and how he overcame such challenges through prayer and meditation. His later writings tell of his devotion to a life of simplicity and the inner man. The writings of Augustine demonstrate for us how the exercise of the spiritual disciplines impacts life actions and provides the foundation for rigorous scholarly pursuits.

Moving to the thirteenth century, we find the influence of Francis of Assisi (1181–1226). His total abandonment for service to the poor is inspiring. Born to a wealthy family, he chose a life of poverty. Francis' life served as a challenge to the corrupting forces of the church in his day. His daily prayers and meditations shaped his benevolent actions which touched the lives of thousands. In Francis' short life of forty-four years, he sought to balance attention between the inner man and outward service. The Franciscan order was founded on the principles of devotion to the inner life and service to others.

One important devotional writing comes from the pen of Thomas à Kempis (1380–1471). *The Imitation of Christ* has been heralded as one of the greatest devotional writings of all time. The text is still being studied for its literary style and contributions to spiritual formation. It is filled with practical and reflective comments on the spiritual disciplines and how they impact daily living. À Kempis lived the life of a monk at the Brethren of the Common Life in Deventer, Germany. His spiritual director was Gerhard de Groote. It has been suggested that *The Imitation* actually consists of the diaries of de Groote. From this work we can reap practical advice on daily living in Christ. *The Imitation* is considered one of the greatest works of its kind.

Thus far, we have only described the quest for the inner life among those who chose to live in monasteries. The greatest body of written material on the spiritual disciplines comes from the monastic movement. This fact has done further harm to the perceived legitimacy and exercise of the spiritual disciplines. The monastic movement tended to move the exercise of the spiritual disciplines out of the day-to-day life of the believer and to place them firmly in the monastery. It did not take long before the disciplines were viewed as otherworldly and of no practical use in daily living for the common Christian. What was being lost by the undue influence of a few extremists and the unintended marginalizing of the monastic writings would not soon be regained.

Martin Luther (1483–1546) spent his early years in an Augustinian monastery. Even though Luther failed to see value in his relationships during his time in the monastery, God used his experiences there to prepare him for a professorial post at the University of Wittenburg and ultimately for the Protestant Reformation. Luther is best known for his theological writings, but his references to spirituality should not be ignored. It was his meditation and study of Romans that finally moved Luther to post his ninety-five theses on the church door at Wittenburg.

Luther's quest to replicate the christological epic in his personal life is often overshadowed by his doctrinal emphasis on faith and grace. His reaction to the abuses of the Catholic Church of his day tends to take center stage and to displace his comments about prayer, meditation, and service. When Luther wrote the introduction to the *Theologia Germanica*,[20] he commented on the need to take the issues of the heart seriously. Foster observes concerning the *Germanica*, "It understands how God uses the patient acceptance of trials, the exercise of spiritual disciplines, and the gentle movings of the Spirit to effect the transformation of the individual into the likeness of Christ."[21]

The Reformation served as a turning point in Christendom in more ways than one. Christian spirituality was largely replaced with an emphasis on personal articulation of a correct doctrine of salvation. The exceptionally strong focus on justification diminished the attention paid to the process of sanctification. Furthermore, Protestants tended to distance themselves from anything associated with Catholicism. As a result, Robert Webber observes, "One of the most crucial ways in which the Protestant break with the past is evidenced is through the loss of much of the spiritual resources of the church."[22]

Luther's monastic influence allows us to see marks of his spirituality, but the task is somewhat more difficult with John Calvin (1509–64). His teachings on the sovereignty of God and doctrine of predestination cause many of us to miss his passion for a deep relationship with Christ. In his *Institutes of the Christian Religion,* Book III, he goes into great detail about the need to pursue holiness and righteous living. We get a glimpse of his passion when he writes, "Doctrine is not an affair of the tongue, but of the life; is not apprehended by the intellect and memory merely, like other branches of learning; but is received only when it possesses the whole soul, and finds its seat and habitation in the inmost recesses of the heart."[23]

We are able to peer deeper into Calvin's desire for the inner life in his *Golden Booklet of the True Christian Life*.[24] Here we read of Calvin admonishing the reader to surrender the intellect to the lordship of Christ and to learn the art of self-denial in the practice of a virtuous life. However, the practical steps to attain this renewed lifestyle are missing in his work. Calvin's admonishments to godly living are both challenging and inspiring, but it is frustrating for the reader when he fails to offer any suggestions on how to attain such a level in one's Christian walk.

It is not until the eighteenth century that we see a glimpse of the spiritual disciplines surfacing in mainline Protestant Christianity. John Wesley (1703–91) strove to bring about a balance between the intellect and godly living through his holy methods.[25] Commenting on the disciplines, he writes, "It was a common saying among the Christians of the primitive church, 'The soul and the body make a man; the spirit and discipline make a Christian': implying that none could be real Christians without the help of Christian discipline. But if this be so, is it any wonder that we find so few Christians; for where is Christian discipline?"[26]

In this century we are seeing a renewed emphasis on the role of the spiritual disciplines. The great theologian Dietrich Bonhoeffer (1906–45) eloquently describes how the quest for the inner life can be practiced in his work *Life Together*.[27] The work is a description of his experiment in Christian spirituality at Finkenwalde, Germany. Here he brought young seminarians out to a secluded location for a limited period of time where they sought to understand better the spiritual reality of Christian community. The work demonstrates a fine balance between the inner journey of the Christian life and the blessing of community. *Life Together* calls for the complete commitment of the Christian in the personal and corporate spiritual disciplines. The "Finkenwaldians," as they were called, would be required to arise in the morning for meditations and prayer, eat breakfast together, study God's Word together, engage in the work of daily chores, and then end the day with evening discussions.

In 1978, a group of forty-five scholars met in Chicago for the purpose of putting together a treatise that would call evangelicals to historic Christianity. The meeting, commonly called "The Chicago Call," resulted in a compilation of papers entitled *The Orthodox Evangelicals: Who They Are and What They are Saying*.[28] One element was a call to spiritual renewal. Robert Webber and Donald Bloesch led this call to renewal. Many of Webber's subsequent writings were filled with challenges for evangelicals to renew their attention to the inner life through the practice of the disciplines and meaningful worship.

Recently a number of writings have emerged about the exercise of the spiritual disciplines. Probably the most popular works have come from the pens of Richard Foster and Dallas Willard. These two men have provided the impetus for the renewed emphasis on the spiritual disciplines among Protestant evangelicals.[29] Foster's book, *Celebration of Discipline*, serves as a selective catalog to the disciplines with helpful suggestions on how to use them in one's life. Willard strongly influenced the thinking of Foster and has written one of the best theological rationales for the need of the disciplines in his work *The Spirit of the Disciplines*. This volume offers a concise and convincing description of our need for complete transformation and gives us practical steps on how to begin the journey.

In summary, we see that the emphasis upon the disciplines looks something like an hourglass. We see that they were commonly practiced during the New Testament era and continued to blossom through the monastic movement, even though they were largely removed from the everyday life of the commoner. The Protestant Reformation brought a restrictive influence on spirituality, which was a reaction against the abuses of Catholicism at that time. Fortunately, we are now beginning to experience a renewal of the disciplines. As we look at the future of Christian higher education, we will do well to consider the role of spirituality in the academy.

Implications for the Future of Christian Higher Education

The Christian academy has two basic spiritual challenges: the personal and the communal. The personal challenge is one of renewed attention to the inner life and the sharing of our inner experiences with others. The challenge to the community is to raise the value of the pursuit of inner life in Christ. That is, we are called to the twofold task of allowing Christian spirituality to find a place in Protestant scholarship and to focus our campuses upon the spiritual reality of community in Christ.

Personal Challenge

Christian scholars are charged with the task of teaching their academic disciplines with a well-informed knowledge base and from a distinctively Christian worldview perspective. This task requires rigorous study and a growing and intimate relationship with Christ. The need for attention to the sanctifying process of Christ is of utmost importance when we are dealing in the arena of ideas. Because of the fallenness of our intellect, we must always be kept in check by the standard of God's Word and the community of fellow believers. The following two personal challenges are offered to promote our personal growth and provide instruction to our students.

First, we must individually strive to become more like Christ in the daily activities of life. Willard reminds us, "Full participation in the life of God's Kingdom and in the vivid companionship of Christ comes to us only through appropriate exercise in the disciplines for life in the spirit."[30] We need to seek to encounter Christ in our daily experiences through prayer, meditation, solitude, fasting, and other avenues that enable us to gain God's perspective of reality. Through the exercise of the disciplines, we will come to view more clearly our work and live our lives Christianly. Our exercise of the spirit in the disciplines will enable us, through Christ, to experience the much needed transformation of our human experience.

It must be emphasized that the disciplines are not an end in themselves. The point is not to introduce a new form of legalism. The focus is on our relationship with Christ. For example, a carpenter uses a wide array of tools to craft a fine piece of furniture. He starts out with a plan and then instinctively uses the right tools to accomplish the task. He intuitively knows that the seven-degree dovetail bit in his router is what he needs to cut the desired joinery in the project, and he instinctively uses the appropriate grade of sandpaper to obtain the desired level of smoothness on the exterior of the project. The carpenter's focus is always on the finished product, not the tools. Likewise, with the spiritual disciplines, our focus is upon nurturing our relationship with God and transforming our actions, not the disciplines themselves.

To further the analogy, the carpenter spent years mastering the tools in order to use them intuitively to craft works of art. It will also take time and some feelings of awkwardness before the disciplines will become a natural part of your inward pilgrimage. Christ admonished us that some things are not accomplished without much prayer and fasting. Over time we, just like the carpenter, will intuitively exercise the spiritual disciplines as a regular part of our inward pilgrimage.

Second, we need to share our inward experiences in the classroom—not for the purpose of being prideful or artificial in our approach but to demonstrate how Christ is working in our intellectual pursuits. Students are longing for professors who are transparently Christian in their scholarship and their lives. Thomas Merton, the great Catholic spiritual mentor, wrote of his regret in not receiving spiritual direction while in undergraduate school.[31] As was mentioned earlier, Augustine abandoned Manicheanism because of the incongruencies between the instructor's teaching and his life. Robert Webber describes the harrowing experiences of his first years as a professor at Wheaton College, "I felt as though I was following after the God on the blackboard, the God in the textbook."[32] He stated that his overreliance on reason had been modeled to him by his teachers, and consequently, that is how he fashioned his teaching style. C. S. Lewis reminds us that "rational argument does not create belief but maintains a climate in which belief may flourish."[33]

Students want to hear us pray, to know that we have fasted in order to find resolve in a particular intellectual crisis, or that in a time of solitude and meditation we have a peace about God's will concerning a particular decision. There is nothing more encouraging for our students than to know that someone they respect as an intellectual giant kneels daily to seek God. Sharing our inner experiences is not intended to be flippant or disingenuous, rather to illustrate how we might use our inward experiences instructively. We can demonstrate to our students that seeking God in the inward experiences is a valid and effective approach to decision making. Students should be taught how to integrate their inward experience with Christ with data as an informed policy-making decision process. Administrators have an opportunity to demonstrate this process in action in the everyday processes of the academic community.

Community Challenge

Our campuses serve first as a community of believers, then as a community of scholars. The founding of our institutions was not primarily for the purpose of scholarship but rather for Christian scholarship. Although similar educational activities take place on both the Christian and non-Christian campuses, our role rests primarily in our relationship with Christ and secondarily in our vocation. For if we give our vocation first place over our relationship with Christ, we will never attain Christian scholarship.

Concerning community, Bonhoeffer writes, "It is essential for Christian community that two things become clear right from the beginning. First, Christian community is not an ideal, but divine reality; second, Christian community is a spiritual and not a psychic reality."[34] We need to come to grips with the fact that Christian community will never attain the ideal for which we desire. This does not mean that we cease striving for excellence; rather, it humbles us under Christ to accept as valid the diversity found in the body of Christ. Many times the lack of the ideal has caused us to forsake the community fellowship during campus chapel or to decline an opportunity of service because it is not organized according to our standards. Christian spirituality is the coming together of the saints in all of our imperfections. Robert Wuthnow, the Princeton social science scholar, argues that the creation of community is one of the greatest challenges for the church in the twenty-first century.[35] Likewise, the future of Christian higher education is dependent on our ability to sustain community in Christ. What follows are four challenges to the academy to foster community.

1. We must engage in community. To worship together, to serve together (locally and globally), to break bread together, to pray together, to fast together, to celebrate together, to submit to one another, and to fellowship together. These are disciplines which Willard calls "disciplines of engagement."[36] For community will be both created and sustained around such traditions of the faith.

2. We should begin to think Christianly about our calendars. Let us focus our academic community not on midterm exams and fall break, but on the celebration of the Christian year. It is now the second week of October, near the end of the season after Pentecost, the time of celebrating the coming of the Holy Spirit and the beginning of the church. It is also only seven weeks before the end of the Christian year and the beginning of Advent, which signifies the anticipation of Christ's coming. The academic year contains two of the most climactic events of the Christian calendar, Christ's birth and his death and resurrection, not to mention the preparatory times for these two events, Advent and Lent, which are rich in meaning and symbolism.

   This is not to say that we disregard the academic calendar, rather that we add the richness of the Christian emphasis on time. Webber writes, "There is nothing wrong with organizing our time around the civil and the academic year. Life simply requires it. But as Christians we have one more way of marking time—a spiritual way, the Christian year."[37] This new way of looking at our calendar will add richness to our lives and our communities, especially as it informs our worship.

3. Our faculty retreats can be used to foster attention to Christian spirituality. This would assist in raising the awareness and importance of attention to the inner life of the scholar. Retreat time could be spent instructively discussing the disciplines and practicing them as a group of believers. It may seem uncomfortable at the beginning, but if sufficient time is given, the retreat would end as a spiritual renewal. The retreats could also be used as times of reflection on such works as Pascal's *Pensées*, Bonhoeffer's *Life Together,* or Thomas à Kempis' *The Imitation of Christ*, all of which could be concluded with discussions centering on the implications these writings have on our scholarship and our particular institutions. These retreats could be facilitated by a contemporary spiritual leader, as was the tradition and the role of past spiritual leaders like Augustine, Francis of Assisi, Thomas Merton, and so forth.

4. The Protestant academy must be challenged to take spirituality seriously as an academic discipline. To this day, the wealth of writing about Christian spirituality is in the Catholic tradition. There is much to be learned and applied from such writings, and such work is of extreme value. Yet, as Foster asserts, "In intellectual honesty, we should be willing to study and explore the spiritual life with all the rigor and determination we would give to any field of research."[38] Not to do so is to deny its ability to impact the human condition and to dispute a reality we confess to be true in Jesus Christ.

Conclusion

The future of Christian higher education starts in the hearts of those who fill the faculty and staff ranks of our campuses. The potential of our scholarship and our institutions will only be fulfilled if the inner life is sufficiently transformed. Much of our heritage as evangelicals is a tapestry of intellectualism and inward experience. The challenge is before us to strive actively for the wisdom that is found in practicing the presence of Christ in our scholarship.

Consequently, we should seek ways to stimulate one another toward personal growth in Christ. We should also engage in community, which will allow us to test our scholarship and benefit from the blessing of being participants in the divine reality of the body of Christ. "Be imitators of God, therefore, as dearly loved children and live a life of love, just as Christ loved us and gave himself up for us as a fragrant offering and sacrifice to God" (Eph. 5:1–2).

This address was delivered as a part of the Conference on the Future of Christian Higher Education at Union University.

Chapter 13

ATTRACT THEM
BY YOUR WAY OF LIFE:
THE PROFESSOR'S TASK
IN THE CHRISTIAN UNIVERSITY

DAVID P. GUSHEE

In an age of relativity, the practice of truth . . . is the only way to cause the world to take seriously our protestations concerning truth.[1]

—Francis Schaeffer

Attract them by your way of life if you want them to receive . . . teaching from you.[2]

—Augustine

My topic is "The Professor's Task in the Christian University." Perhaps the initial thing to be done in reflecting on this theme is to acknowledge an anomaly: It is possible to get through an entire course of study in preparation for a professorial career without ever being required to reflect on the nature and task of the professor.

We would not think of sending elementary schoolteachers into their classrooms without years of quite specific instruction concerning the teaching process and its goals and methods. Nor would we be comfortable sitting in a dentist's chair at the mercy of someone who never was taught precisely how to do dentistry. Nor would we want to work on the fourth floor of an office building constructed by untrained workers. But I managed to get through four degrees in higher education from quite respectable schools without a single class or even part of a class devoted to the art, craft, methods, and goals of teaching—even though I was always clear that teaching was my vocation, and the schools were clear (at least at the doctoral level) that they were preparing teachers. Instead, I was trained in an academic discipline—Christian ethics—and then thrown into the classroom with the assumption that because I know that discipline I am somehow ready to teach college students every day of my working life. I would be embarrassed to make this confession were it not for the fact that my situation on this score is not unique.

So the first observation that needs to be made is that reflection on the professor's task in the Christian university definitely needs to occur, that professors need to do it, not just administrators—and that they need to do it, if possible, before they *are* professors in the Christian university.

Wrong Answers

That said, what is the professor's task in the Christian university? I want to suggest briefly two wrong answers to this question. In naming these wrong answers I am not proposing that many would seriously argue that these answers provide a satisfactory vision of the professor's mission and role. Yet I do want to argue that the vocation of the professor can and frequently does degenerate operationally into one or both of the answers I will name.

Wrong Answer #1: The Professor's Task Is to Do the Professor's Tasks

The first of these is to identify the professor's task with the professor's *tasks*. The professor has an abundance of daily tasks, and these can come to constitute the sum total of the professor's vocation. What are these tasks? Recently I kept track of a fairly routine week and came up with the following list:

- teaching
- writing tests and other assignments
- grading tests and papers
- entering grades in the grade book
- visiting with drop-by students
- answering mail
- supervising student assistants
- responding to administration requests for forms, information, and paperwork
- engaging in hallway conversations

- providing mass academic advising
- going to faculty meetings, university-wide meetings, and committee meetings
- looking through the mail
- answering phone calls, returning phone calls, playing phone tag
- preparing or freshening lectures
- counseling the distraught
- talking with colleagues
- performing departmental functions like ordering library books
- playing basketball with students
- going to chapel at every conceivable opportunity

The upshot of a list like this is that it is more than possible for the average faculty member to work fifty to sixty hours a week doing such professorial tasks without coming within hailing distance of seriously considering the professor's task. Especially in high-teaching-load Christian universities, we are always at risk of getting lost in the tasks and thus losing sight of the task—at risk of losing any kind of broader animating vision of why we do what we do, if we ever had that vision in the first place. It is easy to lose sight of vision because the tasks must be done day by day; every day they impinge upon us, crowding out any deeper sense of purpose or any reflection on that purpose. As my colleague George Guthrie has put it, in academia we are constantly at risk of "drowning in shallowness." Or, to shift images, we are constantly at risk of becoming mere plowhorses, lumbering through our daily tasks with our blinders on and our eyes pointed firmly toward the ground. So the professor's task is not the same as the professor's tasks.

Wrong Answer #2: The Professor's Task Is to Service the Professor's Constituencies

At first glance, a somewhat better way to organize our thinking about the professor's task might be to reflect on the wants and needs of our constituencies. Each day we professors navigate a maze of relationships. Each of our partners in these relationships needs and wants things from us. Thus it is possible to argue that the professor's task is to meet the needs and, where possible, the wants of his or her constituencies. Thus, we could divide up our work by constituency:

- *Students.* Students need and want good and interesting teaching, for which we are well prepared. They also want grading that is fair and timely; and some want mentoring and counseling. We cannot forget our alumni who also keep in touch with us and need us in various ways.

- *Colleagues.* Colleagues want warm, respectful, and collegial relationships; they need us to share the administrative load with them; some want friendship; some seek intellectual companionship; some want to be left alone altogether.

- *Administrators.* Administrators want faculty members who will advance the vision and serve the mission of the school. On a day-to-day basis, however, they need paperwork done on time, forms filled out, grades turned in, class slots filled, committees organized and run, our presence and time at meetings, and so on.

- *Churches.* Churches want faculty members who are active and participating laypeople. From the religion department, they need preachers and interims and guest speakers. Furthermore, they want us to give our attention to the students they send, responsiveness to their requests for time and information, and a trustworthy education.

- *Community.* The local community wants the university to be a constructive player in community affairs and faculty members who will offer their expertise regarding the issues facing the community. The newspaper wants comments and quotes; business and social agencies may want research and other forms of assistance; community service organizations want our involvement, as do civic clubs like Rotary. Here I do not even mention what the national community needs and wants: professors/scholars who can serve as the "mind" and address the issues of the nation.

- *Academia.* The academy wants nothing from any one of us in particular, though our schools usually require more of us than nothing. But from us as a whole, the academy wants and needs reviews, articles, and books; service in professional organizations and task forces; research, grantsmanship, and so on. Some of us, at least, want to offer all this.

A brief consideration of this list reveals its inadequacy as an overall vision of the professor's task. For once again we sense the very real possibility, even probability, of drowning in shallowness. While we cannot ignore the demands our constituencies place upon us, we cannot simply respond to them either. If we do, we become mere plow horses once again, this time with several masters. There are, of course, ways of narrowing these tasks. A wise administrator or department chair will seek to channel the professor to the areas in which he or she can make the most significant contribution and will seek to build a faculty team with complementary strengths. Likewise, as Mark Schwehn and others have suggested, our relationship with students should be seen as the central one, with the demands of other constituencies falling into place around this first priority.[3] Even so, a relationship or constituency-based approach is insufficient. It risks becoming merely reactive, leading the professor to a stance of being driven by the agendas of others (even when those others are students) rather than directed by a coherent agenda of his own.

The Professor's Task: Incarnating a Way of Life

If the professor's task in the Christian university cannot be equated with the professor's tasks or with the demands of the professor's constituencies, is there another way to approach our work and to come nearer to the heart of its meaning? In particular, is there a way of thinking about our task that responds to the needs of the twenty-first century context in which we will soon be doing our work?

I think there is. My thesis is illustrated by an episode I had with a student last year. Jim, one of our finest students here at Union, joined our family for dinner one night last fall. Jim was going to accompany me to a church event that night, and we were in something of a hurry, so dinner only lasted about twenty minutes. After dinner, on the way to this program, Jim said to me, "Dr. Gushee, the twenty minutes I just spent with your family taught me more than anything you have ever said to me." Let me hasten to add that there was nothing remarkable about the evening; it was a typical dinnertime with Jeanie and our three kids. I asked each child to tell me something about the day; we all listened to one another. That's about it. But for Jim, who comes from an intact but unloving and dysfunctional family, that conversation was a revelation. Twenty minutes with us had expanded for all time his moral imagination in the area of family life.

As a Christian ethicist, I spend a considerable amount of my professional time studying contemporary social trends. I am not unfamiliar with current evidence concerning family dysfunction and breakdown, skyrocketing divorce rates, serial monogamy, and other evidences of an unraveling social fabric in this nation. I read this literature all the time and, in fact, have sometimes been critical of the gloomy tone I frequently find in it. Last year, though, through the lives of my students, I saw for the first time just how pervasive the effects of this moral collapse already are.

Day after day, it seemed, young men and young women found their way into my office to talk and weep with me about various aspects of their lives. Perhaps I had been insulated during my seminary years to a certain extent and by the stability of my own family background and personal life. Of course, I thought I knew what was going on in our society. But I was stunned to hear some of the students' stories—physical abuse, verbal abuse, drug and alcohol abuse, crime, neglect, family violence, abandonment, and multiple divorce and remarriage (I think the current record number of parental remarriages suffered by any student of my acquaintance is fifteen). Then there were the varied responses of the students to these experiences. Some were remarkably whole, some were still deeply troubled but in the healing process, and some seemed to be many years away from recovery if ever. One day I remarked to a colleague that I needed a broom in my office to sweep up each day's broken pieces. It was unbelievable to me that at a relatively insulated Christian university like this one that so much brokenness would exist. Surely it can only be worse in the secular university. The students of this generation bear in their bodies and in their souls the scars of our society's disastrous moral collapse.

This is a volume directed to the future. The students who now come our way are the best harbingers of what the future will bring, and what therefore the Christian university will need to offer. On the basis of these experiences with students, who give personal evidence of the social trends we all know about, it is clear to me that what Alasdair MacIntyre once called "the new dark ages" are indeed already upon us.[4]

In a social context such as this, the fundamental task of the Christian professor is nothing other than to incarnate an authentically Christian way of life. We will do this before all the constituencies we have named—but particularly before our primary constituency, our students. The primary contribution we can make to their lives is simply to invest in them, to live healthy, authentic Christian lives in their presence, and perhaps, by God's grace, thus to begin the moral reconstruction of their lives where this is needed. Perhaps we would like to have a more ambitious agenda than this, as many have proposed in the literature of Christian higher education, including this volume. There are many worthy goals for us to seek. But the *kairos* moment in which we find ourselves, I believe, demands a focus on character formation and reformation in the midst of social collapse.

Of course, a focus on character formation as central to higher education is not at all original and not distinctively Christian. It was certainly the animating vision of the Greek philosophers and the schools they established. It appears consistently in historic Christian reflection on education; my title and opening quotation are drawn from one of Augustine's letters. It is a vision that lay at the heart of what even public university education was understood to be about little more than a century ago. But in the days since that time, the vision of education as character formation and of teachers as mentors/models has been displaced in American public life. Some observers are convinced that it has been in part displaced in Christian higher education as well, as our universities have sought faculty on the basis of other-than-characterological criteria and in general are much more reluctant than they used to be to examine their faculty members' lifestyles very closely.

I think that not focusing on character formation is a mistake for Christian universities under any circumstances, but that such a trend, if it exists, is particularly disastrous in our time. Students need to be shown how to live, and students of this generation need such demonstration more than ever before. More than once a student has said to me, "I just don't know how to do that." To do what? To love or receive love; to give or receive loving correction; to form or sustain intimate relationships; to relate constructively to an authority figure; even to engage in an intelligent conversation; and so on. These students remind us of the ancient insight that the virtues that sustain life are learned in community, in particular in that primary and first community, the family. We now witness the results of a grand and disastrous social experiment, which amounts to an attempt to discover whether those life skills and virtues can be learned in the midst of family chaos, disorder, misery, and instability. The results are coming in, and they are what we might expect.

Which Virtues? A Model for Professors

Exactly which virtues should the Christian university professor seek to incarnate? By virtues I mean in this context normative habits of heart, mind, and life for the people of God, as these are revealed in

Scripture and affirmed by the best of Christian tradition. The Christian faith contains a rich body of virtues that are to be sought by all who follow Christ; here I want to focus on those virtues most relevant to the role of the Christian university professor in our time. I propose a five-pronged model, in which a central virtue (and in good Aristotelian style, one or two corresponding vices) is identified in the areas of spirituality, relationships, intellectual life, social engagement, and personal lifestyle. By no means are these the only virtues that could be named in these areas of life; nor, for that matter, are they the only areas of life that could be named. But this model does offer us a place to start.

1. Spiritual Virtue: Authentic Piety

The place to begin is the arena of spiritual life. Surely there can be little question that in a Christian university setting the way in which professors incarnate the Christian faith itself is the single most significant virtue issue we face. I propose that *authentic piety* is the name we should give to the virtue we should seek in this arena.

By authentic piety I mean several things. First, the term implies genuine devotion to God and a living relationship with God. The professor characterized by authentic piety experiences an ongoing relationship with Jesus Christ, a relationship that is at the center of his or her existence. The term *piety* connotes not just an inclination of the heart or mind but also a corresponding set of faith practices and disciplines, such as regular prayer, study of the Scripture, significant participation in the life of a faith community, and service both in the church and in the world. Piety is authentic when such practices are performed not under compulsion or merely by contract but as a genuine expression of devotion to God. Likewise, authentic piety is characterized by honesty in relationship with God; it includes questions as well as answers, doubts as well as certitudes, sorrow as well as joy. Authentic piety is a life pilgrimage rather than a one-time-only transaction. It penetrates to the core of one's being and pervades the whole of one's life and is not compartmentalized or privatized into the so-called religious sector of life.

Authentic piety is a most elusive virtue. It is a gift of God, which must be emphasized; yet it requires continual cultivation. It absolutely cannot be coerced; yet its absence does grievous harm to any Christian institution. It lasts a lifetime; yet it also ebbs and flows, with high points and low. It cannot be fully articulated; yet it can be observed in and through a human life. Authentic piety is at the heart of any

Christian university that retains its identity and feel as a genuinely Christian place; yet many unhealthy substitutes for it exist. This leads us to our vice list. On the one hand, Christian universities and their students suffer profoundly when Christian commitment erodes. Other authors in this volume address this issue. It is certainly the most common threat to the integrity, vitality, and identity of Christian universities, which frequently do all too little to combat it.[5]

The university's leaders cease to be practitioners of authentic piety themselves and to look for it in their staff, administrators, and faculty. Furthermore, hiring and institutional vision casting cease to consider this once critical dimension of life. What remains is either an "on the book" obligation to some form of official Christianity, or not even that. It is interesting to watch and listen to how the Christian faith is described when authentic piety fades and is replaced by quasi-Christian mush. Here I quote a Christian educator who writes approvingly of a religious studies department in which he once served: "[T]he operational definition of faith in this pluralistic context, as the largely unspecified axis of shared sincerity and exploratory spirit around which the other dimensions of human existence revolve, strikes me as the most valid for the college experience. This more open-textured posture is Christian not because it adheres to a specific set of beliefs and/or mores, but because it seeks to foster the educational enterprise within the mediating framework of Christian values."[6]

"Shared sincerity," "exploratory spirit," no "specific beliefs or mores" (read: moral norms)—in my view, this is the language of Christian-becoming-post-Christian higher education. It will not do; it will not serve our students well. It should not be our goal.

On the other hand, one finds the vice of repressive Christian conventionalism. In a helpful 1988 article, Dennis Dirks of Biola University discussed the disappointing performance of students at evangelical schools on moral development tests and instruments. Dirks argues that evangelical universities are prone to the creation of a climate in which what I am calling authentic piety is stifled by a faith environment that is unthinking, merely conventional, safe, sheltered, and homogeneous. At their worst, such institutions terrorize anyone who might raise a question that does not fit neatly inside the little faith box in existence there.[7]

Professors in such contexts are negatively sanctioned and positively rewarded for incarnating this merely safe and conventional kind of faith themselves. This too is poison to authentic piety.

The twenty-first century student may well come from a home in which Christian faith is altogether absent. Many of my students do. Or, she may come from a home in which conventional faith is present and doing its best to kill any seedlings of authenticity or fresh thought. This is also quite common. Thus, our challenge is to incarnate over the course of a lifetime authentic piety and in so doing to open up new horizons of Christian faith for both kinds of students.

2. Relational Virtue: Covenant Fidelity

I want to propose the category of relational virtue and the norm of covenant fidelity as the central virtue for the Christian professor within that category.

The thought that the way in which we handle our relationships with others is a matter of great moral significance is certainly not new, either in Christian or secular moral thought. However, rarely is relational virtue lifted up for focused attention in the literature of Christian higher education. Attention is frequently given to how those who serve in Christian universities relate to their students. But I am arguing here that the entire pattern of our way of relating to other human beings is what is most significant and that the central norm in this arena should be the biblical concept of covenant fidelity.

Those whose lives are characterized by covenant fidelity are people who take seriously the moral obligations created by their relationships with and commitments to other people. They seek to relate responsibly, consistently, and with integrity to all people. Yet they are capable of drawing distinctions between the various kinds of relational commitments they have made and the nature of the obligations these relationships involve.

Let me be more concrete. Christian university professors or administrators will be characterized by covenant fidelity in family life. If married, they will work hard to place marriage and family first, after relationship with God, in their lives. They will exhibit consistent emotional and sexual fidelity to their spouses and will guard the boundaries of that fidelity with great care. They will strive for a growing and flourishing marriage and will work doggedly to remove obstacles that may stand in the way. The Christian university should not be characterized by the high divorce rate found in secular universities and in the broader society. This does not mean that divorce is categorically incompatible with service as a Christian university professor, but it does mean that it can never be accepted casually here as it is elsewhere. The divorced or divorcing professor, for that matter, has opportunity in the midst of great pain to demonstrate covenant fidelity to his or her children and can model patience, humility, and charity in relation to his or her former spouse.

The mention of children and how they are treated reminds us of this dimension of covenant fidelity. Christian professors need to allow their students to get close enough to them to see into their relationships with their children and to benefit from what they see. Many of our students now come from dysfunctional or disastrous family environments, with the treatment they received in childhood leaving considerable emotional damage. The Christian university professor who invests heavily in his or her children, loves them dearly, treats them fairly, participates fully in their upbringing, and so on will leave a mark on such students. In the twenty-first century, the incarnating of covenant fidelity in marriage and family life may be the single most significant contribution the Christian university professor can make to his or her students.

Yet these are not the only relationships our students witness. Covenantal fidelity is at play in the way we relate to our peers and coworkers in university life. Students will notice the manner in which we speak of and speak with our colleagues. When we refrain from gossip, backbiting, and competitive backstabbing, we exhibit covenant fidelity within the context of these important relationships.

We must seek with all our energy to avoid infidelity to our relational covenants at any level of life. Perhaps in a secular university it is possible to bracket off the personal and relational dimensions of the faculty members' lives and to say that as long as teaching and other professional obligations are met, that is all that can be expected of anyone. However, that private/public, personal/professional dualism cannot and should not be permitted in the Christian university. We teach with our lives as well as with our lectures and can reasonably be expected to do so.

3. Intellectual Virtue: Critical Curiosity

Unlike the discussion of relational virtue, as we move to intellectual virtue, we find ourselves in well-traveled terrain. Nearly everyone who writes about the Christian university attends to the life of the mind as it is and as it ought to be in Christian higher education. Thus I do not pretend to originality here as I propose the central intellectual virtue of critical curiosity.

Let us consider first the matter of intellectual curiosity. Many observers of the American cultural scene have noted the relative mental laziness that besets us. With so many toys, games, amusements, and diversions at our disposal, we are not a people characterized by reading, thinking, and reflecting. I remember once talking with a homebuilder, a contractor, who told me that fewer and fewer of his customers are interested in having bookshelves in their home, while just about everyone requests state-of-the-art entertainment centers—a telling sign of the times. Thus we can expect that many of the students who come to us will not hail from homes in which books, serious magazines, and newspapers are read. They will not be accustomed to scintillating dinnertime conversations about the world, culture, and important ideas. (More than likely, the TV will be on.) They will not have come from schools that managed to instill that love of learning that was absent at home. If students are to develop intellectual curiosity, they will have to learn it while they are in our hallowed halls.

Once I attended a remarkable lecture by the Holocaust survivor, author, and Nobel laureate, Elie Wiesel. In a question-and-answer time after his lecture, he was asked to discuss how he managed to survive the horrors he had experienced, not physically, but emotionally and psychologically. His surprising, one-word answer was this: "study." He attributed that commitment to study to his childhood upbringing, in which study of the Torah, Talmud, Kabbalah, and other Jewish holy books—and study in general—was viewed as a holy and joyous obligation. For Wiesel, the fact that there is always another book or article to read is a form of psychological salvation. It keeps him going. He has a relentless intellectual curiosity.

How desperately we need to develop and nurture such intellectual curiosity in our own students! Imagine a situation in which students in our Christian universities read more than is assigned, can't sleep until they track down an answer to a dangling question, are current on national and world events, have a solid grasp of the intellectual heritage of our culture, as well as a cutting-edge sense of where that culture is now heading, read in places like *The New York Times Book Review* and the *Atlantic Monthly,* as well as *Christianity Today* and other Christian media, would rather go to a bookstore than J. C. Penney's. We will not produce students like that if we ourselves are not like that. Only if learning is our way of life will our students develop that same lifestyle. Such curiosity is the precondition for scholarship, both for ourselves and for our students—and such scholarship continues to be all too rare in evangelical university life.

Intellectual curiosity must be critically minded. In my experience, students frequently have a difficult time understanding what we mean when we ask them to be critical thinkers. No one has ever challenged them with such a goal prior to their arrival on our campuses. Their churches more likely encourage an attitude of unquestioning submission to the truth as defined by Scripture and refracted through the lens of a pastor and local tradition. The possibility that any particular Christian's take on truth, including the one they grew up with, is not the same as truth is at times a shocking concept. Alternately, sometimes students respond to the request for critical thinking by trashing everything they read in class, which is equally uncritical when that concept is rightly understood. Critical thinking is the ability to interact with ideas, rather than merely react, to sift them for their truthfulness and value, rather than accept or reject them out of hand. It is a stance characterized by a healthy mixture of stable and confident intellectual commitments, on the one hand, and an open, flexible, humble, reflective teachableness on the other. Using the language of worldview, Brian J. Walsh has put it this way: "Insofar as a worldview is truly open to reality and requires experiential validation if it is to be viable, it is, by nature, in process—open to reform, correction, redirection and refocusing . . . a canonized worldview results in a stifling conservatism, scholasticism, and separatism—none of which is conducive to the atmosphere of a 'liberal' arts college. Being rooted in Jesus Christ gives one the courage to say that we don't have all the answers, nor do we need them."[8]

It has proven remarkably difficult for the modern university, Christian or otherwise, to create an environment characterized by critical thinking. Christian universities, as Dennis Dirks, Michael Cosby, and many other observers have noted, tend to fall prey to the vice of uncritical, parochial, and conventional indoctrination, whereas secular universities either succumb to a parallel secularist indoctrination or a standardless, normless, and truthless relativism. Professors at Christian universities are uniquely positioned to model consecrated critical-mindedness and consecrated intellectual curiosity in order to produce students characterized by the right kind of Christian critical curiosity.[9]

4. Social Virtue: Transformative Engagement

Gordon College sociologist Ivy George has written, "The ultimate aim of Christian higher education is to pursue the world order Christ seeks. This involves a deliberate turning away from familiar models of excellence and leadership and a turning toward doing good and pursuing a different world order."[10] Her words offer an excellent introduction to a fourth arena of concern, social virtue, and reflect the trait I propose for that arena: transformative engagement.

This character quality is linked to all that are previously listed. Authentic piety nurtures in us a heart "after God's own heart," a sensitivity to the brokenness and suffering to be found in God our Creator's world. Those characterized by relational fidelity are aware of the immense costs of its absence. The critically curious are sufficiently attentive to the world as it truly is that they know of its many arenas of suffering, misery, and oppression. From these various streams of insight comes a commitment to transformational engagement in a broken, suffering, and unjust world.

Ivy George is perfectly correct in arguing that "the development of the gentleman or the citizen or even the good Christian leader" cannot be the ultimate goal of Christian higher education.[11] We need a bigger vision for what we are to be and what we are to be about in Christian higher education. What is so frequently lacking is a kingdom vision: that is, this is God's world, over which he is rightfully sovereign; it is a world marred profoundly by human sin; this sin causes innumerable forms of human suffering; God sent Jesus his Son to inaugurate the reclaiming of all creation; the church exists to advance the reign of God into even the darkest and most desperate corners of the human heart and human society—until Christ returns to bring this grand and terrible drama to its climax, once and for all, and to establish the *shalom* God always intended.

Professors who serve in Christian universities need to be animated by this kind of kingdom vision. These are people who wake up in the morning with a desire to spend the day advancing God's reign in every possible way. They are ever on the alert for areas of human need, injustice, and oppression and want to be used by God to bind up the wounds of the broken and to set the captives free. They know that one way that God can use them is through their communication of this passion to their students, who by the hundreds will be sent out into the world as kingdom builders in various areas of human need. As Nicholas Wolterstorff has put it, they want to "teach for justice."[12]

Note that I do not believe this vision for social transformation in accordance with God's will can be confined to the Christian studies people, the ethics people, or the sociology department. It is a scriptural mandate for all God's people and is thus a vision that should move the whole people of God, including Christian educators and their students. Note as well that this social virtue is not confined to cognition but extends to the arena of action. We ought to be characterized not only by the right beliefs about human suffering and God's redemptive intent but also by concrete forms of transformational engagement, which our students can then observe and in which they can participate with us. As Wolterstorff argues, "There is no better way for teachers to cultivate a passion for justice in their students than by themselves exhibiting that very passion."[13]

The vice in opposition with this virtue is clear and all too pervasive. The Christian university campus is frequently characterized by a profound truncation of moral vision. God's broad kingdom purposes are understood far too narrowly, if they are a matter of concern at all. Students are not challenged to leave their hermetically sealed Christian bubbles and to engage the wider world with transformational moral activity. The Christian life is about "my soul," "my happiness," "my relationships," "my walk with God," not about God's world, broken people made in God's image, social justice that is God's will, starving children over whom God weeps, genocide and war that destroy God's children, and God's intent to respond to all of this through the committed, wise, and sacrificial efforts of his redeemed people. How desperately we need a broader and more wholistic understanding of the Christian faith, the purpose of the Christian college, and the normative character and tasks of the faculty in this regard. Again, Nicholas Wolterstorff: "The . . . Christian college must open itself up to humanity's wounds."[14]

5. Personal Virtue: Purposeful Self-Discipline

By way of closing, I ask you to consider with me what I am calling the personal virtue of purposeful self-discipline. Our students come to us during a developmental stage in which they are wrestling with the purpose of (that is, God's call upon) their lives. Some come from homes in which parent or parents had a job but not a purpose in life. They have witnessed adult lives lived as a bored drift from day to day, the boredom punctuated only by the latest gadget or video or CD. All of them know friends who have no clue what they are to do with their lives and no particular answer to the question Steven Garber asks in *The Fabric of Faithfulness:* "Why do you wake up in the morning?"[15] They may be asking that question themselves.

There are few gifts more valuable we can offer our students than the evidence of a purposeful life. If they can look at us and see men and women who know exactly why they get up in the morning and are eager to do so, they will more than likely learn to do the same. They may come to share our particular purpose in life, or it may take a different form, but they will have a purpose. Of course, as Christians we cannot avoid the issue of which particular purposes in life are actually worthy of pursuit. Hitler woke up every morning with a clear sense of purpose—to destroy his racial enemies. Academicians all over the world wake up in the morning with a desire to publish rather than perish, to get promoted, and so on. Not every purpose, not every *telos*, is morally worthy. Yet, if our purpose is genuinely to use our lives to advance God's kingdom, and other purposes are clearly constrained by this one, we are on the right track.

So the thought of a drifting, purposeless Christian college professor ought rightly to offend us. And the thought of a no-holds-barred, do anything to climb over your back on my way to the top Christian college professor, offends us as well. But a steady and committed pursuit of God's kingdom through the ministry of Christian higher education is altogether fitting.

Such a pursuit requires the virtue of self-discipline. Purpose and self-discipline go together, the latter serving the former. The development of self-discipline, like the discovery of life purpose, is a critical developmental task of the college student. Learning to work hard and steadily, to treat one's body in a way that will enable it to flourish, to establish constructive personal habits in the areas of diet, exercise, rest, scheduling, and so on—these are among the most important components of the task. We can be certain that our students will notice the extent to which we ourselves are self-disciplined in personal lifestyle— that is, if we allow them to get close enough to us to see.

Conclusion

My task in this paper has been to explore the nature of the professor's task in the Christian university. I have argued that this task cannot be reduced to the myriad daily tasks of the professor, and that this is an ever-present danger. I have also claimed that our task should not be viewed merely in terms of servicing our various constituencies. Instead, I have suggested that incarnating an authentically Christian way of life with and before our students lies at the heart of our vocation. While this suggestion is not a new one, I have claimed that in the context of the moral and family disintegration of late twentieth-century North America, the task of character formation in Christian higher education takes on a new urgency. I have proposed five interdependent arenas of character—spiritual, relational, intellectual, social, and personal—and one central virtue in each area—authentic piety, covenant fidelity, critical curiosity, transformative engagement, and purposeful self-discipline. I am not saying that the professor must be perfect, because this is impossible, but I refuse to concede that such a vision of faculty character is an unattainable fantasy. Perhaps most importantly, I hope that I have communicated along the way what a joyous and wonderful calling it is to serve in Christian higher education and to have opportunity to "attract by our lives" the precious human beings who are our students.

This address was delivered at the Conference on the Future of Christian Higher Education at Union University.

Chapter 14

INTEGRATING FAITH AND LEARNING IN A CHRISTIAN LIBERAL ARTS INSTITUTION

ARTHUR F. HOLMES

Over the last two or three years I have been reading in the history of Christian involvement in higher education, from the second century on through the Middle Ages and the Reformation into the Enlightenment. I find three recurring concerns, which are distinctive contributions of the Christian college: the shaping of character, the integration of faith and learning, and the usefulness of liberal learning as preparation for service. These three emphases, I want to suggest, should become the focus of your education; they should determine where you concentrate your energies, your attention, and your time while you are here.

Develop Character

There is a recent book about college students by the chaplain and a faculty member at Duke University, a book called *The Abandoned Generation.*[1] Its thesis, well documented from observations and experience, is that the moral and personal development of students has been abandoned in today's secularized university. A few years ago, when Allan Bloom of the University of Chicago published *The Closing of the American Mind*, he complained that today's students talk as if there is no such thing as right and wrong, nor such a thing as truth or falsity, and that they have no worldview on which to ground such ideas.[2] This is the plight of today's abandoned generation, for whom the Christian college still seeks character development.

What is character? The word itself, taken literally, has to do with engraving—carving into one's being a moral identity that is ineradicable. Character does not mean an unthinking conformity to the expectations of parents or society or church; it does not mean good intentions that are never implemented; it is not just an outward show but rather something inside working outward—something solid, consistent, the same day in and day out. If I am weak-kneed and cannot stand on my own feet, you say I have weak character. If I behave well but inwardly am jealous, hateful, self-centered, you should call me a hypocrite. If I am well-intentioned but have no follow-through, I'm irresponsible. What are you? How would you describe your character? Or perhaps more appropriately, how would your roommate or closest friend describe it? Who are you, really? How do you characterize your moral identity?

Developmental psychologists describe the moral identity of entering students as "diffused," or "dualistic." To be diffused is to be all over the map, without focus, never one consistent self. To be dualistic is to be double-minded, pulling in different directions at the same time. You still don't have it all together. Is that true of you? These psychologists also try to track the changes that take place as we grow through the college years toward integrated personality and moral integrity. Integrity is not just honesty; it means oneness, a consistent oneness that is always the same through and through. It is character. The Bible speaks of the righteous, people who produce the fruit of the Holy Spirit. All of this feeds into the concept of character. What I say to you, then, is this: Make it your business here in college to develop your character.

But how? Character formation is, after all, the work of God's grace in a human nature he created and we perverted. It is the process that theologians call sanctification, making the sort of righteousness reckoned to us in justification a reality in our lives. But what God does in grace he does through means in which we participate. So, given the kind of human nature God has given us, and given the grace of God, how do we develop character?

Let me propose two things, the first of which has been recognized at least since Aristotle and clearly has parallels in biblical teaching. You develop character by developing habits. Character traits are essentially habits of the inner life that have outward consequences. Do you remember Robert Bellah's book *Habits of the Heart?*[3] Virtues are good habits of the heart; vices are bad habits of the heart. We develop these character traits by the heart-habits we shape. With children, we provide discipline and instruction to start them in the right direction. Bringing up a child in the way he should go means cultivating in her the right habits. But as we achieve more maturity, it depends much more on us. We have to *choose* the right and the good; we must reflect, examine ourselves, make the right choice again and again until it becomes, as we say, second nature. It becomes a habit. Augustine, too, calls us to this kind of inner self-examination and resolve, to develop a properly ordered love, a pattern of life, a habit of the heart.

Did you ever read Benjamin Franklin's autobiography? In it he writes of his efforts to develop good habits. They were not altogether successful—after all, are yours or mine? What he did was to list on a piece of paper the various vices he saw in himself and wanted to over-come. As he made progress against a particular vice, he would take his pen and put a check mark against it: a number of vices received check marks in the course of time. When he realized he was slipping and showing a particular vice again, he took his pen knife and scratched the mark out so as to start over again. Then as he made progress again, he would have to make a check mark once more; but again he would have to scratch it out, and soon the paper was full of holes, all the way down his list. Yet he kept struggling to cultivate those habits of the heart.

Like Franklin, we need repeated self-examination, repeated moni-toring of what sort of character we have. We need to choose the right repeatedly and follow through on the commitments we make. When I was a child, my parents hung a plaque in my bedroom with a text that has stuck with me ever since: "Watch ye! Stand fast in the faith! Quit you like men! Be strong!" (1 Cor. 16:13). I looked at that plaque every morning as I grew up. I could hardly avoid it right there in my bed-room. I believe it made an indelible impression. It still says to me: "Examine yourself; cultivate the right habits."

Ignatius, the founder of the Jesuit order, in the instructions he left for the guidance of that order, insisted that commitment to scholarly excellence is vitally important for developing moral excellence. A syn-ergy exists between how we discipline our minds and how our charac-ter develops. If you don't have the intellectual discipline it takes really to study, how can you expect to have the moral discipline it takes to be a good person? Both take discipline. Both take self-scrutiny and sys-tematic, methodical work. So develop the right habits both in your studies and in your heart. That is the first step.

The second is this: In order to have integrity, to be one and the same person, you must possess a unifying, consuming devotion to what is supremely good. This is another of Augustine's emphases. Love the Lord your God with all your heart and mind and strength. That should also be the unifying virtue in every one of your lives, for where your treasure is—whatever you value most, whatever you love most—there will your heart be also. It must be this habit of the heart that unifies the life.

How can a Christian college help in all this, if indeed it is part of the *mission* of Christian higher education? First of all, recognize that your studies can help. In ancient Greece, even before the beginnings of the Christian church, the primary purpose of education was character development, transmitting the values of the cultural heritage of the time. Greek education was known as *paideia,* the word from which we get our terms *pedagogy* and *pediatrician. Paideia* meant, initially, that you would read Homer. You would meet his heroes, see their virtues at work, observe the consistency of their character. Greek young people not only read Homer, they recited Homer; they reenacted his heroes' exploits, recited their speeches, feeling the emotions and sharing the passions until heroic values and virtues became part of them too. By identifying inwardly with their heritage, the ancient Greeks made its values their own.

As the so-called liberal arts of the day developed, they studied dialectic, or elementary logic, because in learning to think critically and examine what is said and make intelligent judgments, they learned to discern between right and wrong or true and false. They were taught rhetoric because communication skills helped them spell things out for themselves and for others, and helped clarify what they should do. They were taught astronomy because astronomy made plain that everything had a proper place in the world, a contribution to make, a responsible role within the total picture of the cosmos. They learned geometry which, as one of them said, "sowed the seeds of justice" with its emphasis on equality and proportion. And they learned music, because music can calm the passions, harmonize the soul, and tune it to virtue. Of course, this was not a blanket judgment about all music, as you know if you have read Plato's *Republic.* The Greek's concern for its effects on character guided their use of the arts. Thus, we see that the liberal learning of the ancient Greeks deliberately addressed the development of character.

Think about that in terms of your own studies. Every subject is value laden. In God's creation, there are no bare facts devoid of purpose, value free. The fact/value separation is a myth that has come down to us from the Enlightenment. Literature comes replete with the moral traits of its characters, history likewise, and the humanities as a whole. The social and behavioral sciences address issues that are loaded with human values and moral concerns. Science and technology have a resounding social impact and raise new moral questions all the time. Professional studies introduce you to occupations requiring specific character traits for effectiveness. Give attention, then, to the moral impact of your studies. Studies can help you shape the habits of your heart.

Community life can help as well. Here I am thinking of residence halls and student activities. The book I mentioned at the outset, about the abandoned generation, moves from description and diagnosis to recommendations for affecting student character. The author's recommendation is to develop smaller communities within the larger campus, because it is by participating in the life of a more closely knitted community that people develop moral identity, a character of their own. Another college educator, David Hoekema, likewise observes that now that the *in loco parentis* (in place of parents) approach with its paternalistic rules has gone, we must develop small communities on campus with which students can identify.[4] Mark Schwehn, in his book *Exiles from Eden* (an ominous title), complains that character development is no longer a concern in academia.[5] His recommendation? Develop small communities. At Valparaiso University in Indiana, Schwehn headed an honors college appropriately called "Jesus College," the purpose of which is to develop character in the context of disciplined study. Stanley Hauerwas has written repeatedly on topics like this, making the point that as we enter into the life of a community and make its story and its values our own, we begin to assimilate something of its character.[6] The president of the college I attended repeatedly said, "It's always too soon to quit," until that adage became part of the heritage of every alumnus of the college. "Stick-to-it-iveness" became a virtue that was expected of us.

Community life can help. So examine your residence hall life. Examine your extracurricular activities. What ideals do they embody? What ideals are you acquiring there? What character-building potentials of community life on this campus could you tap into?

A Christian college provides you with many possible models and mentors. In ancient Greece, mentorship was not the sole responsibility of the teacher. A wealthy family would carefully choose a slave who could be entrusted with the guidance of a young person going out socially into the world. This *paidagogos* was a guide, a companion, a counselor, a disciplinarian. The word is used in the New Testament with reference to Scripture as the *paidagogos* that nurtures us in righteousness. We need *paidagogoi,* models and mentors, in our lives. Who could serve in this role for you? A friend? Your family? Another student? Who would you want to emulate and be like? What teachers stand out in your mind? I referred just now to Ignatius, the founder of the Jesuit order. He said that the responsibility rests primarily on the teacher to set an example that will inspire moral and intellectual excellence along with spiritual commitment. Who models this for you?

Think of possible models in Scripture. Moses was learned in all the wisdom of the Egyptians and became the lawgiver of a nation, memorialized now in the United States Supreme Court in Washington. Solomon is an exemplar of wisdom he acquired through hard work, gathering proverbs from across the world of his day. He said, "Much learning is a weariness to the flesh." Daniel, who studied Babylonian language and literature along the way, now stands for courage. I suspect his studies helped him. And Paul, who stands out as a model of faithfulness in his tasks, studied the Torah faithfully as a Jew. Take advantage of the biblical models, and take advantage of the opportunities and models you have here to develop character. Finally, keep the following in mind. In the late second century, Clement of Alexandria wrote a book called *The Paidagogos,* in which he presents Jesus Christ as our *paidagogos,* the model and mentor who guides and prepares us for eternal life.

I think the Christian college can help in this process of Christian growth, by the studies that are involved, by the community life that is possible, and by the models and mentors, living and historical, that God provides right here. In the second Epistle of Peter you will find this advice: "giving all diligence, *add* to your faith virtue; and to virtue knowledge; and to knowledge temperance [self-control]; and to temperance patience; and to patience godliness; and to godliness brotherly kindness; and to brotherly kindness charity" (2 Pet. 1:5–7 KJV). Add what to your faith? Add character, one virtue after another. Work on it. What virtue do you most need? Work on it. Cultivate the mental and emotional habits that underlie it. Work on it. Make this virtue an expression of your overall love for God, heart and mind and every strength. Giving all diligence, don't be negligent, but develop your character.

Integrate Your Learning

In addressing the topic of developing character, we focused on habits of the heart and the integration of personality as constituting character. Here we will focus on the habits of the mind and the integration of faith and learning. We would do better to call it "reintegration" because the problem is not that we deal with two unrelated things and somehow or other have to force a shotgun wedding. Rather, we need to reintegrate a union that was broken apart in the course of history.

Some of you have read George Marsden's _The Soul of the American University,_ a book that made the front page of _The Chronicle of Higher Education._ It traces an historical process by which the American university lost its putatively Christian soul. It is the story of how Enlightenment secularization affected our institutions of higher learning, a process that tore faith and learning apart. The very nature of the Enlightenment was its emphasis on the light of reason alone, discarding the voice of tradition, rejecting the input of any authority, ignoring the input of revelation in the arts and sciences until only a thoroughly secularized kind of learning remained. The rule of reason meant the rule of science, so the methods of science became standard for every discipline. Science was supposed to be presuppositionless, so all learning must be presuppositionless, pursued therefore in a theological vacuum. That is why we should really be talking about the _re_integration of faith and learning.

Another reason for using the term _reintegration_ is that most of us come to college as compartmentalized thinkers, with our Christian experience and belief in one compartment and our knowledge of the sciences and humanities in another. We tend to be dualistic in our thinking. But compartmentalized minds need to be reintegrated because that is not the way God intended us to be. He is Creator and lord of all, and he wants that to pervade our thinking about every bit of the "all." So again I prefer to speak of _reintegrating_ rather than integrating faith and learning.

I also find it helps to think historically about reintegration, because it is not something that sprang up anew in the twentieth century. "Integration" has become a cliché in Christian college circles over the last twenty or thirty years, but it has actually been in operation for centuries.[7] It began with the beginnings of Christian higher education in the Hellenistic world of the second and third centuries when

Christians were exposed to the kind of education that had begun in ancient Greece. Christians went to Hellenistic schools, and some taught in them, so they were familiar with Greek literature. Augustine, two centuries later, tells how his inadequate Greek prevented him from enjoying Homer as he did Virgil. Homer and the Greek poets, you see, were the educational vehicle for transmitting the cultural heritage of the past. That, too, was how they learned history. The seven liberal arts had already emerged by Hellenistic times. The trivium contained three ways to wisdom: grammar, which was the study of literature and language; rhetoric; and dialectic, or critical thinking. Then the quadrivium, the fourfold way to wisdom, included arithmetic, geometry, astronomy, and music—the mathematical disciplines. These liberal arts were the way to an earthly wisdom that Christians found quite valuable. But it was not enough; and in any case, what has it to do with Christianity?

If you have read Homer and other of the Greek or Latin poets, you realize that some of their poetry is not appropriate for impressionable adolescents, scurrilous things about the gods and idolatry and pagan morality that some Christians today still object to their children reading. Tertullian, the North African church father, forbade Christians to teach in pagan schools because teaching Greek literature might be taken as an endorsement of pagan practices. But he approved of young people attending pagan schools because they did not have to agree with everything they were taught. Others took a different approach. Basil of Caesarea, for instance, in "A Letter to Young Men on Reading Greek Literature," wrote that you can learn a great deal from it, including some valuable moral principles. But since it is so mixed, he advised them not to rely entirely on pagan teachers for their education.

By then, Christians were adding to Greek education and its human wisdom an additional kind of Christian education in divine wisdom. They greatly appreciated both the Greek poets and the Greek philosophers, particularly the Stoics and Plato. Augustine would later devote almost an entire book in his *City of God* to the things he found valuable in Plato: Plato believed in one God who formed the universe and that this God is an immaterial being; he believed that the soul is immaterial, that God made all things good, that we should seek the good, and so on. But how did these pagans know so much? That question occupied Christian thinkers because they were so impressed with the truth in pagan learning. How *did* these pagans know so much?

Justin Martyr responded that in some way they and we must participate in the same source of truth. He picked up on the Stoic concept of _logos_, a rationality that orders the whole universe in intelligible ways, seeds of which are evident in the rationality of our minds. Plato and the others must somehow have participated in the divine _Logos_, whom Justin now identified with the _Logos_ of John's Gospel. Some church fathers drew attention to chapter 1, verse 9: "the light that enlightens everyone that comes into the world." Their exegesis is questionable, for that text could better be translated, "When this light came into the world, . . . he enlightened everyone." It is not the preexistent _Logos_ but rather his incarnation that enlightens the world. Be that as it may, the Alexandrian church fathers most fully developed the _logos_ theology.

Origen had been the grammar teacher in a pagan school. His father had died when he was young, a martyr, so Origen went out to work as a teacher. And when the bishop needed somebody to replace Clement as the head of the catechetical school, he appointed Origen at the ripe age of nineteen. He continued to provide instruction in the faith, but realizing that Christian young people needed more if they were to hold their own in that city of learning, he also started teaching the liberal arts and philosophy and built on those disciplines with intensive biblical and theological studies. Clement had said, "All truth is God's truth, no matter where it's found, and the task of the church is to regather those fragments, even from the most unlikely places, and to reunite them to the body of the whole from which they have been torn." This statement reflects a reintegration of truths of faith with truth from other sources, a reintegration of faith and learning. Alexandria is where it began, and we therefore stand in a long and important tradition. But the question persists: How could pagans know so much?

As a former grammar teacher, Origen followed the Greek approach to literature—or literary criticism, as we call it. It was threefold: a straightforward historical reading of the story, moral applications, and an allegorical interpretation for mythological elements. Origen simply carried that approach over to the interpretation of Scripture. It was current before him: The first-century Jewish Alexandrian theologian, Philo, wrote a little piece titled "On Mating with Hagar the Egyptian." You remember the story of Abraham and Hagar. Philo provided an allegorical interpretation for Alexandrian Jews: Abraham was unable to produce fruit in his union with Sarah until _after_ he had been with Hagar; in the same way, a Jew will be unable to be fruitful in studying divine wisdom until he has been fruitful in the study of the Greek wisdom of Hellenist Egypt. Clement of Alexandria, two centuries later, picked up the allegory and added, "But be careful you don't get so enamored with the handmaiden that you neglect your lawful wife." Origen in his turn finds another allegory. The Israelites of the Exodus took from the Egyptians the wealth they needed to go out into the wilderness and worship God. So may Christians take from the pagans those treasures of learning that belong rightfully to God. Augustine repeated Origen's allegory and talked about plundering the Egyptians. We may not like that kind of biblical interpretation, and hopefully we have since learned a little bit in that regard, but you see the point. All truth is God's truth, no matter where it is found. Ultimately it all comes from him, it all belongs to him, so we need to gather it all together and bring it as an offering to God, a reintegration of truths of our faith with truth we learn in other ways in God's creation.

This tradition of reintegration was maintained through the centuries. Before he became a bishop, Augustine was an educator who taught rhetoric and the liberal arts. Some of his earliest writings record his discussions with students about the theological basis of the trivium and quadrivium, their basis in *logos* theology. A revival of learning resulted from Charlemagne's initiatives, and schools were established in monasteries and cathedrals. Leaders of this movement went back to that liberal arts tradition again. Throughout the Middle Ages, Christian thinkers reintegrated truths of faith with truths of reason, with *logos* theology as the basis: The *Logos* who created and ordered the cosmos also made us in his own image, rational beings able to contemplate his wisdom and his goodness.

But problems arose. After all, it is one thing to say "reintegrate," but what if claims to truth conflict? Plato spoke many truths, but Plato didn't believe God ultimately created the universe, that is to say, gave it existence. Plato believed that God ordered the basic "glop" from which things emerged; he was an "orderer," not an "originator." Plato did not believe in creation ex nihilo. Aristotle did not either. Aristotle's God could not act or work at all but was simply a final cause whom everything in creation tries to imitate. All Aristotle's God ever does is eternally to contemplate his own contemplating. He cannot even know anything other than himself, for if God knew changing things, then he himself would change in knowing changing things. A perfect Being cannot change.

How can you integrate that philosophy with Christian belief? That actually became an issue in the thirteenth century. After Aristotle's writings were rediscovered in the Muslim world and began to be known across the Pyrenees in France, a philosopher named Averroës saw that Aristotle was incompatible with his Muslim theology but still thought both were true. A theory of twofold truth developed. Averroës suggested that to the sophisticated, Aristotle is right, but for the simple-minded Muslim, theology is right. As Averroism became known in Christian universities in France, Bonaventure, who had taught in the University of Paris and then became the leader of the Franciscan Order and a teacher in the Franciscan monastery schools, responded that without illumination from God we cannot expect pagan thinkers to know the truth about God. So he turned his back on Aristotle. However, across town at the University of Paris, Thomas Aquinas argued that much in Aristotle was very helpful to Christian thought. Aristotle was wrong on some things but could be corrected. So in developing arguments for the existence of God, Aquinas began with Aristotelian premises about cause and effect, contingency and necessity, and so forth, and then proved the non-Aristotelian conclusion that God is the efficient cause who brings things into being. That's quite a coup. What about God being unable to know his creatures? Well, Aquinas borrowed from Augustine a view known as "exemplarism," that Plato's "forms" (which his God used in fashioning the world of nature) are really God's eternal counsels, exemplars for his creation. So Aristotle's God is no longer just thinking on his own thinking but thinking about his creation. Aquinas reintegrated Christian theology with Aristotelian learning by correcting what was wrong in Aristotle.

This reintegration of pagan Greek philosophy and Christian theology was the general purpose of the scholastic method that developed in the medieval universities. It was largely a method of disputation, debate, and argumentation that grew out of the work of an eleventh-century teacher named Abelard, who published a book called *Sic et Non* (pro and con). The book was a collection of biblical passages for and against various points of Christian doctrine, a resource manual for student debates in theology. It was not exactly calculated to win friends, and Abelard got into a lot of trouble. He was accused of being unconcerned about student moral and spiritual development, and he was accused of teaching heresy. The controversy raged for twenty years until he was finally condemned by the church council in Soissons and very accommodatingly died two years later.

Using the scholastic method, the teacher either expounded some book or else supervised disputations over points of controversy. Why? What if you want to draw on pagan learning and recognize where it falls short? You need some critical thinking, some good logic and debate. When you read Thomas Aquinas, the format is again like a manual for debate. He poses a question; he lists objection 1, objection 2, objection 3. Then he says, "On the contrary . . ." and, "I answer. . . ." Then "Replies to objection 1," "Replies to objection 2," "Replies to objection 3," and you have in the space of one or two pages the grist for a debate on any topic you like. The objections and replies cite both pagan and Christian writers in struggling for a defensible answer. It is hard intellectual work.

The claim that all truth is God's truth needs to be kept in this larger context. It may explain how these pagans could know so much, even though they also teach many things that are untrue. You must learn to distinguish truth from falsity, show what is true and what is not, and then interrelate the truth logically as a whole.

The outcome of the work of the medievals is tremendous. They interrelated all they knew from the pagan past and the Christian past into an all-inclusive worldview, a massive hierarchical scheme where everything in existence is arranged according to degrees of goodness, beauty, truth, and unity. It is like some cosmic choreographed dance to the glory of God. Everything in creation to some degree reflects his goodness, wisdom, and power. The arts and sciences manifest his wondrous work, and the whole vision becomes a symphony of praise. As students did their academic work in the medieval monastery schools, they voiced their thoughts and feelings out loud: "God is good!" or "Praise God!" This spontaneous praise of God was part of the liturgical life of the monastery. Likewise, our academic work can become contemplation and worship of God. This doxological theme is another ongoing emphasis in the history of Christian higher education.

Think about Paul's statement in Colossians: "in [Christ] are hid all the treasures of wisdom and knowledge" (2:3 KJV). What does this mean? It clearly does not suggest that the truth is hidden from us, for Paul has just said a mystery was finally revealed by Christ's coming. Consider rather the term *treasure*, a value judgment about wisdom and knowledge. Origen also used that word in likening liberal learning to the "treasures" of Egypt. Is all the value of liberal learning then related to Jesus Christ?

Who is the Christ that Paul is talking about in Colossians? Virtually the entire first chapter is about him, the Creator of everything who sustains its existence, providentially orders its operation, enters it in grace, and will eventually renew his creation. He is involved in everything. All wisdom and knowledge, then, eventually point us to him. That is their greatest treasure.

Paul goes on to say, "Beware of philosophy," or rather "beware of _that_ philosophy," for the definite article in Greek works like a demonstrative pronoun: "Beware of _that_ philosophy which is according to the traditions of men and the rudiments of this world, rather than that which is in accordance with Christ." Paul contrasts two worldviews, one in which wisdom and knowledge are related to Christ, the other in which this world's traditions prevail. Paul is after a reintegration of faith and learning that will restore to the Creator that which is rightfully his, redeemed thinking that properly honors Jesus Christ.

So we must recognize and respect the value of truth no matter where it is found. We must integrate our understanding of Scripture and theology with what we learn from other sources, relating biblical revelation to general revelation. That calls for interdisciplinary thinking in which theology is a leading voice in the dialogue between the disciplines; it calls for worldview thinking across the curriculum; and it calls for worshipful learning. Education is a sacred calling. If Haydn's _Creation_ can truly sing: "The heavens are telling the glories of God," then my mind should sing that the arts and sciences do, too.

Prepare to Serve

The three topics in this essay represent three recurrent objectives of Christians in higher education throughout the centuries. We come now to the third, what at longer length I like to call "The Usefulness of the Liberal Arts in Preparation for Service to Church and Society." So far we've been talking of Christian college education in terms of what it can do to me in helping with the development of character, the integration of faith and learning, and the shaping of a Christian worldview. But now we come to the question that I suspect brought you to college in the first place: "What can I do with it?"

I intentionally left this question until last because I don't think it should be the first question you ask about college. The real question to ask about college is, "What can it do _to_ me?" But the secondary question, "What can I do with it?" is nevertheless frequently the one with

which people start thinking about college, the one perhaps that motivated you to think about college at all. "What can I do with it?" asks
about the usefulness of a Christian liberal arts education.

Shortly after 1600 Francis Bacon, while advocating educational
reforms, declared that "knowledge is power." While that saying has
become proverbial, like many other worthwhile sayings it has been lifted entirely out of context. You see, Francis Bacon was a sincere
Reformed Christian who recognized that God mandated us, from the
beginning of human history, to serve him as stewards of his creation.
So when he said that "knowledge is power," Bacon spelled out specifically what he did *not* mean as well as what he *did* mean. He said very
explicitly that the power over nature that knowledge provides should
not be used for self-aggrandizement—to make me more powerful. He
was also explicit that it is not for national aggrandizement—to make
England supreme. Rather, power over nature's resources should be
used to improve the human condition, to remedy some of the effects of
the fall. Knowledge should make us better stewards of the creation
mandate, better servants of God and of those in need. Knowledge gives
us that power.

The danger of a "utility of education" approach, if that were the
whole story, is that it doesn't say *for what* it should be used. For what
purpose should you go to college? That is the problem with utilitari-
anism in ethics: What is the good you want to maximize? And the
problem is just as acute in education: What is it to be used for? To what
end? Like Francis Bacon, the Christian must come to grips with that
question. So I pose the question to you as you think about your education: What do you intend to do with your schooling?

Knowledge is indeed powerful stuff, but for what ends? Christian
ends? Christian purposes? Is it preparation for service, or preparation
for selfish ends? Which is it to be? Throughout the centuries, the
church emphasized the usefulness of liberal arts education. Augustine,
in his work called *On Christian Doctrine* but better translated *On
Christian Teaching,* explains how the various liberal arts contribute to
our understanding of Scripture and thereby to the church's ministry to
others. And the Protestant Reformation helped bring about reforms in
higher education, which produced the Puritan colleges, on which
church-related colleges in this country were originally modeled. In
those Puritan colleges, liberal arts education was intended to produce
what they called "eloquent wisdom." That phrase, too, has become
proverbial, and I like it. Eloquence combines communication skills

with an aesthetic quality. It is an eloquence that is effective in reaching people because of its grace and clarity and cogency. But eloquent _wisdom!_ For the liberal arts, the wisdom of the ages transmitted through liberal learning are not primarily just a matter of breadth. From their beginning in ancient Greece, they have been the means for transmitting a heritage of wisdom from the past, understandings and values passed on from generation to generation. So human wisdom is eloquent, but the divine wisdom we learn from Scripture and from Christian thought through the ages is also eloquent. The usefulness of liberal learning lies in its eloquent wisdom.

We frequently narrow down the usefulness of education to job training. But I want to emphasize that education as just job training is far too limiting, far too shortsighted. I have three reasons for that conviction.

1. _Jobs take far more than job training._ If you have worked very long at a job, you know that. I worked at teaching philosophy for forty-three years, and it took a lot more than job training. So let's distinguish training from education. Training is focused on specific functions or tasks, while education focuses on the development of a person—what it can do _for_ you, not what you do _with_ it. But jobs take more than training for specific functions. Jobs take _people,_ people who have developed, grown, and matured; people who have acquired understandings, who comprehend what they are doing and why and how; people who understand people and can communicate with them; people with organizational skills and decision-making ability; people who can become leaders; people who see the whole picture rather than always functioning with tunnel vision. Jobs take more than job training; they take people.

The provost of Massachusetts Institute of Technology a few years back told of a New York accounting firm that interviewed forty candidates for accounting positions. Of those forty, they hired ten. Of those ten, they noticed that four had college minors in one of the creative or performing arts, who brought to their jobs creative thinking, flexibility, and a capacity for personal presentation. Now, the MIT provost reported, that accounting firm consistently uses background in the arts as one of its criteria in screening candidates for jobs in accounting.

Some years ago one of our students, a senior philosophy major, went to Chicago to hunt for a job. He walked into a firm that dealt on the futures market. "What was your major in college?" "Philosophy." "What can you do with that?" He had heard this sort of questioning before, so he said, "I can think; I can analyze a complex problem; I can work my way through difficult, technical literature and know what it's saying; and I have some capacity for making decisions as to what ought to be done." They hired him. He went to work in the futures field and found that every person in the firm had been a philosophy major. I learned later that the president of the firm was also a former philosophy student of ours and not the best one either. But he knew what he was doing.

The point is that it takes more than job training to do a job. It takes transferable skills, qualities of mind, understandings that only liberal arts education can provide. Especially important are the understandings of ethics and contexts and people that a distinctively *Christian* liberal arts education provides. So the first reason education as job training is too shortsighted is that jobs take far more than job training.

2. *A career is more than a job.* Through a lifetime career you can go through all sorts of career changes: job mobility, advancement, and midlife career changes. As corporations downsize, the list of career changes is likely to grow longer. A career is far more than a job, so you need far more than job training.

Christian liberal arts is not primarily job training, though it may train you for some jobs. Rather, Christian liberal arts is *career* preparation. In helping to build moral character, it addresses far more than job preparation. While any job may take moral character, a career takes still more. And it takes the ability to learn as you go, a lifetime of keeping abreast of changes in your field, and learning independently to do things you were never taught. You may look at me and say, "Hey, that man's been teaching in one job for forty-three years." No, not in one job. I found I had to teach in areas I had never formally studied and to undertake tasks for which no courses I ever took prepared me. I never took courses on how to understand students—an immense job in itself. I never took courses on how to teach; college teachers never used to have formal preparation in teaching. I never took courses on how to chair a department, how to be a leader, how to be a campus politician, how to be an acting dean, how to become involved professionally in national organizations, how to cultivate a publisher, how to write a book. A career takes *far* more than job training because a career is far more than just having jobs.

Perhaps one of the most important things that one learns about, or should learn about, in a Christian college is the purpose and meaning of work. Unless you have considered what work is intended to be about, you don't really know how to choose a job. You don't know what questions to ask. You don't know what you are looking for. If you think you're only working to make a living, you will sometimes wonder if it is all worthwhile. Unless you have a theology of work, a biblically informed understanding of the purpose of work and the ethics of work, of the human problems involved in work relationships and the workplace, and a biblically informed understanding of how to make your point with eloquent wisdom in representing employee interests to employers—unless you can translate into these areas your understanding of what it is to be a human person created in the image of God, a sinner in a messed-up world, a world that nonetheless is governed by divine providence where the grace of God can work in complex human problems—without that sort of preparation, you're not really ready for work. So I say that a theology of work is tremendously important. Work is stewardship; work is service; work is a calling, a divine vocation. These purposes of work are all tremendously important.[8]

The early reformer William Tyndale said, "There is no better work than to please God. To pour water, to wash dishes, to cobble shoes, to be an apostle, is all one." The ultimate purpose of all work is the same: to please God. John Calvin said that talents are not just spiritual graces but everyday abilities to invest your years in. There is "no employment so mean as not to be truly respectable and important in the sight of God." And Martin Luther: "Everything is spiritual if God's word is added to it and it is done in faith." Do you get the point? Work should be addressed to God. "Whatever you do, do your work heartily, as for the Lord" (Col. 3:23 NASB). And then no work is too mean to have dignity.

I'm afraid that when we think of the usefulness of education for the workplace, we think of how high and mighty a job can be or how much better college graduates' salaries are. But that misses the meaning of work. If one thing is worse than reducing education to job training, it is reducing work to making money. If you do that, you are not educated—at least, not Christianly educated. You've missed the point of a Christian worldview. Thus, while jobs take far more than job training, a career is far more than a job.

3. _Life is more than a career._ Life's responsibilities are far more diversified, far more complex than any career. Life brings us responsibilities in relationship to God, in relationship to the physical world of which we are a part, in relationship to other people, and in relationship to ourselves. We live out our relationships to God, other people, and the physical world in our families and friendships, in the community,

in local and national governmental structures, as citizens, in the workplace, and of course, in the church. *This* is your life. Life is far more than a career.

I look back on my life and see the challenges my family had to face, the challenges of making a marriage work, making ends meet, raising two sons in the troublesome sixties, the adjustments at becoming empty nesters, and so forth. It demanded understanding and convictions about the purpose of marriage and family as God intended them to be, the ability to rethink things we had taken for granted, plus moral character, decision making, wisdom, and in it all the capacity to forgive and be forgiven.

You might say similar things about community, church, and civil life and the tasks they require of us. For life is *far* more than a career, and education is preparation for *life*, not just a job or a lifetime career. Christian higher education is preparation for living Christianly in a complex, contemporary world, living out our relationship to God and nature and other people within the family and workplace and community and church. It's preparation for life.

Prepare for service rather than putting self-advancement first. Life is serving other people. If you do not believe that, wait until your first baby arrives and you're up half the night every night for the first three months cleaning up messes. I think that marriage and parenthood are designed to teach us that life is serving other people. So learn how to serve.

That's what Christian higher education is useful for, for serving the church and society and arts and sciences, for understanding these spheres of service and developing the skills and character they will require of us. The humanities we study are about life. The social sciences are about life. The natural sciences are about the world in which we live. Education is about life. And the integration of faith and learning relates to it all, to all of the arts and the sciences, to all of the professions; it relates to family life, to economic life, to citizenship, to church life.

So prepare to serve. That's why you are in college. Jobs take more than job training. A career is more than a job. Life is more than a career. A Christian liberal arts education will prepare you for a career. It may help prepare you for many jobs, but it will prepare you more effectively for life.

This address was part of the Staley Lectures delivered at Union University.

The Grandeur of God and Real Education: A Strategy for Integrating Faith in a Post-Christian Culture

David S. Dockery

This chapter will focus on one of the key distinctives of Christian higher education. It is a call for all of us to think together about real education, that is, education grounded in reality with a vision of wholeness. It is an invitation to reflect on the meaning of education that prepares us for service in the world. Beyond that it is time for us to think about the significance of the distinctive role of a Christian university in our rapidly changing world. Ultimately this chapter is a call to reflect upon the grandeur of God as the foundation for real education. Too often we hear people say we need an education for the real world, yet I would contend that what we really need is a real education that prepares students to serve effectively in a fallen world.

Paul as a Model

In the seventeenth chapter of Acts, we find guidance for this task from the apostle Paul. Verses 16–31 report that Paul has arrived in Athens. Here the apostle encounters the culture of his day, which we might define as a highly educated and sophisticated pre-Christian culture.

Athens was the cradle of democracy, the foremost of the city-states at the height of the Grecian empire (5th–3rd centuries B.C.). But when Paul visited Athens, the city was no longer a leader in terms of military or political power. In terms of cultural influence however, Athens remained unsurpassed. Its contributions in sculpture, literature, philosophy, and rhetoric were unparalleled. Athens still carried the distinction of being the native city of Socrates (470–399 B.C.) and Plato (427–347 B.C.), and the adopted home of Aristotle (384–322 B.C.) and Zeno (335–263 B.C.). Cicero (106–43 B.C.) observed that "in spite of its decline in political power, Athens still enjoyed such renown that the now shattered and weakened name of Greece is supported by the reputation of this city." As commentators like John Stott and John Polhill have observed, there is something enthralling about Paul in Athens, the great Christian apostle amid the glories of ancient Greece. Though times had changed, Athens still had an unrivaled reputation as the Roman empire's intellectual center.[1]

Paul, while waiting for Timothy and Silas to join him in Athens, became a keen observer as he walked around to see the sights of the city. Even today, the Parthenon and other architectural remains in Athens, though in partial ruin, have a special splendor for any first-time visitor.

Paul was no uneducated or uncultured visitor; quite the opposite. He had been blessed with a massive intellect and was a graduate of the great institutions of his day in Tarsus and Jerusalem. No doubt he valued and appreciated the city's great history, art, architecture, literature, and wisdom.

Yet it was not these things, according to our text, that grabbed his attention. He was distressed to see that the city was literally smothered under a forest of idols (see Acts 17:16). More gods were in Athens than in all the rest of the country. The Roman satirist who claimed that it was easier to find a god than a person in Athens was hardly exaggerating. Innumerable temples, shrines, altars, and statues could be found, some so large they could be seen from forty miles away. Paul was not blind to their beauty, but he was grieved that they did not honor the one true God, the Father of the Lord Jesus Christ.[2]

The cultural trends that shape much of our world today are similarly influenced by the rise of neopaganism and the various and diverse forms of spirituality.[3] Thus I believe Paul can become an insightful guide to enable us to respond to this changing post-Christian world around us.

Paul's Message

I find it fascinating that Paul was able to proclaim the greatness of God not only in the religious places (the synagogues) and the market places (17:17), but also in the center of the intellectual world (17:19).

We would certainly expect the apostle Paul to be comfortable proclaiming the greatness of God in the synagogue, and we are not surprised that he moves easily into the marketplace, but to take the concept of the grandeur of God into the Aereopagus, the intellectual center of the city, might be surprising to some. But to those who recognize that Paul saw all of life from a God-centered perspective, this is no surprise. Listen as we hear him reflect on God's greatness in Romans 11:33, 36:

> Oh, the depth of the riches of the wisdom and knowledge of God!
> How unsearchable his judgments,
> and his paths beyond tracing out! . . .
> For from him and through him and to him are all things.
> To him be the glory forever!

Similarly, on the campus of a Christian university, it should not surprise anyone to learn that the greatness of God is faithfully proclaimed in chapel. It probably would surprise few that the greatness of God is often proclaimed in campus activities, whether in a campus ministry event, a mission trip, a conversation in the cafeteria, or a late-night dorm Bible study. But what about the other places on campus, particularly the classroom? Should we expect to find references to the greatness of God in the heart of the intellectual center of the campus?

Without spending a great deal of time interpreting Paul's address to the intellectual leaders in Athens, let us summarize what I believe are the five key themes of his address.

First, _God is the Creator of the universe_ (v. 24). This view was quite different from the pantheism of the Stoics or the world of chance of the Epicureans. Paul's view is also different from those today who would deny that God is _both_ the personal Creator of everything that is and the personal Lord over all he has made. It is absurd to think that the One who spoke creation into being and holds it together by the word of his power (Col. 1:15–17; Heb. 1:2–3) can be housed in shrines built by human hands (Acts 17:24).

Yet Christians often trivialize God by not recognizing his grandeur and his greatness. In a recent issue of _First Things_, we find a quote from Charles Misner talking about Albert Einstein.[4] Misner, himself a noted scientist, said:

I do see the design of the universe as essentially a religious question, that is one should have some kind of respect and awe for the whole business. Its very magnificence should not be taken for granted. In fact that is why I think Einstein had so little use for organized religion, although he strikes me basically as a very religious man. Einstein must have looked at what the Christian preachers said about God and felt that they were blaspheming. He had seen much more majesty than they had ever imagined, and they were just not talking about the real thing.[5]

Einstein died in 1955, and Christians have only continued to trivialize God. Donald McCullough, in his work *The Trivilization of God,* has suggested that we run the risk of creating a manageable deity by turning God into some divine self-help recipe.[6] Einstein was saying that secular scientists have seen more of the grandeur of God in the world of God than most Christians have seen in the Word of God. Do we have a proper respect for the Creator God? Do we have a superficial view of God and the world? When people hear us talk, do they say "they're just not talking about the real thing?"

Paul could proclaim the grandeur of God as Creator because he was amazed at the magnitude of creation. And today we know far more about this creation than those in Athens ever imagined.

Scientists know that light travels 5.87 trillion miles a year—that is a light year. Our galaxy is about 100 million light years across, which means that our galaxy is about 587 million trillion miles across. Within the optical range of our best available telescopes today, about one million such galaxies have been discovered. And in our galaxy there are about 100 billion stars and our sun is a small one. Our sun is about six thousand degrees centigrade on the cooler surface and it travels about 155 miles per second through the galaxy and will complete its revolution in two hundred million years.[7]

When we study these things and recognize that there is a personal God who spoke this world into being and holds it by the word of his power (Col. 1:15–17; Heb. 1:2) shouldn't we respond with awe at the grandeur of God?

Paul's second point was that *God is the providential sustainer of all life.* God is not the one who needs to be sustained, but he is the one who gives life and breath to everyone and everything else (Acts 17:25). So today we declare not our independence from God but our dependence on God. We recognize that he does not depend on us, but we on him.

Paul's third point was that _God is the Ruler of all nations_ (17:26) and fourth, _He is the Father of all human beings_ (17:26-28) by virtue of his role as Creator. Thus we are all created in his image and can respond to him and relate to one another. We can think, reason, love, worship, and communicate because we are created in his image. Paul explained these things by an appeal to God's truth made known in God's general revelation of nature, human experience, and history.[8]

In redemptive terms, God is the Father of _only those who are in Christ_, and we are his children only by redemption and grace, yet in creation terms God is the Father of all humankind, and all are his creatures, depending on him for life. In addressing these key themes about God, Paul strategically quoted from the Greek philosophers and poets to expose their own inconsistency.[9] Thus he brings the Christian faith to bear on the Greeks' thought patterns.

Paul's Strategy

This strategy of integrating faith and knowledge is at the heart of real education, viewed from the vantage point of the grandeur of God. Paul understood cultural categories of the time and used them to express the reality of divine revelation.[10] Paul had obviously studied and learned the philosophical and literary matters of his day and was able to use them as building blocks in his communication. He demonstrated an appreciation of Athenian culture and was able to bring truth to bear upon the prevailing zeitgeist of that culture. The key aspect of his strategy involved the integration of his Christian faith with those cultural issues that allowed him to adjust the cultural assumptions of that pre-Christian context in light of God's eternal truth, particularly through his understanding of God as a transcendent, creating, sustaining, and self-disclosing God who has made humans in his image. Finally he provided evidence of coming judgment, which will take place because of God's ultimate manifestation of himself through the resurrected Christ (17:31).

Toward a Model of Real Education

You might ask: What do these events from two thousand years ago have to do with education today at Christian colleges and universities? I would contend that we can learn much from Paul's strategy. As Paul understood his culture, so must we seek to understand our own. By demonstrating an understanding of our contemporary post-Christian culture, we are then able to engage that culture with a measure of credibility, whether the arts, the sciences, the social sciences, the humanities, the business world, educational theories, or healthcare issues. Therefore, Paul's words to the three groups identified in Acts 17 enable us to see that the grandeur of God is to be made known in places of worship, in the marketplace, and yes, even in the academy and intellectual centers.[11] The essence of the Christian faith is that God is Savior, but we fail to understand the comprehensiveness of the Christian faith unless we also see God as Creator, Sustainer, Ruler, Father, and Judge, which are the foundational blocks of a Christian worldview.[12]

When we recognize these marvelous truths, we say "Great is the Lord and greatly to be praised. Give thanks to the Lord, make known his deeds among the people, for his name is to be exalted."[13] Paul proclaimed the whole of nature and of history and appealed to philosophy and literature, those elements I believe to be at the heart of a liberal arts curriculum. He emphasized the greatness of God, not only as the beginning and ending of all things, but as the One to whom we ultimately will give account. Paul emphasized that these things are known by and in God's creation.

Many people today are rejecting the Christian faith, not because they perceive it to be false, but because they believe it is superficial or trivial. People are looking for an integrated worldview that brings coherence to all learning and helps make sense of life's experiences[14]—some of which are quite confusing.

The comprehensiveness of Paul's message and the insights of his strategy are magnificent; yet the motivation for what he wrote cannot be overlooked. You and I often do not think as Paul thought, see as he saw, feel as he felt because we do not understand the grandeur of God as Paul did. Authentic Christian thinking appreciates the greatness, goodness, and glory of God—lifting up his sheer wonder and size and majesty. Right thinking about God challenges the presuppositions of North American culture, both secular and Christian, which in their contemporary forms seem to be primarily and pragmatically focused on the right to happiness. Concentrating on the grandeur of God calls on us to deny these false ideas and instead to exalt God's majesty and greatness.[15]

When Paul walked around Athens, he did not just notice the idols, but he observed, considered, and reflected upon their significance. In our observations, we often look too quickly and read too fast.[16] We need to learn to see and read and then think and reflect from a God-centered perspective. After we have sought to be students of culture, we are then able to appreciate the good, the true, and the beautiful, and confront the false values that are lodged and displayed within our culture. Therefore, the challenge of integrating the Christian faith and all learning involves perception, appreciation, engagement, and then, when necessary, confrontation—in that order.[17]

In many, many ways, our post-Christian Western culture in general, and American culture in particular, resembles the pre-Christian Athens of Paul's day, particularly the focus on the new, the novel, and the world of chance emphasized by the Epicureans. Ours too is what Alexander Solzhenitsyn has called a "culture of novelty." C. S. Lewis, in his famous work _God in the Dock_, in which he highlights the value of classic works, maintained that we are obsessed with the new and the novel. Truth and values in our culture of novelty seem to be of little concern or consequences. Paul models for us and thereby invites us to integrate Christian truth in culturally relevant ways and to communicate and live this truth in the midst of an incredibly superficial world.[18]

Superficiality is present when people deal with issues apart from the true reality that ultimately gives them meaning. One can be an expert in one area and fail to connect that area with reality, namely God himself, resulting in a superficial understanding. Unfortunately, most of that to which we are exposed on a daily basis falls into this category-—whether in literature, the media, in music, in film, in many educational enterprises, in social interaction, and, God forbid, sometimes even in church.[19] All of this is because of the trivialization of God. What is left is only superficial, for it fails to see God as the ultimate reality behind everything.

Thus, in every class our goal must be to engage the subject matter, the true and various options associated with it, and issues of our day in the various areas of learning, while recognizing that our great God is central in every discipline. Harold Heie maintains that such integrated knowledge is a realizable ideal for any academic discipline. Thus, "the integration of [faith and] knowledge," he claims, "is the most distinctive task of Christian liberal arts education—always was, is now, always will be."[20] The integration of faith and learning is a unity involving not only the study itself, but the motivation for the study. For God is behind it all and over it all, whether it is math, art, science, or literature. I know some understand that the grandeur of God is important to chapel and to campus ministries, but what about sociology? history? business? grammar?

"Why learn grammar?" someone might ask, whether English, Spanish, French, or whatever language. Every faculty member would quickly respond that you cannot communicate as an educated person without proper grammar and syntax. Some students may say that does not really matter—as long as it's close, most people can get it. To which would come the reply from the faculty at any recognized academic institution:

1. You need to understand grammar to communicate because you will not succeed in your occupation if you cannot communicate well.
2. You will not advance in the community if you cannot communicate in a way that is grammatically acceptable.
3. You will not have healthy self-esteem if people look down upon you when you fail to communicate well because of poor grammar.

Those three things are all true and pedagogically sound. But I agree with John Piper who says that one should expect even more at a Christian university. This we should hear:

1. First, it is important to understand grammar because you should want to communicate well, since communication itself is a gift from God.
2. Beyond that, you need to recognize that you are able to communicate because you have been created in the image of God. We thus have the ability to think and communicate in linguistic symbols. Communication is a possibility among the diverse linguistic cultures of the world and is possible cross-culturally and cross-temporally because human beings everywhere created in the image of God have memories of the past, considerations of the present, and expectations of the future.
3. Third, we should want to communicate well, since from the beginning language was God's idea—because "in the beginning was the Word, and the Word was with God, and the Word was God" (John 1:1 KJV).
4. Finally, we should seek to communicate in a way that is grammatically appropriate because God is dishonored when we take lightly his good gifts to us.[21]

Unless we understand the impact of the grandeur of God in every discipline on this campus, even in something as basic as grammar, then it is not education offered with and from a Christian worldview for the glory of God. Some of you might say this seems to turn everything into religion. To which we would respond, no! Rather we are, as Charles Wesley penned in his hymn, uniting the pair so long disjointed, knowledge and vital piety. This uniting of faith and learning then is "Real Education," with a capital R. That is the call of the hour and the distinctive approach to Christian higher education where all teaching and all learning must take place with a view toward reality found only in the glory and grandeur of God.[22]

This address was given at the Fall 1998 convocation at Union University.

Chapter 16

REACHING THE POST-CHRISTIAN UNIVERSITY: LESSONS FROM HARVARD

KELLY MONROE

My title is "Reaching the Post-Christian University: Lessons from Harvard." Once upon a time, the Coalition of Christian Colleges and Universities could have included the following members: Harvard College, dedicated in 1636 *In Christi glorium*—for Christ's Glory; Yale College, dedicated *lux et veritas*—the light and truth of the gospel; and Dartmouth College, dedicated *Voces clamantium en deserto*—a voice crying in the wilderness.

Likewise, Stanford, Duke, Wellesley, Columbia, Mount Holyoke, Tufts, the colleges in Cambridge and Oxford, Yen Si in Korea, Xavier in India—these are a few among many great institutions inspired by Jesus Christ.

Do we now call these schools "post-Christian"? Do we call them "secular"? Do we call them dormant because good seeds have been planted and are buried deep beneath the surface, usually invisible, as seeds are, but still alive and potentially fruitful? Perhaps they're waiting for sunshine and water and good soil.

You've likely pondered these questions as well. Most importantly, what does Jesus think of these schools dedicated to him that future generations of students would find life in him? What happened to them and in them to cause their decline? How do we learn from all the ways the Philistines have stopped up the well of living water that makes education truly liberal and liberating? I refer the reader here to several books, including George Marsden's.

Beyond some critique, I'd like to spend most of this time exploring God's faithfulness and power to reinvigorate, to redeem, to re-create. I want to learn from Martha in John 11. When Jesus finally arrived in

Bethany four days after her brother Lazarus had died, she ran out to greet him on the outskirts of the village, we're told. Disappointed and probably weeping she said, "If only you'd been here, my brother wouldn't have died. But even now, I know you can do all things." I love that—"even now, you can do all things."

God at Harvard?

The founders of Princeton, for the first 150 years while it was called the College of New Jersey, dedicated their school with these words: *vitam mortuis reddo*—I restore life to the dead. "Even now," said Martha, "I believe you can do all things." Even now, you are the resurrection and the life.

Post-Christian universities need people of faith to say, "Even now you can do all things," particularly when the picture is bleak. Let's take as a case study America's first college, Harvard College. The earliest by-laws read: "Let every student consider well the main end of his life and studies is to know God and Jesus Christ, which is eternal life (John 17:3), and therefore to lay Christ in the bottom as the only foundation of all sound knowledge and learning. Seeing the Lord giveth wisdom, everyone shall seriously by prayer and in secret, seek wisdom of Him." Note the dynamic relationship between faith and reason.

Likewise, a 1789 Massachusetts law instructed Harvard professors to impress on the minds of youth committed to their care the principles of piety and justice and a sacred regard for truth. Love of their country, humanity, and a universal benevolence; sobriety, industry, and frugality, chastity, moderation, and temperance, and those other virtues which are the ornaments of human society.

Today many students do not even know the meaning of these words. A later iteration of Harvard's motto became *Veritas Christo et Ecclesia*—Truth for Christ and the Church. Today the popular motto is simply *Veritas*. Christ and the church are completely deleted. We now have a truth that is liberated from any particular meaning; a truth that is unanchored and adrift.

We're told now that truth, if it exists at all, is perhaps a social construct to accomplish an agenda of those in power. The truth is subjectively determined. But if there is such a thing as truth, at most it's some vague and impersonal ideal of tolerance or a vision of electronic global unity. Today our constant challenge and privilege, whether we're in a secular or a Christian school, is to revive and to nurture the knowledge of truth as a Person—as the Life-Giver. As the relentless lover. The author who enters the play. Truth who awakens wonder and the mind. Truth who is a revolution of tenderness for the least and the last and the lost and all of humble heart. Truth that connects us to the heart and mind and power of God by his Holy Spirit within us. Truth who exchanges his wholeness for our brokenness, who loves us enough to die for us. Truth who rises from the grave because his love is stronger than death. Even now.

Emptiness

The ancient and progressive knowledge of Jesus is no longer preserved institutionally. Now it's only found in the margins and in the grassroots among students and very few professors in extracurricular Bible studies and discussion groups and local churches. *Veritas* is no longer equated with Jesus Christ. A few years ago Billy Graham asked our former president, Derek Bok, "What is the biggest problem of college students today?" He answered with one word: "emptiness."

In the past three years at Harvard, we have had among undergraduates alone (a college of six thousand students) at least eight suicides, one after the murder of a roommate. Furthermore, two seniors embezzled $100,000 raised by their dorm for children with cancer; the new president took three months off for exhaustion after his first year; and one of the papers, *The Gazette,* proudly reported that "secularism is taught in every classroom."

In my research of Christian history at Harvard—I'm not a historian but have been working on this for ten years or so—I've discovered dozens of major gifts and endowments given by alumni for over three hundred years explicitly for Christian purposes, that students would continually know the gospel and understand the meaning of Harvard's history. These funds for lectureships, professorships, buildings, and scholarships have either disappeared mysteriously or have been grossly misallocated. For three years we've been asking about these funds, and still we've gotten no answers internally, so we're beginning to have to speak like this about the problem externally as well, in order to get wise counsel. Emptiness.

More personally, I grew up the child of a father who was a psychology professor at the University of Chicago and then Ohio State. He was absorbed in the worldview of behavioristic psychology and relinquished his own childhood religion. My father and his colleagues knew the ideas of Freud and Marx and Jung and Dewey and Derrida and Foucault, but not the ideas of Jesus, not the words and person of Christ, much less Augustine, Luther, Calvin, Pascal, Edwards, Wesley, and so on. When friends shared the gospel with me in high school, I didn't meet an unembodied concept, but a Person who knew me and loved me, the Life-giver, and a few people who looked a lot like him.

I began to observe my dear father's academic world, which is bound by conformity and fear. Far from liberal education, it struck me as very illiberal; that is, it's closed to a wide spectrum of ideas. The academic ideas seemed to work in the classroom, but not in real life. And the ideas didn't seem worthy of students and their real questions in that so many of the presuppositions and ideas were dehumanizing, expressing a low view of human life apart from a personal Creator.

Eventually I saw our family, as well as many others in his department, disintegrate. It was not a big surprise. In fact, it was inevitable apart from the love of God because otherwise the center cannot hold. I saw that ideas have consequences, that falsehood leads to despair and fragmentation, and that truth leads to love and unity and beauty.

We can each add to the tragic litany of the consequences of secularism in colleges across the nation. We can lament the century of despair following Nietzsche's famous announcement that "God is dead." But last year the Harvard Graduate Christian Fellowship made T-shirts that read, "Nietzche is dead." They were signed, "God."

I sense a hunger on campuses as I travel, and today I sense something new. Just look at recent alumni magazines of some colleges. Here's one from Brown University. The cover page says "Looking for God," and then it has a photograph of graffiti that reads "True or False: God is the shortest distance between zero and infinity in either direction" (sounds more like M.I.T.). The Princeton Alumni Weekly: "Searching for God; Students Talk about Their Journeys of Faith."

I sense something new. So let's spend the rest of the time looking at what God is doing to restore us to himself. Even now. *Vitam mortuis reddo.*

Whether we are at Union University or the University of Beijing, God wants every student, every faculty member, every staff member, for himself. He wants every generation. He wants children, not grandchildren. He wants to excite every center of learning. He is constantly creating and recycling and making dead things come back to life.

Finding God at Harvard

I will use my experience at Harvard as a kind of case study of God's work of renewal. When I arrived in 1987, I met no Christians at the Divinity School. It's a very lonely place for Christians. But I began to meet believers in otherwise isolated pockets of the university—or as one person said, the "multiversity connected only by a central heating system." I found Christians in the departments of astrophysics, philosophy, business, math, botany, law, public health, and so on. And God began to knit us together as a community, as the idea of university—unity in diversity—took hold, once again. Let me share a short section from the book *Finding God at Harvard,* to describe this coming together as a community.

> For the first time since coming to Harvard, I felt joy. The reach of this gospel amazed me. Musicians, physicists, historians, architects, and athletes sharing the goodness of God in friendship, the life of the mind. Life. We discussed our research. We considered our vocation as our calling from God. The place, as Frederick Buechner said, where our deep joy meets the world's deep hunger. Like many retreats to come, this was the time for hours of beach soccer and ultimate frisbee, Bible study, laughter, prayer, and the confluence of old and (for me) new friends. The retreat marked a turn of seasons. Wood smoke scented cool air. Autumn leaves changed the season of the observers, though we sensed the promise of spring. Just as ours was a time out of time to prepare for a world which, we believed, would soon become alive to us.
>
> This was my introduction to an iconoclastic subset of graduate students out of Harvard's ten thousand who seemed more interested in making a life than in making a living. They are attracted to Jesus because Jesus knows that our danger is not in too much life, but in too little. They come from many countries to integrate great ideas with life and service. Truth for the art of life. They are people, as Charles Malik says, "of being."

This community is orchestrated by God with the help of an extraordinary servant-leader (InterVarsity Christian Fellowship) named Jeff Barneson. Jeff kindly invited me to work with him, and I became like a cyclist drafting off his rear wheel and energy. Our graduate Christian fellowship became a kind of symphony where different sounds come together in beauty and harmony. To use yet another metaphor, the fellowship is an extended family that is counter-culturally more involved in service than in power.

We began to find ways to be together, such as worshiping in the middle of Harvard Yard on Easter and praying. God was gathering coals for a fire. Mission trips and community service in North America and Latin America provided opportunities to build small businesses, reform prisons, and construct churches and medical clinics. This, by the way, was begun ten years ago by a student from Wheaton (Peter Clark) who came to the Kennedy School of Government. The influence of students who graduate from your colleges and come to our university for graduate school is catalytic, and we just want to thank you. So keep sending them.

So we've had ten summers during which God was enlarging our hearts for the poor, helping us to see our own poverty apart from him, and expanding our imagination for service. In various ways, we began asking the Holy Spirit how to be the body of Christ in the world, how to be his eyes, his feet, and his hands; some even asked to become poor with the poor.

We have seen God build a community centered in worship, service, and witness. The growth of this community is now recorded in the book, *Finding God at Harvard*. Often people do a double take and ask, "Can I find that book in any fiction section?" I'll just say that this book is not theory, but testimony. We wanted to go beyond the genre of critique and analysis to actual witness in the middle of a hard place. We wanted to break through the insecurity and sterile academic language, which is the mode of expression within the secular academy in general and actually to learn to speak in honest human language. James Houston says we need to become postintellectuals, that is, real human beings who are being saved by grace and can speak the language of the mission field but are not limited to it.

This was a seven-year project, a sort of coming together, and very much a "coming out of the closet," if you will, of alumni and professors and students. I'll just give you a few examples. One is Nicholas Wolterstorff from Calvin and now at Yale in philosophy. More than a modern abstract essay on theology and the problem of evil, he writes of his own personal crisis, the unimaginable loss of his son in the mountains of Austria, in relation to the sovereignty and the suffering of God. If Truth is a Person, we need such personal accounts of him rather than rarified essays on theodicy.

Another example is the story of Glenn Loury, an economist and ethicist who bravely wrote that while teaching ethics at the Kennedy School at Harvard, he was addicted to drugs, committed adultery, and repeated to himself that "life has no meaning, life has no meaning." Again, this was while he was teaching ethics to graduate students, many of whom would soon go on to Washington to serve our country.

Then someone shared the gospel with him. He told him how Jesus came to give us life and have it abundantly; that when the Son sets you free, you are free indeed; and that he who is forgiven much loves much. The story ends with Glenn Loury's account of being born again.

Another example is the story of Robert Coles who was a Pulitzer Prize winner for his work on children in crisis. A self-important Harvard M.D./Ph.D., he went to New Orleans in the early 1960s and encountered on the way to work a mob of adults waiting on a corner outside an elementary school. He thought, _Oh, this is interesting_. The mob was protesting and ranting and raving, and he decided to stop and see what was happening. It turned out that they were waiting for a little six-year-old African-American girl named Ruby Bridges. Norman Rockwell painted her walking to school. Ruby was among the first to be racially integrated into the school system in New Orleans. The white parents responded by taking their children out of the school for an entire year, but Ruby's parents both worked two jobs cleaning for white folks and so she was the only child in the school for an entire academic year—just Ruby and her teacher. And the mob was there every morning and every afternoon to persecute Ruby as she walked to and from school.

Being a good academician, Robert Coles said, "Hey, I bet I could get a grant to study this little girl." And so he did, from the American Psychiatric Association, to see how she would respond to this persecution. And he couldn't understand why she seemed to be sleeping well and to be so healthy. He studied her for weeks and just couldn't understand. One day he arrived in the classroom early. He saw her coming in and saw her stop and talk to the mob of people, which she had never done before, in her little white dress and little white bows in her hair.

When she came into the classroom, Robert Coles said, "Ruby, I noticed that you were talking to those folks today." And Ruby said, "No sir, I've never spoken with them before." And he said, "Well, I'm sure I saw you speaking with them just now." And she said, "No, well, maybe it was that I was late today and I usually say my prayers for them before

I come to school, but today I was a little late, and so when I heard them I just stopped then, and I just wanted to talk to God about them today."

"Well, Ruby, you're saying that you pray for these people." "Yes, sir. Every day and every night with my parents and on Sunday in church." "Well, why should you be praying for them?" "Well sir, I guess I think maybe they need praying for, don't you?"

And he went on with his sort of psychiatric interrogation and finally said, "Ruby, what do you say when you pray for these big white people?" And she said, "Well, my minister told me that when Jesus was here they used to call him names, kind of like what they call me, and they used to say they were going to kill him, kind of like what they say to me, and that, well, that before they did actually kill him he said some things back to God, and he said 'Father, forgive them, because they don't know what they're doing.' And so that's what I pray every morning and every night and on Sundays. I say, 'Father, forgive them because they don't know what they're doing.' Except today I was late, and so I forgot until I heard them again."

Well, this was a six-year-old girl who couldn't read or write her name yet, nor could her parents, but they had whole chapters of Isaiah and Proverbs and the Psalms memorized. These are the world's finest people, meek to use the word, teaching a self-important Harvard M.D./Ph.D., on his way to getting a Pulitzer Prize, about grace and about dignity, about forgiveness that breaks the cycle of evil in the world. Robert Coles said, "You know, at Harvard I got straight A's on all my moral philosophy exams, but I never knew the name of the woman who cleaned my dorm room for four years." So he learned from Ruby a lot about the art of life and about the extraordinary grace and dignity of what appear to be very ordinary people.

Lastly I'll mention the story of Harold Berman who taught at Harvard Law School for thirty-seven years. He is now at Emory, and he wrote somewhat of an academic essay on the nature of Judeo-Christian versus pagan scholarship. I thanked him and explained that *Finding God at Harvard* was a personal book about our own journeys and faith rather than theory. I asked, "Could you add something of your own story to this?" (Harold Bermann was raised in a Jewish family.) And he said, "Well, let me think about it." A few weeks later I got this in the mail:

In my own case, the truth that set me free first appeared to me at the outbreak of World War II when I was 21 years old. [Remember, this is a Jewish man.] I was in Europe where I had been studying European history for a year. While I was in Germany, Hitler announced on the radio that Germany had invaded Poland. It was literally the outbreak of the World War, and many of us fled for France. I thought that Hitler's invasion of Poland would lead to the total destruction of human civilization. I felt as one would feel today if all the major powers were to become involved in a full-scale nuclear war.

I was shattered, in total despair. There, alone on that train, Jesus Christ appeared to me in a vision. His face reminded me of one of the Russian icons that I would later see, heavily scarred and tragic. Not suffering, but bearing the marks of having suffered. I suddenly realized that I was not entitled to such despair, that it was not I, but another, God himself, who bore the burden of human destiny and that it was rather for me to believe in Him even though human history was at an end.

When the train arrived in Paris that morning, I walked straight to the Notre Dame Cathedral, and I prayed a personal prayer to God for the first time in my life. My wife, who is Protestant, asks me how I could have become a believer in Christ without having read the Gospels. My answer is that that is how the first disciples became believers. Truth is a Person. And so this experience of amazing grace not only made me a Christian believer against my will and against my heritage but also freed me from that pride and illusion of intellect which is the besetting sin of academic scholarship.

The Veritas Forum

In 1992, three years into the writing of this book, we gathered the writers and tried a sort of live version of the book called the Harvard Veritas Forum at the Law School. The idea was to create a space, a forum where every question can be asked about the possibility of truth in relation to Jesus Christ, again so reviving the original idea of _veritas_ in relation to Jesus Christ. We expected a hundred people, and seven hundred people came. The ethos of the forum was not a defense of Christianity but an exploration. The Forum is not combative but rather a sort of coming alongside of the questions of students, most of which are no longer allowed in the classrooms, by the way (which is also why Christian colleges and universities are much more liberal in the best sense).

We were asked questions like the occasional, "Why do my socks disappear, and where do they go?" and "Why does the parking patrol always find my car?" (a big problem in Cambridge). We were also asked questions of greater significance: "What are our origins? What is it to be human? Do faith and science conflict? What about chaos and entropy and evolution? How can I trust that the Bible is historically accurate? How can love last?" Beneath that last question is a broken heart. And whether it's wealthy college students or inner-city kids who are killing one another or suburban kids who are killing themselves, if Truth isn't a Person whose nature is love, then there is no answer for that question, nor hope for our society or our own hearts.

Other questions we were asked were: "If God is love, why do I suffer? Why is Christian faith based on a blood sacrifice? That seems so primitive. Aren't all religions equal?" To this last question, the speaker answered, "Yes, except in matters of creation, human worth, God's love and power, caring for the poor, hope, happiness, and human destiny of heaven and hell." My favorite question was, "Why does beauty mean something?"

After the questions were asked, writers could answer them from their own struggles and discoveries rather than with theoretical, abstract answers. And then the skeptics and others would come along with something to contribute. Hopefully they felt welcome, that they were in a place of hospitality, a space for healing and dialogue, where everyone felt the need for the others in this journey together.

To me, what's intriguing about the Veritas Forum is not that it's something new. I think the church has always been asking questions about truth. This is what we are all doing all the time, so I feel a little silly for even being up here telling you what you probably already know, but it's countercultural for us.

What is intriguing about the Veritas Forum is the apologetic of community and the unity and beauty of truth in relation to Jesus. In other words, there might be a thousand people at the Veritas Forum looking at a panel of writers on stage—fourteen or fifteen of them in a conversation with this large group, in which any question is fair game. And students and faculty are scratching their heads and thinking, *There's an astrophysicist, a philosopher, a historian, a mother of four, a grandmother, and a painter; why do they all agree with one another? How often do three Harvard people ever agree with one another about anything? That's not how you get a dissertation published. You say something new, whether or not it's true.*

And yet why do all of these people agree with one another on the very basic nature of reality? And why do they seem to love one another and the students? Why do they seem joyful even though they have suffered? Why do they sing together? Again, we want to fan into flames the university, which reunites disciplines and cultures and generations, where we see the gospel as the only fabric of real integrity, the starting point for the living of life. Madeline L'Engle said, "Rather than arguing about why Christianity is superior to other world religions, I'd rather put forth a light that is so lovely that all in its presence would be drawn to it." This is what we hope the Veritas Forum and the Christian presence on every campus can be—to inspire freshly every generation of students.

I am privileged to be a part of the Veritas Forum as it has emerged in other universities. I don't think it's a new idea but a new name and a new kindness of God to do this one more time. And it's just like him to be faithful to every generation in various ways.

What are your students asking? Are they hearing God's answers? Do they see how all things hold together in Christ? Justice and mercy, faith and science, flesh and spirit, mind and heart, forgiveness and healing, healing and anointing, anointing and service. Are they discovering the tenacity and integrity of the gospel? How is Jesus real to them? Do they feel his affection for them? Do we feel his affection for us? Though the Word became flesh, do I just make him words again?

I think the gospel cannot be institutionalized with complete success in seals, mottoes, stone, and ivy, since truth is a living Person who loves and is alive. I ask myself: "Is he still flesh and blood to me? Is his Spirit still breathing the breath of life into me? I'm learning that the first casualty of the culture war may not be truth, but love. Students need Truth, who is by his very nature loving and personal. They want authenticity—the real thing—embodied Truth lived out as an art called love. Students want knowledge that involves relationship. They want truth that begets transformation, not just information. And so it's no surprise that students are still curious about Jesus—maybe more so than ever".

So how is God at work at Harvard and in other hard post-Christian places? I've mentioned a worshiping community that's like a symphony or, to use another metaphor, like a garden out of which fruit and flowers grow. Our word *seminary* came from an older word meaning "seedbed." I mentioned a graduate student ministry with tomorrow's faculty and professional leaders, a ministry of playing together, enjoying God's creation, escaping the self-important ivory tower into a world of trees and ocean and forest and animals and children and poverty and solitude—all the things we can forget about in the busy city. This, in its best moments, is a community of hands-on service and mission where students get a chance to convert their lofty ideas into actual work with and learning from the poor, whose wisdom comes at a high price.

We are continuing a conversation with administrators about the university's need for accountability to its Christian community, its Christian heritage, and its lack of systemic integrity properly to allocate endowments and vision.

How is God at work? Through witness and engagement. Through Bible studies in the yard in each of the graduate schools. Through the book I've mentioned. Through taking the risk of moving beyond technique to actual witness. Through the Veritas Forum. And I'd like to add a question in case any of you have ideas or counsel on this. Is there a relationship of the spiritual renewals in your schools the past few years with the spiritual quests and renewals in secular schools? We hear about spiritual renewal in some of your schools, and it's been inspiring. But I don't know if the spiritual renewal in Christian and secular schools represents two separate streams or if they are related to each other.

Finally, I'd like to add a few notes of thanksgiving and encouragement for what you in Christian colleges are doing. I encourage you to stand firm with full confidence in your mission and to enjoy the ways in which various disciplines, cultures, and generations come together as a symphony that brings glory to Jesus Christ and beauty to the earth.

I want to suggest that the post-Christian university and society need you. We need models of college life that are alive, models that are secure and confident in the Lord Jesus. We need to see schools where the center still holds, where wells of living water still nourish. We need to know students who are healthy and not destroying their bodies and their souls. We need to see a continual renewal and reformation and revival not attributable merely to alumni giving but to the Holy Spirit's power to make all things new, to make the rocks and stones cry out. This requires our utter dependence on him rather than on our own intelligence. And I'd ask you to have mercy on these places that are starving, understanding that their pride is often a sign of their poverty.

In *Finding God at Harvard*, we quote C. S. Lewis in his book *The Abolition of Man:* "It's not that the heads of secular intellectuals are bigger than ordinary, but that the atrophy of their chests beneath makes them seem so."

I would encourage you to build friendships with administrators and faculty in post-Christian colleges and universities, to be a lifeline to them. I ask you to practice hospitality where discouraged others can find healing and hope and joy—even now.

I will end by reading from the Epilogue of _Finding God at Harvard._

> In my search for God at Harvard I expected to find something new. Something beyond Jesus. But instead, I have found more of him. I have begun to see how the pure light of God's truth refracts and falls in every direction with color and grace. I found the memory of this truth in the color of crimson, in the ivory yard gates, and in the symbols on the college seal. I began to see him in the work and eyes of fellow students, in rare books, in a friend's chemistry lab, in recent astrophysical abstracts, and in the lives and legacies of founders and alumni who, whether living or beyond this life, would befriend and teach us . . . .
>
> I have only about three notes to contribute, but I join in. We sing while hanging drywall with Habitat for Humanity in Boston and while ski-hiking Tuckerman Ravine. We sing while quilting in Cambridge and while building a school for kids with polio in the rain forest of Peru. We sing while riding low in the back of a dusty pickup truck across war-torn El Salvador. We sing at the weddings and funerals of friends. The Lord is our song, and so we sing.
>
> With the eyes to see we find a great cloud of witnesses to which we all belong. We sing with them, warmed by the knowing that all manner of things shall be well one day. We remember the prophet Jeremiah, to whom the Lord said, "Do not say that 'I am only a youth.' Be not afraid, for I am with you to deliver you." And so we find courage in ages past, the age to come, and this age which, by grace alone, is ours.[1]

This address was delivered at the Conference on the Future of Christian Higher Education at Union University.

Chapter 17

VALUES THAT MAKE A DIFFERENCE

BOB R. AGEE

In the midst of some recent reading about leadership, I was struck by the realization that the students who are attending our colleges today are not just preparing to enter the job market in the late 1990s. Students who are here today will become a part of the reservoir of prospective leaders for the twenty-first century.

Think about it, students: You are destined to be a part of the launch of a whole new millennium—a fresh thousand years. You are in the midst of preparing yourselves for a lifetime of meaningful work and service as the new century dawns. In a few short years, you will enter the world of work to establish your role and reputation in the life of whatever business, industry, institution, or organization you have chosen. You will be a part of the leadership cohort that will assume the responsibility for shaping the early days of that new century.

What kind of leaders will you dare to be? What kind of leaders are we going to need for the twenty-first century?

During a conference on leadership several years ago in which leaders from a wide spectrum of fields spoke, several speakers identified needed characteristics of those who would aspire to be leaders. An executive with the aerospace industry suggested a profile for the effective Christian leader for the twenty-first century. She proposed that such a leader will be:

- a person of unquestioned integrity
- people oriented
- creative
- committed to excellence
- an expert communicator
- a team leader and team builder
- one who exercises leadership through consensus and
- a person with a global vision

197

A leader from the business arena identified eight characteristics he said are vital for leaders: integrity, courage, dedication, vision, humility, openness, creativity, and motivation.

The dramatic changes that have taken place during the last quarter of the twentieth century call for a new breed of thinkers and doers. Our world needs for you to dare to commit yourself to try to make a difference in whatever profession you choose and wherever God plants you.

So then, what will it take to be an effective leader in the early decades of the twenty-first century? Here are six key ingredients.

1. *Effective leaders for the twenty-first century will be people who have developed a deep understanding of and sensitivity to this ever-shrinking global village.* The American business and educational community can no longer ignore the importance of globalizing education and emphasizing cross-cultural understanding. The United States is the only major industrialized nation in the world that has been content to remain functionally literate in only one language, and sometimes we are not very adept at using it. We can no longer be content to introduce students only to Western civilization when the emerging leaders in world events are coming from the Orient, the Middle East, and a host of little known developing nations. We can no longer play Rip Van Winkle and sleep through an exploding knowledge revolution and the emergence of a global economy the likes of which this country has never imagined. If our nation is effectively to exercise its place of leadership in the world, there must be men and women entering the work force now who have begun to develop a deeper awareness of their world and who are willing to think through and be more sensitive to how to function more effectively in this ever-shrinking globe. Do not limit your thinking to the limited confines of where you live now or where you have traveled thus far. Determine to develop the abilities and sensitivities to be able to function effectively in a global marketplace as your arena to make a difference.

2. *Leaders for the twenty-first century must be people of VISION.* Over the years I have tried to motivate students by calling for people to catch a vision for excellence. The passion of my soul has been that faculty, staff, and students would dream ever-expanding dreams of being better than they ever thought possible and dreams of doing more and better than they ever previously conceived. Institutions and leaders of institutions who are willing to dream dreams and see visions for a better tomorrow will be those who will make a profound impact for good in their world. Those institutions and their leaders who never dare to

dream, who never issue a challenge today for a better tomorrow, simply live like sponges off their world and seldom contribute much to make it better. Students, you are part of a heritage that has practiced reaching beyond the now, daring to think new thoughts and being courageous enough to try new approaches. The seven last words of any organization or institution are: "We never did it that way before."

I have heard it said that there are three kinds of people in the world: those who make things happen, those who watch things happen, and those who sit around and wonder what happened. People of vision are those who have learned to look beyond themselves to see and sense the needs around them and who can visualize programs and structures to try to meet those needs. People of vision are those who have developed the capacity to believe that work can be done better, that institutions can perform better, and that their world can be better. We must have leaders for the twenty-first century who dare to dream dreams and see visions for a better tomorrow.

3. *Leaders for the twenty-first century must be people who have made a deep and abiding commitment to biblically based moral values.* Virtually every book you read on leadership or on organizational behavior emphasizes the importance of identifying and committing oneself or one's organization to a strong set of core values. Core values provide the true north on your life's compass that will keep your sense of direction right. There seems to be an enormous amount of interest in the marketplace in seeing our society recover some of the ethical values that form the foundation of a lasting democratic society. Sir Walter Moberly, in his work entitled *The Crisis in the University,* written in 1949, warned the American educational community about its efforts at making education "value neutral." He pointed out that under the false flag of being value neutral we were indeed imparting values that could undermine the foundations of a free society. He warned that neglect of moral and spiritual foundations and the neglect of the effort to develop character in the lives of students would be costly to the individual and to democracy.[1] So many of the questions today are not questions about whether we can do things; they are questions about what is right to do.

Moral values have suffered from several destructive prevailing moods. At some juncture within the scholarly community, we decided that all truth was relative and there were no standards or absolutes. Cynics talked about religion as being merely a social invention designed to provide ritual, ceremony, and context for meaningful, orderly community. The Bible was reduced to being viewed simply as another piece of religious literature to be seen as having no more authority or as being no more inspired than any other great and noble work. The prevailing mood advocated that right and wrong are relative to any given situation. As a result, our society has found itself adrift without a rudder in this sea of relativism while issues of justice, "ordered liberty," self-discipline, the dignity of human life and property, personal morality, and ethical behavior have fallen by the wayside. The twenty-first century will call for leaders who have made the commitment to strong biblically based morality and ethics and whose lives are characterized by deep and abiding integrity. This shrinking world cries for men and women who will seek to embody the lifestyle, spirit, and attitudes that will be marked by integrity and become that cohort of leaders to whom the masses can look with confidence and respect.

4. *Leaders for the twenty-first century will be people who are committed to a strong positive work ethic.* Far too many people in the work force are looking for a position and not a job. I've talked with numerous young professionals in recent years about what they want to do with their lives, and almost without exception, I hear them talk about wanting a job in a place where they can have some fun, make plenty of money, and don't have so much work to do that they can't do what they want to do. There is a pervasive yearning for success and position without having to work hard to get there. Leaders are people who don't watch the clock, who don't count the hours, and who aren't content with doing the minimum that's expected. Leaders are those who care deeply enough about the potential outcome of an effort that they pay the high price in sweat, long hours, hard work, and whatever else it takes to make the desired outcome come to pass.

Part of our heritage as evangelical Christians is what historians refer to as the "Puritan ethic." One aspect of that heritage is an emphasis on working hard, remaining diligent to give a day's work for a day's pay. That emphasis includes taking pride in the quality of our work, so that when we do our work, we can look back on it and know that we have done our best.

5. *Leaders for the twenty-first century will be people who are committed to excellence in every area of their lives.* In the book *A Passion for Excellence,* the authors cite three characteristics of institutions, industries, or organizations that achieve and lead: an emphasis on quality, innovation, and people centeredness.[2] People who are content with the way things are never become leaders; they are institutional mainte-

nance people. People who lead have an obsession with the improvement of performance, process, and product. We need people who are willing to think new thoughts and try new approaches, always looking for ways to improve conditions, performance, process, and product.

The place to begin developing a commitment to excellence is here and now. Your college education provides the context for you to develop the disciplines of mind and life that will make a difference in your tomorrow. God has entrusted to you the priceless capacity to learn and grow. There is so much more to you than what you have yet developed. Your future is almost limitless. Yet you can make the decision to be careless with that capacity, neglect the development of mind and skills, and choose a lifestyle of meaningless mediocrity. Why be content with being anything less than the best you can possibly be? Make excellence your ambition, and begin your pilgrimage now. The God we serve deserves nothing less than our best.

6. *Leaders for the twenty-first century will come from those who are committed to seeking to know the mind and will of God for their lives and for their world.* That's what singles out Christian leaders from all the rest. In the early pages of the Book of Joshua, Joshua called the people together to talk about moving across into the Promised Land and beginning a whole new era for the people of God. He reminded them that they had never passed that way before. He then issued the call for them to: "Sanctify yourselves: for tomorrow the LORD will do wonders among you" (Josh. 3:5 KJV).

That's exactly where we are today, facing a whole new era in human history, inheriting a world in transition, facing the task of constructing new paradigms, and trying to make old structures better. Christian leaders for the twenty-first century will try to discover what God wants for his world and will do whatever they can to move that world toward what God wants. Christian leaders will see a growing world and its needs, and they will be people of vision who are willing to think new thoughts while attempting new solutions to humankind's age-old problems.

I like the perspective of journalist Hal Wingo when he contended:

Let us turn our thinking in the direction of a God for the twenty-first century who may dazzle us into dizziness with all that is to come but who in the process shows himself to be an even more remarkable Creator than we had dared to dream. The future, with its capacity to turn today's fantasy into tomorrow's reality, may be awesome, but isn't the mind of God greater than Steven Spielberg's? Our task is to dare the twenty-first century to show us its stuff. And we will show it a people whose God is not through with this world yet.[3]

Our world needs leaders who dare to walk with God, seeking his mind and his leadership in every dimension of life, seeking to please him and to live out his will and purpose for their lives and for their world.

Conclusion

Three kinds of attitudes will prevail as people move into this new century:

1. What can I do to make a living so that I can survive and exist during the twenty-first century?
2. What can I do to function more effectively in the twenty-first century?
3. What do I need to do to provide effective leadership in the twenty-first century?

All three are legitimate questions. Those who are content to be preoccupied with the first question will not make much of an impact on their era. Those who are willing to tackle the second two questions and work at the answers can make a difference in their world.

Today I am issuing a challenge and a call to the Christian students and faculty.

To the faculty I issue the call and the challenge to do more than teach your subject matter. You are some of the finest Christian scholars in this land. You are among the best at what you do. Let us renew our commitment to excellence and dare to believe that we can impact students in such a way that they will care more deeply about their world and will be willing to embrace and embody those characteristics that will make them effective Christian leaders for the twenty-first century.

To the student body I issue the call and the challenge to rise to the demands of the twenty-first century. Dare to dream new and better dreams for a better tomorrow. Dare to believe that you can make a difference in your world. Dare to seek the mind and will of God in the decisions you make and in the persons you become. Dare to expend yourselves in the process of alleviating suffering, helping a hurting humanity, and in making your world a better place in which to live.

Dare to see yourselves as kingdom outposts in whatever profession or vocation you enter. Hear the words of President Theodore Roosevelt.

> It is not the critic who counts; not the man who points out how the strong man stumbled, or where the doer of deeds could have done better. The credit belongs to the man who is actually in the arena; whose face is marred by dust and sweat and blood; who strives valiantly; who errs and comes short again; who knows the great enthusiasms, the great devotions, and spends himself in a worthy cause; who at the best knows in the end the triumph of high achievement; and who at the worst, if he fails, at least fails while daring greatly; so that his place shall never be with those old and timid souls who know neither victory nor defeat.[4]

God grant that we will have the courage and the faith to dare greatly for the twenty-first century!

This address was delivered at a chapel service at Union University.

Chapter 18

More Than Survival

HARRY L. POE

Higher education in the United States faces a major dilemma that has several dimensions. The symptoms crop up in a variety of ways, but generally higher education no longer has a purpose governed by a vision. Almost three thousand years ago an ancient Semitic writer said that without a vision, people perish. The increased specialization of disciplines within higher education over the last hundred years has bred fragmentation of knowledge rather than integration. Fields of knowledge increasingly pull apart and fail to deal with the relationship between different spheres of knowledge.

At the same time, professional education has been given up by the professions that once controlled membership in the guild by apprenticeship. The academy has now assumed the function of training in place of the earlier apprenticeship model. The professions now train their members through higher education. As a result, the academy has become torn between the liberal arts, which see as their mission the development of critical thinking, and the professional departments, which see as their mission the development of competent practitioners or professionals. Educational institutions tend to be full of conflict between these parties over the purpose of higher education.

Institutions also experience conflict between teaching faculties and administrative staff in terms of priorities, which are always judged in terms of how much money is spent by whom. In this climate, decisions about curriculum and basic academic directions often become political and economic decisions. This dynamic appears in a wide range of institutions, including state universities, private liberal arts colleges, state technical schools, private religious colleges, and well-endowed private universities. A wide range of moral and political agendas come into play in deciding what ought to be taught, how it ought to be taught, what emphasis ought to be given, and what kind of values, if any, should permeate the academy.

Society as a whole now demands a greater stake in the "product produced" through higher education. Increasingly, this business or economics model of education controls. What product does a university or college produce? Who is the customer? Am I getting value for my dollar? Education has come to be regarded as an "investment" by different interests: the state, private enterprise, philanthropists, and religious groups, as well as parents and students.

The way out of the growing indolence of the academy has become clouded because the academy no longer has a clear purpose and overarching ideal of what it should be doing. It has no clear reason to be.

The Collapse of Christendom

Higher education in the West came about as an invention of the church, and its purpose was intrinsically related to its form and function. The church created higher education to deepen students' faith, knowledge of God, and understanding of God's creation. Education existed as a part of the church. God provided a basis for understanding the relationship of all knowledge. Because all things came from God, all things could be legitimately studied and understood as a gift from God. This basic view of the purpose of education created the stack pole or the *universitas*, the basis for universal knowledge.

Different religious orders created their own *collegium* or college, which was a religious community. The members of each community who completed their initial period of instruction advanced to the rank of novice, or *bachelor*. Thus, the first degree of progress was the bachelor of the arts of knowledge. Of course, a bachelor became synonymous with an unmarried man because only a man could enter the male religious orders charged with preserving the knowledge of God and civilization. Those members of the community who advanced in their instruction might become a *master* of the order. The different houses of learning had a master as their head. Different religious orders would have a master as their head. The head of the Knights Templars was the Grand Master. Thus, those pursuing knowledge advanced in their *degrees*. The Masons as well as the academy have preserved this terminology from the medieval orders to measure one's advancement in knowledge and one's status within the community. The very few who became *doctor* were those authorized to teach the religious *doctrine* of the church. All ways of knowing came under the umbrella of theology and doctrine, but those who studied were all monks. The official uniform of the academy to this day continues to be the monk's simple gown and hood.

The Collapse of Value and Vision

The academy holds onto the traditions and terminology of the church, but it has separated itself from its ecclesiastical foundations. The form and tradition remain, but without the purpose. Without purpose, the academy (or any other institution from a business to a government agency) drifts toward mere tradition. Without vision, functionality no longer has a relationship to a value. In the absence of true values, the academy constructs pseudovalues, such as "quality."

The academy now speaks of itself as offering "quality" education. What does that mean? We do it the way we have always done it, of course. We define ourselves as the standard. The way we do it is the best way to do it because we are the standard. To depart from the way we do it would mean to diminish our "quality." For instance, a student must be in class fifteen hours per semester for every "hour" of credit they receive. Why? Because that formula makes quality education. Why? Everybody knows that. Of course, the real reason the academy started requiring fifteen hours of class time for every hour of credit was because the Carnegie Foundation wanted "a day's work for a day's pay" from faculty. Institutions that did not follow that formula did not receive money from the Carnegie Foundation. As a result, the schools in the United States adopted a formula driven by economic pressures related to stakeholders external to the institution itself.

The academy also regards the method of instruction as a sign of quality. One lectures because education has come to be regarded as the dispensation of a body of knowledge that comes best by hearing. The lecture actually represents a veiled imitation of the sermon wherein "faith comes by hearing." The lecture hall of the academy duplicates the ecclesiastical model of dispensing the knowledge to the congregation. Why does the academy still do it that way so long after the divorce from the church? Because lectures are a sign of quality. Why? Because we have always done it that way. Professors replicate the method of instruction they experienced, not because it is the best way to learn, but because it is the only way they know. Without a clear vision and purpose, they have nowhere to turn but to tradition, even with the exposition of the most radical social ideas.

The problem of higher education relates to its retention of the forms of the medieval church, but without a purpose to give it unity and meaning. We do the same old things, but without any overarching reason to do them. This situation manifests itself in the fragmentation of the disciplines of learning within the institutions and a fragmentation of personal life and society in a country where this model of education prepares people to live fragmented, meaningless lives.

Without vision, schools will pull themselves apart and lapse into habitual internecine turf warfare spawned by budget battles, but they will survive as institutions. Institutions have an amazing capacity to continue to exist regardless of how far they have moved from their founding purpose. Existence becomes the reason for existing. Institutions take on a life of their own, devoid of any purpose. Jesus referred to this institutional phenomenon two thousand years ago when he said that a person does not put new wine in old wineskins because the old skins cannot tolerate the dynamic ferment of the new. Higher education in the West finds itself in that position today. The university has divorced itself from the old purpose, which revolved around a universal vision of knowledge. With the emergence of post-modernity, however, the university no longer holds to the idea of universal knowledge, universal values, and universal norms. In their place, the university champions fragmentation.

Growing Dissimilarities

As fragmentation grows and institutions pursue particular visions for themselves, colleges and universities will grow increasingly dissimilar in their appearance. The lack of consensus about the purpose of the university occurs at the same time an explosion in educational experimentation has begun. The experimentation began in the late 1960s and early 1970s with ideas like the "open university." Driven largely by student disinterest in following the prescribed curriculum, a number of loosely structured programs emerged following the spring riots of 1970, which allowed students to earn academic credit toward graduation for a variety of life experiences they deemed valuable. By the mid-1980s, private colleges and public universities struggled to balance budgets, while sources of revenue shrank in the face of skyrocketing costs. In this climate, the experiments in education led to innovative approaches to nontraditional education. The educational institutions discovered a huge market of people who never finished college but found their careers stalled until they could earn a college degree—any college degree. Increasingly, the nontraditional pool of students has grown in proportion to the total number of students. Through the use of adjunct faculty and accelerated courses, which dramatically reduce the number of contact hours for courses, allowing students to complete a degree in as few as eighteen months, colleges have found the goose that lays the golden egg.

The revolution in technology that began with the introduction of the personal computer in the early 1980s has led to a transformation of college culture by the late 1990s. Those schools that do not have sophisticated campus networks and student access to the Internet stand at a decided disadvantage in recruiting students. The technology has bred another revolution in teaching methodology as faculty incorporate technology in the traditional lecture class, but also as technology becomes an alternative, and in some cases a replacement, to the traditional textbook. The Internet has also opened the possibility of distance education in which students have a "virtual" class experience with peers around the country or the globe. The traditional student-faculty interaction occurs not in real time and space in a classroom, office, or commons area. Instead, interaction takes place over the Internet, through compressed video and immediate audio exchange.

Private colleges, publicly funded universities, well-endowed universities, successful grant-writing research universities, publicly funded technical schools and community colleges, and religious schools grow increasingly dissimilar as they pursue different educational visions. The kind of institution that once characterized itself as *in loco parentis* often takes little or no interest in the personal life, character development, and moral habits of those who pay tuition. *Alma Mater* has taken a laissez-faire attitude toward the raising of her children since the Boomers of the late 1960s and early 1970s rebelled so successfully against any attempts to restrict or control the college lifestyle. Religious institutions have come to experience this reorientation of mission as much as secular schools. Schools with historic ties to denominations have to rethink what it means to be a "Christian" school in this era. In most cases it means little more than that a denomination started the school in the last century. Sometimes it means that a course on Bible or religion is part of the core curriculum. One looks hard to see much difference between the college experience at the average denominational school and a state school except in terms of the size of the school.

The pragmatic, hard-nosed businesspeople who raised the Baby Boomers and sat on the boards of trustees of religious schools saw nothing particularly Christian about an English course or a history course. Decisions at such schools tended to be driven by economic considerations. Yet religious worldviews filter through every discipline of knowledge, as one of my friends who had a peripheral church experience as a child found when she went to college. Her English professor taught that "God" was nothing more than the "Spirit of the age." The Baroque period was characterized by a certain "spirit" of the culture, and the Romantic period had a different "spirit." This "Spirit of the age" is what God is. She accepted this view as her gospel. This was the first experience she had with someone discussing religion at an intellectual level, but her experience suggests that worldview comes into play with how one teaches a course. One cannot simply dismiss a discipline as not being "religious." All knowledge is religious.

Today's Student

At a time when the average university has draped itself in the self-authenticating trappings of scholarly tradition while pursuing a policy of marketing a product and surviving at any cost, a different kind of student enrolls in the traditional undergraduate program than did so twenty years ago. College students today are the children of Baby Boomers. They were raised by the most self-centered generation the country has yet seen. In that regard, these young people were not raised so much as they were allowed to raise themselves. While their parents reveled in the higher standard of living that a two-income family can enjoy, these children took up the slack at home. These are the children who a few years ago were referred to as "latchkey children." They cared for themselves after school, and the television set was their baby-sitter and nanny. This generation became the first emotional beneficiaries of quick, no-fault divorce as the divorce rate climbed to the 50 percent range during their formative years.

In terms of values development and worldview, this generation grew up without any significant exposure to religion. In their study of marginal church members, Penny Marler and Kirk Hadaway point out that 75 percent of Baby Boomers had a significant "base line" experience of at least two years in church while growing up. The Baby Busters reversed this statistic with only 25 percent having a significant "base line" experience in church.[1] No one was left to take the Echo Boomers to church. While the Boomers rebelled against their parents' religious conventions, the Echo Boomers have no such emotional involvement pro or con with religion. Boomers said, "I had to go to church when I was little. I'll let my children decide about religion for themselves." While the sentiment has a certain egalitarian flare, in practice it meant that the parents denied their children a basis for deciding about faith because they were never exposed to the option.

The Path to the Future

Christians build institutions. These institutions usually result from the activity of a movement that emerges from a period of spiritual vitality or awakening. The institutions are well intended as a means of carrying on the work or contribution of the genius of that period of vitality. This effort at bottling spiritual vitality has never worked. It did not work with the monks of Cluny in the early Middle Ages, and it did not work with the YMCA. Spirituality cannot be institutionalized. This observation lies at the heart of the problem of maintaining a Christian college or university. If an organization with such a clearly defined purpose as the YMCA can go from being the leading organization for evangelizing young people to the largest franchised health club, then one should not expect that a college with such diverse interests can long remain Christian. Institutions assume the character and agenda of the financial interests that support them.

Christians often complain about how the "liberals" or the "secular world" has "stolen" our great institutions. The litany usually begins with Harvard and Yale, then proceeds to some of the great regional universities with denominational backgrounds like the University of Chicago (Baptist) and Duke University (Methodist). Very rarely do they complain about the loss of the great hospitals and children's homes. Therein lies the problem. At the present time, few people have a concern for these ministries. Great Christian institutions have never been "stolen." They have always been thrown away by Christians who had no particular interest in them. So much attention has been given to the litany of great colleges and universities lost to the Christian faith that little attention has been given to why some institutions continue to remain Christian beyond the generation that founded them.

Carl Lundquist, for many years president of Bethel College and Seminary and president of the CCCU, often explained why he had no plans for raising an endowment for Bethel by declaring, "The churches are our endowment!" This statement may sound rather cavalier and irresponsible at a time when the economic picture of colleges and universities in the United States looks so gloomy to the ones who must balance the budget. The statement, however, reflects a commitment of accountability to the churches that founded the school to serve the mission of Christ. A healthy endowment has the potential to free a school from any accountability to its founding purpose and mission. Very few Christian institutions have survived prosperity. The institutions flourish, but somehow Christ gets left behind.

Poverty by itself, however, is no particular virtue. Even more important than the economic issues are the relational issues at work when Lundquist declared that "the churches are our endowment!" Bethel was kept Christian by the care of the churches of the Baptist General Conference. Apart from the official lines of governance, the churches "owned" Bethel. They did not govern it; they felt responsible for it. They cared about the kind of experience young people had at Bethel. They held the school accountable. The school in turn took the churches seriously. Bethel was part of a family that went beyond the formal denominational structures.

Denominational structures and formal lines of funding, reporting, and trustee selection do not guarantee the continuation of a distinctive Christian mission for a college or university. Denominational politics easily reduce to a game of avoiding accountability. The informal relationship serves a more important function than the formal relationship in keeping a college connected with its purpose and mission. As long as the churches care about Bethel and as long as Bethel cares what the churches think, Bethel will continue to have a distinctively Christian mission.

A vision for the future of Christian education can only emerge from a clear grasp of the founding purpose of an institution to serve Christ in relationship with churches. Christian colleges and universities that successfully deal with the dramatic challenges of higher education in the United States at the turn of the new century will focus on the strategic issue of how to fulfill the purpose for which they were founded. Christian colleges and universities that drift away from their purpose will tend to focus on the tactical issues that confront every institution in the education industry today. Preoccupation with the unending stream of trend shifts without a governing universal basis for knowledge and integration will leave such schools devoid of identity and powerless to form the character of students. In such situations, the only universal value is the dollar. Operating from this perspective, trustees are in danger of making "wise decisions" for the survival of the institution. Unfortunately, survival is not a very lofty purpose.

Christian colleges and universities have the curious need to risk death in order to fulfill their mission. This phenomenon will only accelerate with the increasing influence of a post-Christian, post-denominational, postmodern world. The report of the National Commission on the Cost of Higher Education has recommended that governments develop new approaches to academic regulation that emphasize performance and differentiation and that academic communities develop accrediting processes that emphasize effectiveness. With the collapse of the old academic tradition and the emergence of radically different educational models, the right to grant degrees may no longer be available to institutions in the future the way it has been in the past. In most countries, the government controls the granting of degrees. In the past, many Christian colleges have not accepted government aid in any form to avoid entanglement with governmental restrictions. How would Christian schools respond if they could no longer grant degrees? The answer to this question would quickly identify where an institution stands with respect to its foundational purpose and mission. Does the school exist to grant degrees or to do something else?

REFLECTIONS ON THE FUTURE OF CHRISTIAN HIGHER EDUCATION

DAVID P. GUSHEE

"The eye is the lamp of the body. If your eyes are good, your whole body will be full of light. But if your eyes are bad, your whole body will be full of darkness. If then the light within you is darkness, how great is that darkness!" (Matt. 6:22–23).

You can tell the difference by looking in their eyes.

I write at the desk of my modest guest room in the ancient university city of Oxford, England. I have been here for a board meeting of the Oxford Center for Mission Studies, an exciting international Christian initiative in graduate theological education. After the meeting concluded, I spent the day touring this famous town and trying to get a sense of what life is like here, what kinds of men and women now study at what is arguably the most famous university in the world.

I walked into the Eagle and Child, the Oxford pub made famous by its once-regular literary customers, most notably C. S. Lewis and J. R. R. Tolkien. Upon entering, my first sights and sounds were of two dissolute-looking college-age friends cursing a blue streak at each other over their ales and through their cigarette smoke. They did not appear to be angry; this simply seemed to be their customary way of relating to each other. They had no compunction about filling the air with every unprintable word imaginable. Their eyes were very weary, dark with an ironic coldness.

Oxford University was originally established for Christian purposes, and the vestiges of its medieval Christian vision are everywhere apparent. But that was at least two intellectual/spiritual/moral revolutions ago, and the light of Christ no longer shines in the eyes of the people I see on these historic streets.

I attended the College of William and Mary, perhaps the single American university with the closest historical ties to the British university system. Sir Christopher Wren, one of seventeenth-century England's greatest architects, designed the college's original building (the Wren building). Originally founded with the purpose of training ministers, William and Mary has long been a secular public university in the Virginia system.

When Ken Elzinga writes of the spiritual and moral emptiness that afflicts the University of Virginia, William and Mary's sister and rival institution, I know whereof he speaks. I entered college in 1980, and those were wild days. The dorms sponsored keg parties as a way of welcoming their freshmen inhabitants. The drinking age was eighteen then, and the university was proud to tell us during orientation that it had put *in loco parentis* to rest during the 1970s.

So we could drink all we wanted. We could visit in any dorm room on campus at any time of the day or night and do whatever we wanted there. We eighteen-year-olds were on our own, licensed to exercise the total freedom that was appropriate to our new station in life. And so the rowdy inhabitants of Spotswood Hall got drunk most every night. Vomit was a regular feature of the bathrooms and halls. One memorable night, a group of young gentlemen exercised their freedom by uprooting a vending machine from its place and tossing it to its demise three stories below.

Casual sex was common, as were pregnancy tests, sexually transmitted disease tests, and the occasional abortion. Young couples routinely displaced roommates as they moved in with each other. Campus parties at times came to resemble pagan bacchanals—indeed, certain events were explicitly linked to this particular ancient tradition. The light in many eyes began to dim, succumbing to darkness.

Yet, the classroom experience was scintillating. Professors had almost nothing to do with students, but their performance in the classroom—despite secular assumptions—was generally superb. They pushed us—and themselves—hard. The pressure was at times sanity threatening. But those who survived it were exceedingly well prepared for the rigors of any educational or professional challenges that lay ahead.

As I reflect both on two years of teaching at Union University and on the essays and papers collected in this volume, my thoughts return to my own college experience. I think of the young men and women who lost their moral compass while studying at one of the nation's great public universities. I remember with sadness the dear friend who entered college as a fellow Christian leader and ended as a convinced secularist whose taste in music ran to the hard rock group AC/DC. Thanks be to God, I survived—though not unscathed. But I did survive, in large part, due to the steadying influence of the Baptist Student Union and the local congregation that embraced and cared for me and other college students. Not everyone was as fortunate.

A first-rate college education need not be bought at the price of our students' souls. It is more than possible to offer young men and women access to the finest minds in the nation and to the rich intellectual heritage of our culture—*and* to offer them an environment that is morally and spiritually nurturing. The place where this marvelous combination can and sometimes does occur is the Christian college. It seems to me that the future of Christian higher education hinges on whether we can create and sustain many such colleges in the century ahead. I want to close this volume by reflecting very briefly on the two related tasks before us: preserving our souls (spiritual/moral integrity) while advancing our minds (intellectual/academic quality).

Several of the papers reflected on the central issue of how to preserve the soul of our Christian universities: that is, those Christian universities that have not already gone the way of the YMCA, as Hal Poe so astutely observes.

Robert Sloan points to several ways in which Christian universities and their sponsors seek to institutionalize Christian identity, then focuses on the faculty as the linchpin. Poe reminds us that identity loss happens not because somebody undertakes a plot to steal a Christian university but because a university's inhabitants simply don't care enough to preserve its identity against those forces which corrode it.

No single site within a Christian university is responsible for guarding its soul, its identity and integrity. It is a total community responsibility. While perhaps this responsibility is vested ultimately in the trustees and the president, the soul of a Christian university depends on whether the light of Christ can be found there—from students to faculty, janitors to registrars, trustees to the public relations office. And that en-*light*-enment in turn depends on the overall spiritual vitality of the faith communities from which these people are drawn. Authentic Christian existence cannot be coerced, mandated, borrowed, or imitated. Christ must be real and must be Lord for each and for all. That light in the eyes is either there or it is not.

There is no more important challenge in the Christian university than the preservation of its soul. And yet a caution is needed. A fixation on identity and boundary guarding is not in itself a sign of vitality. We must be fully and intelligently aware of the particular identity "pressure points" and how to defend ourselves against identity threats. We need the kind of informed critical engagement with destructive cultural/intellectual/spiritual forces that is evidenced throughout this work. But identity preservation is not enough. It is a defensive agenda. It is a wall-building, or if you prefer, a foundation-preserving, act. But walls and foundations are not the reason we exist. Clear identity is the *presupposition* of our kingdom-advancing mission, not the mission itself.

An institution—or, for that matter, an individual—constantly fixated on boundary and identity issues is not healthy. We would worry about a person whose primary form of public communication was an articulation of his identity: "I am David Gushee. I am a man. I am married and have three children. I live in Jackson, Tennessee. I am a Christian." Yet that is what we are in danger of doing both in the discussion of Christian higher education and in our broader engagement with the culture. I think that by now the forces that dominate secular American culture know that evangelical Christians are not happy with them and proclaim a very different identity. "Fine," I can hear them saying, "Now do you have anything positive to contribute?" It is a question we need to be able to answer better than we are doing right now.

This leads to some concluding thoughts on the question of how to nurture the intellect of the Christian student and the mind of the Christian university as a whole.

Here is where the issue of faculty comes most acutely into view. The great challenge, as Joel Carpenter indicates, is to nurture truly first-rate evangelical scholars who can engage secular intellectuals on equal terms—indeed, scholars who can, at least at times, actually set the intellectual agenda in their fields. This level of scholarship cannot be done solely within the confines of the evangelical subculture. Indeed, a ghettoized Christian scholarship is of little value. Excellence in Christian scholarship requires engaging the main currents of thought in one's field. Evangelical scholars face the challenge of reading and knowing not only the work of like-minded scholars but also that of intellectual adversaries and every other significant voice.

It is certainly possible for evangelical scholars to enjoy a thriving publishing and lecture circuit career without ever breaking out of the boundaries of the evangelical Christian subculture. I have noticed this in my own field of Christian ethics, in which dozens of evangelical works are published each year that exhibit little contact with the broader world of religious and philosophical moral reflection. Such works may have many uses but unfortunately make a negligible impact on the direction of the field or the broader culture. While these persons do make a contribution to the church and its mission, this is not the ideal of Christian scholarship for which we should strive.

But when we do cross out of the subculture and do so with genuinely high-quality scholarship, we are sometimes (though not always) going to be pleasantly surprised at the reception we receive. We will find that there are unexpected friends and allies in secular universities and sometimes even in other religious traditions. But the price of admission to this broader intellectual conversation is first-rate scholarship on our own part.

The nurture of such scholarship is worthy of the most strenuous and costly efforts on the part of many different players: college and seminary faculty and administration, philanthropists, foundations, congregations, campus ministries, and evangelical advocacy groups of all types. As Karen Longman suggests, the best and brightest minds moving through our Christian universities need to be shepherded intentionally through the undergraduate and (frequently secular) graduate school process, aggressively recruited to teach in our universities, detoxified of the secularism likely imbibed in the educational process and in other ways carefully nurtured in professional development.

These scholar/teachers should be encouraged to participate in meaningful scholarship and intellectual engagement and should be rewarded for doing so. Every effort should be made to invest in sufficient salaries to keep the most productive and significant among them from being plucked away by the secular universities that become interested in them. All of this involves vigorous fund-raising efforts on the part of administrators. But fundamentally it involves the willingness of millions of evangelical Christians to demonstrate with their checkbook their high regard for scholarship and the "Christian mind." This in turn requires that Christian universities regularly demonstrate their integrity, usefulness, and value to the individuals and groups we ask to provide such support.

Once both Europe and North America produced great Christian universities in which both soul *and* mind were full of light, the light of Jesus Christ. At the beginning of a new millennium, the darkness that is the bitter result of our soulless age is all too apparent. If we can seize the opportunity that lies before us, Christian higher education has a very bright future indeed.[2]

Oxford
Holy Saturday
April 11, 1998

ENDNOTES

Introduction

1. See Russell Chandler, *Racing Toward 2001* (Grand Rapids: Zondervan, 1992); Guy Benvensiste, *The Twenty–First Century Organization: Analyzing Current Trends and Imagining the Future* (San Francisco: Josey Bass, 1994); also see *Current Thoughts and Trends* 12:5 (May 1996): 8. Many ideas in this essay have been adapted from James E. White, *Rethinking the Church* (Grand Rapids: Baker, 1996).

2. See Ron Johnson, *How Will They Hear If We Don't Listen* (Nashville: Broadman & Holman, 1994); Gene Edward Veith Jr., *Postmodern Times: A Christian Guide to Contemporary Thought and Culture* (Wheaton: Crossway, 1994); and Kenneth Myers, *All God's Children and Blue Suede Shoes: Christians and Popular Culture* (Wheaton: Crossway, 1989).

3. See Jean Bethke Elshtain, *Democracy on Trial* (New York: Basic Books, 1995); see also Neil Postman, *Technopology: The Surrender of Culture to Technology* (New York: Vintage, 1993).

4. William H. Willimon and Thomas H. Naylor, *The Abandoned Generation: Rethinking Higher Education* (Grand Rapids: Eerdmans, 1995); Thomas H. Naylor, William Willimon, and Magdalena R. Naylor, *The Search for Meaning* (Nashville: Abingdon, 1994); see also Walter Truett Anderson, *Reality Isn't What It Used to Be: Theatrical Politics, Ready-to-Wear Religion, Global Myths, Primitive Chic, and Other Wonders of the Postmodern World* (San Francisco: HarperCollins, 1990); William Mahedy and Janet Bernardi, *A Generation Alone* (Downers Grove: InterVarsity, 1994).

5. Barry Alan Shain, *The Myth of American Individualism* (Princeton: Princeton University Press, 1994); Shain echoes Jeffrey C. Goldfarb's analysis in *The Cynical Society: The Culture of Politics and the Politics of Culture in American Life* (Chicago: University of Chicago

1991); also see Alasdair MacIntyre, *After Virtue* (Notre Dame: University of Notre Dame Press, 1984).

6. See D. A. Carson, *The Gagging of God* (Grand Rapids: Zondervan, 1995).

7. See David F. Wells, *God in the Wasteland* (Grand Rapids: Eerdmans, 1993); Penny Marler, *Unchurched Faith* (Nashville: Abingdon, 1996); and also the regular reports from the George Barna Research Group of Glendale, California.

8. See Arthur F. Holmes, *All Truth is God's Truth* (Grand Rapids: Eerdmans, 1977); S. D. Gaede, *When Tolerance Is No Virtue: Political Correctness, Multiculturalism and the Future of Truth and Justice* (Downers Grove: InterVarsity, 1993); James E. White, *What Is Truth?* (Nashville: Broadman & Holman, 1994); Brian J. Walsh and J. Richard Middleton, *The Transforming Vision: Shaping a Christian World View* (Downers Grove: InterVarsity, 1984); Alister McGrath, *Evangelicalism and the Future of Christianity* (Downers Grove: InterVarsity, 1995); idem, *Intellectuals Don't Need God* (Grand Rapids: Zondervan, 1993).

9. See Michael Hammer and James Champy, *Reengineering the Corporation* (New York: Harper Business, 1993); James Champy, *Reengineering Management* (New York: Harper Business, 1995); Michael Hammer, *Beyond Reengineering: How the Process-Centered Organization Is Changing Our Work and Our Lives* (New York: Harper Business, 1996); and Hedrick Smith, *Rethinking America: Innovative Strategies and Partnerships in Business and Education* (New York: Avon, 1995).

10. Ibid., 17.

11. See David Ricks, *Big Business Blunders: Mistakes in Multi-National Marketing* (Chicago: Irwin, 1983). The illustrations are adapted from James E. White, *Rethinking the Church* (Grand Rapids: Baker, 1996).

12. George Bernard Shaw, cited in Allan Cox and Julie Liesse, *Redefining Corporate Soul: Linking Purpose and People* (Chicago: Irwin, 1996), 91.

13. See the story in Joel Barker, *Future Edge* (New York: William Morrow, 1992), 15–19.

14. See the warnings concerning things we do not want repeated in our Christian colleges and universities in James Tunstead Burtchaell, "The Decline and Fall of the Christian College," *First Things* (April 1991): 16–29.

15. Borrowed from John C. Maxwell, _Developing the Leader within You_ (Nashville: Thomas Nelson, 1993), 25–26.

16. See Steven Garber, _The Fabric of Faithfulness_ (Downers Grove: InterVarsity, 1996); also see former President Derek Bok's discussion of the importance of values/moral education in our universities in _The President's Report 1986–87_, Harvard University; also Arthur Holmes, _Shaping Character: Moral Education in the Christian College_ (Grand Rapids: Eerdmans, 1991).

17. My ideas for this introductory essay have been largely shaped by George M. Marsden, _The Soul of the American University_ (Oxford: Oxford University Press, 1994); Mark A. Noll, _The Scandal of the Evangelical Mind_ (Grand Rapids: Eerdmans, 1995); and Marsden, _The Outrageous Idea of Christian Scholarship_ (Oxford: Oxford University Press, 1997)

Chapter 1

1. Jack Jones, "Slouching Toward the Millennium," _Los Angeles Times Magazine_ (24 Dec. 1989), 8.

2. See James A. Mecklenburger, "The New Revolution." _Business Week_ (special advertising section), ED23, (no date); also James D. Meindl, ed., _Brief Lessons in High Technology: Understanding the End of This Century to Capitalize on the Next_ (Stanford, Calif.: Stanford Alumni Association, 1989).

3. Jacques Ellul, _The Technological Bluff_ (Grand Rapids: Eerdmans, 1990); Neil Postman, _Amusing Ourselves to Death_ (New York: Penguin, 1986); idem, _Technopoly: The Surrender of Culture to Technology_ (New York: Vintage, 1993).

4. See Ronald H. Nash, _The Closing of the American Heart: What's Really Wrong with America's Schools_ (Dallas: Probe, 1990).

5. Leith Anderson, _A Church for the 21st Century_ (Minneapolis: Bethany House, 1992), 17.

6. See Gene Edward Veith, _Postmodern Times: A Christian Guide to Contemporary Thought and Culture_ (Wheaton: Crossway, 1994).

7. Jean-Francois Lyotard, _The Postmodern Condition: A Report on Knowledge_, G. Bennington and B. Massumi, trans. (Minneapolis: University of Minnesota Press, 1984).

8. E.g., Jacques Derrida, _Of Grammatology_, G. C. Spivak, trans. (Baltimore: Johns Hopkins, University Press, 1976).

9. Michel Foucault, "Truth and Power" in *Power/Knowledge*, ed. Colin Gordon (New York: Pantheon, 1980).

10. Stanley Fish, *Is There a Text in This Class? The Authority of Interpretive Communities* (Cambridge: Harvard University Press, 1980).

11. Diamond Rio, "It's All in Your Head," *Diamond Rio IV* (1996).

12. George Barna, as cited by David Winfrey, "Barna's Polls Find Reason to Rejoice and Worry," *Western Recorder* (17 Sept. 1996): 1.

13. See Craig Blomberg, *Matthew*, New American Commentary (Nashville: Broadman & Holman, 1992), 335.

14. T. S. Eliot, *Christianity and Culture* (New York: Harcourt Brace, 1940), 22.

15. Ibid.

16. John R. W. Stott, *The Contemporary Christian* (Downers Grove: InterVarsity, 1992), 114–26.

17. George Marsden, *The Soul of the American University* (Oxford University Press: New York, 1994).

18. Russell Chandler, *Racing Toward 2001* (Grand Rapids: Zondervan, 1992), 108.

19. Mark Schwehn, as cited in Daniel Cattau, "Education: A Problem Could Be a Solution," *Progressions, A Lilly Endowment Occasional Report*, 2:1 (1990), 20.

20. Dorothy Bass, as cited in Carol Elrod, "Church Historian Analyzes Causes of Mainline Church Malaise," *Religious News Service* (15 Nov. 1988); also see similar comments in James David Hunter, *Evangelicalism: The Coming Generation* (Chicago: University of Chicago Press, 1987).

21. Clark Kerr, *The Uses of the University* (Cambridge: Harvard University Press, 1995).

22. Ibid. Kerr opposes the classic dream of John Henry Newman, *The Idea of a University* (Notre Dame: University of Notre Dame Press, 1982 {1873}).

23. Bill Readings, *The University in Ruins* (Cambridge: Harvard University Press, 1996).

24. See Thomas J. Peters and Robert Waterman Jr., *In Search of Excellence* (New York: Warner, 1982).

25. Cited by Roger Dow and Susan Cook, *Turned On* (New York: Harper Business, 1996), 6.

26. David Damrosch, *We Scholars: Changing the Culture of the University* (Cambridge: Harvard University Press, 1995).

27. See Arthur F. Holmes, *All Truth Is God's Truth* (Downers Grove: InterVarsity, 1977).

28. See D. Bruce Lockerbie, *A Passion for Learning* (Chicago: Moody, 1994).

29. Justin Martyr, *Second Apology*, XIII; see Harry L. Poe, *The Gospel and Its Meaning* (Grand Rapids: Zondervan, 1996), 90–95.

30. Clement of Alexandria, *Miscellanies*, I. 13.; see David S. Dockery, *Biblical Interpretation Then and Now* (Grand Rapids: Baker, 1992), 75–102.

31. Augustine, *On Christian Doctrine*; see Poe, *The Gospel and Its Meaning*, 67–70.

32. See Marsden, *Soul of the American University*; also Kelly Monroe, *Finding God at Harvard* (Grand Rapids: Zondervan, 1996).

33. John Calvin, *Institutes of the Christian Religion*, 2.2.15.

34. Cited in D. Bruce Lockerbie, *Thinking and Acting like a Christian* (Portland: Multnomah, 1989), 92–93.

35. Francis Schaeffer, *The Church Before the Watching World* (Downers Grove: InterVarsity, 1971).

36. As reported by Lockerbie, *Thinking and Acting like a Christian*.

37. See Millard J. Erickson, *The Evangelical Heart and Mind* (Grand Rapids: Baker, 1993); George R. Knight, *Philosophy and Education* (Berrien Springs, Mich.: Andrews University Press, 1989); John R. W. Stott, *Involvement* (Old Tappan: Revell, 1984); Mark A. Noll, *The Scandal of the Evangelical Mind* (Grand Rapids: Eerdmans, 1994)

Chapter 2

1. James T. Burtchaell, "The Alienation of Christian Higher Education," in *Schooling Christian,* ed. Stanley Hauerwas and John Westernoff (Grand Rapids: Eerdmans, 1992), 129–83.

Chapter 3

1. George M. Marsden, *The Soul of the American University* (New York: Oxford University Press, 1994).

2. This section of my presentation is highly dependent upon many hours of fruitful discussions as well as the excellent work of my colleague, Dr. Michael Beaty, in his readable and highly insightful piece, Michael J. Beaty, "An Apology for the Christian University," 17 *Faculty Dialogue* (1992): 39–51.

3. Douglas Sloan, *Faith and Knowledge: Mainline Protestantism and American Higher Education* (Louisville, Ky.: Westminster/John Knox Press, 1994). Cited in Michael Beaty, J. Todd Buras, and Larry Lyon, "Faith and Knowledge in American Higher Education," *Journal of the Conference on Faith and History* 29 Vol. 1 (Winter/Spring 1997): 73–81.

4. This story is recounted in Beaty, Buras, and Lyon, "Faith and Knowledge in American Higher Education," 75.

5. See David Solomon's excellent article, "What Baylor and Notre Dame Can Learn from Each Other," revised and reprinted in *New Oxford Review* (December 1995): 8–19.

6. The implications, in my view, are enormous. Samuel P. Huntington, *The Clash of Civilizations and the Remaking of World Order* (New York: Simon and Schuster, 1996).

7. Though one must finally reject his materialistic naturalism, the importance of "the unity of truth" has been magisterially set forth in Edward O. Wilson, "Back from Chaos," *The Atlantic Monthly* 281 (1998): 41–62, and Edward O. Wilson, Richard Rorty, and Paul R. Gross, "Is Everything Relative?: A Debate on the Unity of Knowledge," *Wilson Quarterly* 22 (Winter 1998): 14, both of which are summarized in Wilson's new book, *Consilience: The Unity of Knowledge* (New York: Alfred Knopf Publishing, 1998).

8. James Tunstead Burtchaell, "The Alienation of Christian Higher Education in America: Diagnosis and Prognosis," in *Schooling Christians: "Holy Experiments" in American Education*, ed. Stanley Hauerwas and John H. Westerhoff (Grand Rapids, Mich.: Eerdmans,1992), 129–83; see also George M. Marsden, *The Soul of the American University* (New York: Oxford University Press, 1994), 287.

9. Richard John Neuhaus, "The Christian University: Eleven Theses," *First Things* 59 (January 1996): 20–22.

Chapter 4

1. Data on 10,521 CCCU students collected by UCLA's Higher Education Research Institute report as part of the CCCU's Collaborative Assessment Project, "Taking Values Seriously: Assessing the Mission of Church-Related Higher Education" (1994 First-year students).

2. Edward (Chip) Anderson, "Spiritual Approaches to Promoting Student Persistence," a paper presented at the National Conference on Student Retention, Orlando, Florida, July 1996.

3. Paper presented at the 1997 CCCU conference of chief academic officers by Dallas Willard (April 3–5), 1997, Phoenix, Ariz.).

4. Donald O. Clifton, Paul Nelson, *Soar with Your Strengths* (New York: Dell, 1992).

5. J. Marcia, "Identity Status in Late Adolescence: Descriptive and Clinical Applications," Identity Development Symposium, Groningen, The Netherlands, 1979.

6. Laurent A. Parks Daloz, Cheryl H. Keen, James P. Keen, and Sharon Daloz Parks, *Common Fire: Leading Lives of Commitment in a Complex World* (Boston: Beacon Press, 1997).

7. For information on this research project, see John Van Wicklin Ronald A. Burnell, and Richard E. Butman, "Squandered Years: Identity-Foreclosed Students and the Liberal Education They Avoid" in *Assessment in Christian Higher Education* (Lanham, Md.: University Press of America, 1994).

Chapter 6

1. Joseph T. Bayly, "I Saw Gooley Fly," *HIS*, Vol. 20 (February 1960), 4–6, Inter–Varsity Christian Fellowship.

2. Attributed to Arthur Holmes of Wheaton College, *Christianity Today* (8 Oct. 1990): 90–91.

Chapter 7

1. Carl F. H. Henry, *Twilight of a Great Civilization: The Drift Toward Neo-Paganism* (Wheaton: Crossroads, 1988).

Chapter 8

1. Daniel Yankelovich, *Coming to Public Judgment: Making Democracy Work in a Complex World* (Syracuse University Press, 1991).

2. Ravi Zacharias, *Can Man Live without God?* (Dallas: Word, 1994).

Chapter 10

1. *D. Martin Luthers Werke: Briefwechsel* (Weimar Hermann Bohlaus Nachfolger, 1933), vol. 3, pp. 81–82. Translation mine.

2. John R. Searle, "Reiterating the Differences: A Reply to Derrida," *Glyph* 1 (Baltimore: John Hopkins University Press, 1977), pp. 198–208.

THE FUTURE OF CHRISTIAN HIGHER EDUCATION

3. Jacques Derrida, "Limited Inc. abc . . ., *Glyph* 2 (Baltimore: John Hopkins University Press, 1977), pp. 162–253

4. William James, "Pragmatism's Conception of Truth," in *Pragmatism and Four Essays from the Meaning of Truth* (New York: Meridian, 1955), p. 132.

5. Thomas C. Oden, *After Modernity . . .What? Agenda for Theology* (Grand Rapids: Zondervan, 1990), pp. 41–42.

Chapter 11

1. Quoted in George M. Marsden, *The Soul of the American University: From Protestant Establishment to Established Unbelief* (New York: Oxford University Press, 1994), 437.

2. Kuklick is quoted in Carolyn J. Mooney, "Devout Professors in the Offensive," *Chronicle of Higher Education* 4 (May 1994): A-18.

3. Alan Wolfe, "Higher Learning," *Lingua Franca* March/April 1996): 70–77; Wolfe, "A Welcome Revival of Religion in the Academy," *The Chronicle of Higher Education* (19 September 1997): B-4,5.

4. Daniel Coit Gilman, *University Problems in the United States* (New York: 1898), 178; quoted in Marsden, *Soul of the American University,* 143.

5. Paul Blanshard, *American Freedom and Catholic Power* (Boston: Beacon Press, 1949).

6. Philip Gleason, *Contending with Modernity: Catholic Higher Education in the Twentieth Century* (New York: Oxford University Press, 1995), 302.

7. Gleason, *Contending with Modernity,* 320.

8. Reinhold Niebuhr, *The Contribution of Religion to Cultural Unity,* Hazen Pamphlets 13 (n.p., 1945), 10; quoted in Douglas Sloan, *Faith and Knowledge: Mainline Protestantism and American Higher Education* (Louisville, Ky.: Westminster/John Knox Press, 1994), 112.

9. Quoted in Sloan, *Faith and Knowledge,* 4.

10. Sloan, 206.

11. Quoted in Gleason, *Contending with Modernity,* 121.

12. 1 Peter 3:15.

13. Quoted in Gleason, 319.

Chapter 12

1. Stan Grenz, *Revisioning Evangelical Theology: A Fresh Agenda for the 21st Century* (Downers Grove: InterVarsity, 1993), 45.

2. R. J. Foster, *Celebration of Discipline: The Path to Spiritual Growth* (San Francisco: Harper and Row, 1978), 1.

3. R. J. Foster and J. B. Smith eds., *Devotional Classics: Selected Readings for Individuals and Groups* (New York: HarperCollins, 1990), 29.

4. Ibid., 8.

5. I discuss this issue at some length in the literature review of my dissertation, "Integration of Faith and Learning Among Christian Evangelical Colleges and Seminaries: An Alumni Assessment Model" (Ph.D. diss., Peabody College of Vanderbilt University, 1994).

6. Dallas Willard, *The Spirit of the Disciplines: Understanding How God Changes Lives* (New York: HarperCollins, 1988). Willard offers a rather extensive discussion of this matter.

7. Ibid., 51.

8. All Scripture is quoted from *New International Version* (1973).

9. J. Sire, *The Universe Next Door: A Basic World View Catalog* (Downers Grove: InterVarsity Press, 1988), 36.

10. John Calvin, *Institutes of the Christian Religion*, trans. John Allen, (Grand Rapids: Eerdmans), 3.11.3.

11. Ibid., III, 3, 6.

12. Willard, ix.

13. Darrell Reinke, *The Spirituality of Western Christendom*, ed. Rozanne Elder (Kalamazoo: Cistercian Publications, 1976), 165.

14. Willard, 5.

15. D. L. Wolfe calls this "pseudointegration" in "The Line of Demarcation Between Integration and Pseudointegration," in H. Heie and D. L. Wolfe, eds., *The Reality of Christian Learning: Strategies for Faith-Learning Integration* (Grand Rapids: Eerdmans, 1987), 3–11. Wolfe would argue that this example would demonstrate a false understanding of the Christian worldview and reality.

16. Willard, 77.

17. Ibid., 92.

18. Ibid., 10.

19. B. Christensen, *The Inward Pilgrimage: An Introduction to Christian Spiritual Classics* (Minneapolis: Augsburg Fortress, 1966), 17.

20. Martin Luther, *Theologia Germanica of Martin Luther*, Bengt Hoffman, trans. (New York: Paulist, 1980).

21. Foster and Smith, 153.

22. Robert Webber, *Common Roots: A Call to Evangelical Maturity* (Grand Rapids: Zondervan, 1978), 219.

23. Calvin, III, 1, 4.

24. John Calvin, *Golden Booklet of the True Christian Life* (Grand Rapids: Baker, 1952).

25. See H. A. Snyder, *The Radical Wesley and Patterns for Church Renewal* (Downers Grove: InterVarsity, 1980).

26. In Willard, 16–17.

27. Daniel Bloesch and James Burtness, trans., and G. B. Kelly, ed., *Life Together, Prayerbook of the Bible*, Vol. 15 *Dietrich Bonhoeffer Works* (Minneapolis: Fortress Press, 1966).

28. R. Webber and D. Bloesch, *The Orthodox Evangelicals: Who They Are and What They are Saying* (Nashville: Thomas Nelson, 1977).

29. There has always been a wide array of materials on Christian spirituality to consult in the Catholic tradition, with one of the most popular being Thomas Merton. Outside of the United States, readers would want to consult the Protestant works of Emily Herman (Australia), Ole Hallesby (Norway), and Evelyn Underhill (England).

30. Willard, 26.

31. In C. J. Healey, *Modern Spiritual Writers: Their Legacies of Prayer* (New York: Abba House, 1989), 50.

32. R. E. Webber, *Evangelicals on the Canterbury Trail: Why Evangelicals Are Attracted to the Liturgical Church* (Waco: Word, 1985), 25.

33. Ibid., 79.

34. Kelly, 35.

35. Robert Wuthnow, *Christianity in the Twenty-first Century: Reflections on the Challenges Ahead* (New York: Oxford University Press, 1993).

36. Willard, 158.

37. R. Webber, *The Book of Daily Prayer* (Grand Rapids: Eerdmans, 1993), 4.

38. Foster, 3.

Chapter 13

1. Francis Schaeffer, *The God Who is There*, quoted in Steven Garber, *The Fabric of Faithfulness* (Downers Grove: InterVarsity, 1977), 108.

2. Quoted in John Leinenweber, *The Letters of Augustine* (Liguori, Mo.: Triumph Books, 1992), 99.

3. Mark Schwehn, *Exiles from Eden* (Oxford: Oxford University Press), 58–59.

4. Alasdair MacIntyre, *After Virtue* (Notre Dame: University of Notre Dame Press, 1984), 263.

5. Robert T. Sandin, "To Those Who Teach at Christian Colleges," *New Direction for Higher Education* 79 (Fall 1992): 46.

6. Jerry H. Gill, "Faith in Dialogue: Toward a Definition of Christian Higher Education," *Encounter* 56 (Autumn 1995): 345.

7. See Dennis H. Dirks, "Moral Development in Christian Higher Education," *Journal of Psychology and Theology* 16 (1988).

8. Brian J. Walsh, "Worldviews, Modernity and the Task of Christian College Education," *Faculty Dialogue* 18 (Fall 1992): 31.

9. Cf. Kenneth W. Shipps, "Church–Related Colleges and Academics," *New Directions for Higher Education* 79 (Fall 1992): 30.

10. Ivy George, "In a New Educational Order: Teaching and Curriculum," *Christian Scholar's Review* 21 (Spring 1992): 304–11.

11. Ibid.

12. Nicholas Wolterstorff, "Teaching for Justice," in Joel Carpenter and Kenneth W. Shipps, eds., *Making Higher Education Christian* (Grand Rapids: Eerdmans, 1987), 201–16.

13. Ibid., 213.

14. Ibid., 209.

15. Cf. Garber, *Fabric of Faithfulness*, throughout.

Chapter 14

1. William H. Willimon and Thomas H. Naylor (contrib.), *The Abandoned Generation: Rethinking Higher Education* (Grand Rapids: Eerdmans, 1995).

2. Allan Bloom, *The Closing of the American Mind* (New York: Simon and Shuster, 1987).

3. Robert N. Bellah, ed., and contrib, Richard Masden and William M. Sullivan, (contrib.) *Habits of the Heart: Individualism and Commitment in American Life* (University of Califiornia Press, 1996).

4. David Hoekema, *Campus Rules and Moral Community: In Place of in loco parentis* (Lanham, Md.: Rowman and Littlefield, 1994).

5. Mark R. Schwehn, *Exiles from Eden: Religion and the Academic Vocation in America* (University of Notre Dame Press, 1981).

7. Cf. Arthur F. Holmes, *The Soul of the Christian University* (Calvin College: Stob Lectures, 1997).

8. See for example Lee Hardy, *The Fabric of this World* (Grand Rapids: Eerdmans, 1990).

Chapter 15

1. See John R. W. Stott, *The Spirit, the Church, and the World: The Message of Acts* (Downers Grove: InterVarsity, 1990), 276–91; see also John Polhill, *Acts* (Nashville: Broadman & Holman, 1992), 365–78.

2. For a thorough description of the Athenian idols and temples, see O. Broneer, "Athens, City of Idol Worship," *Biblical Archaeologist* 21 (1958): 2–28; G. T. Montague, "Paul and Athens," *The Bible Today* 49 (1970): 14–23.

3. See D. A. Carson, *The Gagging of God: Christianity Confronts Pluralism* (Grand Rapids: Zondervan, 1996); also Stephen L. Carter, *The Culture of Disbelief* (San Francisco: Basic Books, 1993); Charles Colson, *Burden of Truth: Defending the Truth in an Age of Unbelief* (Wheaton: Tyndale, 1997).

4. Cited by Richard John Neuhaus in *First Things* 18 (Dec. 1991): 63.

5. Ibid. I am indebted to John Piper for bringing this quote to my attention.

6. Donald W. McCullough, *The Trivialization of God: The Dangerous Illusion of a Manageable Deity* (Colorado Springs: NavPress, 1995).

7. See John Marks Templeton, ed., *How Large is God?* (Radnor, Penn.: Templeton Foundation, 1997); Hugh Ross, *The Creator and the Cosmos* (Colorado Springs: NavPress, 1993). On these matters also see the fascinating interview with John Polkinghorne, *Books and Culture* 4 (September 1998): 30–33.

8. See G. C. Berkouwer, *General Revelation* (Grand Rapids: Eerdmans, 1955); and Paul Helm, *Divine Revelation: The Basic Issues* (Westchester, Ill.: Crossway, 1982).

9. See Kenneth O. Gangel, "Paul's Areopagus Speech," *Bibliotheca Sacra* 127 (1970): 308–12.

10. See William J. Larkin, *Culture and Biblical Hermeneutics* (Grand Rapids: Baker, 1988); and Sherwood Lingenfelter, *Agents of Transformation* (Grand Rapids: Baker, 1996).

11. See Alister McGrath, *Intellectuals Don't Need God, and Other Modern Myths* (Grand Rapids: Zondervan, 1993). Also see Scott R.

Burson and Jerry L. Walls, *C. S. Lewis and Francis Schaeffer: Lessons for a New Century from the Most Influential Apologists of Our Time* (Downers Grove: InterVarsity, 1998), 251–72, who give twenty-one guidelines for engaging twenty-first century culture.

12. See James W. Sire, *The Universe Next Door: A Basic Worldview Catalog* (Downers Grove: InterVarsity, 1997), 16–38.

13. See John Piper, *Desiring God* (Portland: Multnomah, 1986).

14. J. P. Moreland, *Love Your God with All Your Mind: The Role of Reason in the Life of the Soul* (Colorado Springs: NavPress, 1997), 173–86; also see Harold Heie and David Wolfe, eds. *The Reality of Christian Learning: Strategies for Faith-Learning Integration* (Grand Rapids: Eerdmans, 1987).

15. See the call for Christians to enlarge their view of God in the recent interview with J. I. Packer, "Children of a Larger God," *Leadership* 14 (Summer 1998): 108–13.

16. James W. Sire, *How to Read Slowly* (Wheaton: Harold Shaw, 1978).

17. See Heie and Wolfe, eds., *The Reality of Christian Learning: Strategies for Faith-Learning Integration.*

18. Cited in J. Daryl Charles, "Engaging the (Neo)Pagan Mind: Paul's Encounter with Athenian Culture as a Model for Cultural Apologetics," *Trinity Journal* 16 NS (1995): 47–62. See also C. S. Lewis, *God in the Dock* (Grand Rapids: Eerdmans, reprint 1994).

19. Os Guiness, *Fit Bodies, Fat Minds: Why Evangelicals Don't Think and What to Do About It* (Grand Rapids: Baker, 1994). Guiness constructs a compelling case that a leading problem among evangelicals is anti–intellectualism, creating polarization between heart and mind, false pietism, and a populist pragmatism. Also see D. Bruce Lockerbie, *Dismissing God* (Grand Rapids: Baker, 1998) who surveys literary giants of the past two centuries who have challenged God for the heavyweight championship of the universe. A. C. Swinburne is a classic example with his startling words, "I kneel not" in "Hymn to Prosperine."

20. Harold Heie, "Integration and Conversation," in *The University Through the Eyes of Faith*, ed. Steve Moore (Indianapolis: Light and Life, 1998), 63.

21. Adapted from John Piper, "How Not to Blaspheme God," Conger Preaching Lectures (unpublished; delivered at Beeson Divinity School, Samford University, Birmingham, Alabama, 1998). Piper's

insights have been most helpful as I have reflected on key themes in this chapter.

Chapter 16

1. Kelly Monroe, ed. Finding God at Harvard: Spiritual Journeys of Thinking Christians (Grand Rapids: Zondervan, 1996).

Chapter 17

1. Sir Walter Moberly, The Crisis in the University (London: SMC Press, 1949).

2. Tom Peters and Nancy Austin, A Passion for Excellence (New York: Random House, 1985).

3. Hal Wingo, quoted from a speech delivered at the National Congress on Leadership (Gatlinburg, TN: June 4–7, 1986).

4. Theodore Roosevelt, from an address delivered at the Sorbonne in Paris (April 23, 1910). Reprinted in The Works of Theodore Roosevelt: The Strenuous Life vol. 13 (New York: Charles Scribner's Sons, 1926), 510.

Chapter 18

1. Paper presented at a conference by Penny Marler and Kirk Hadaway, Religious Marginality in America: Understanding: "Marginal Members," sponsored by Hartford Seminary's Center for Social and Religious Research with the support of the Lilly Endowment, Inc., 1993.

2. Portions of this chapter appeared as "When Survival Becomes the Highest Purpose" in The Campus Minister 19:2 (Fall 1997), 14–20.

David P. Gushee

Director of the Center for Christian Leadership and
Associate Professor of Christian Studies, Union University

Arthur F. Holmes

Professor Emeritus
Wheaton College

Karen A. Longman

Vice President for Professional Development and Research
Coalition for Christian Colleges and Universities

Kelly Monroe

Founder of the Veritas Forum at Harvard University

Harry L. Poe

Vice President for Academic Resources and Information Services
Union University

Claude O. Pressnell, Jr.

Executive Director
Foundation for Tennessee Independent Colleges and Universities

Robert B. Sloan, Jr.

President
Baylor University

Norm Sonju

Business leader and former
General Manager of the Dallas Mavericks

CONTRIBUTORS

Bob R. Agee

Executive Director
Association of Southern Baptist Colleges and Schools

Robert C. Andringa

President
Council of Christian Colleges and Universities

Joel A. Carpenter

Provost
Calvin College

David S. Dockery

President
Union University

James T. Draper, Jr.

President
LifeWay Christian Resources of the Southern Baptist Convention

Kenneth G. Elzinga

Cavalier Professor of Economics
University of Virginia

Millard J. Erickson

Visiting Distinguished Theologian, Truett Theological Seminary
at Baylor University

Stan D. Gaede

Provost
Westmont College

Timothy George

Dean of Beeson Divinity School
Samford University